BUS

Transform Your Business into e

Going Beyond
the Dot Com Disasters

E-Business Solutions

An Academic Press Series

Bennet P. Lientz and Kathryn P. Rea
Series Editors

The list of titles in this series includes:

Start Right in E-Business
Dynamic E-Business Implementation Management
Breakthrough Technology Project Management, 2nd ed.
Grow Your E-Business for Success

Transform Your Business into e

Going Beyond
the Dot Com Disasters

Bennet P. Lientz
University of California, Los Angeles
Los Angeles, California

Kathryn P. Rea
The Consulting Edge, Inc.
Beverly Hills, California

ACADEMIC PRESS
A Harcourt Science and Technology Company

San Diego   San Francisco   New York   Boston   London   Sydney   Tokyo

Academic Press
A Harcourt Science and Technology Company
525 B Street, Suite 1900, San Diego, California 92101-4495, USA
http://www.academicpress.com

Academic Press
Harcourt Place, 32 Jamestown Road, London NW1 7BY, UK
http://www.academicpress.com

Library of Congress Catalog Card Number: 2001088195

International Standard Book Number: 0-12-449982-1 (Paperback)

PRINTED IN THE UNITED STATES OF AMERICA
01   02   03   04   05   06   CO   9   8   7   6   5   4   3   2   1

Contents

Part I
E-Business Strategy

Chapter 1
Introduction

Chapter 2

Assess Your Business and IT Goals and Activities

Chapter 3
Develop Process and Transaction Plans

Chapter 4

Define Your E-Business Vision and Objectives

Chapter 5

Build Your E-Business Strategy

Part II
E-Business Planning

Chapter 6
Perform Industry, Competitive, and Technology Assessments

Chapter 7

Determine Your E-Business IT Architecture

Chapter 8

Develop Your Outsourcing and ASP Approach

Chapter 9

Perform Marketing for E-Business

Chapter 10

Create Your Organization Approach for E-Business

Chapter 11
Establish Your Project
and Program Management Approach

Chapter 12
Define Your E-Business Implementation Strategy

Part III
E-Business Transformation

Chapter 13
Implement Quick Hits

Chapter 14

Coordinate Your E-Business Implementation

Chapter 15

Manage Your E-Business Operations

Preface

There have been probably over 500 books written on e-commerce and e-business. New ones come out all the time. Why another book? This book is different in the following areas:

- Written after dot com hype and disasters—gathering lessons learned from their experiences.
- Focuses on implementation, beginning with business goals through implementation and expansion.
- Recognizes that e-business is an on-going program, not a one-shot project. It is not like reengineering, ERP, and Y2K—one-time activities. It is a different animal.
- Learned lessons from some of the over 50% of e-business efforts that fail, including recent dot com failures.
- Provides a down-to-earth common sense approach that proceeds step by step and does not require you to hire an army of outside helpers.
- Avoids the normal success stories. Because e-business is a program and not a project, such success stories may glow in the short term and then die out in the long term.
- Gives attention to problem areas where people go wrong and advises how to avoid, prevent, and overcome these.
- Does not pay attention to the fluff of the Web pages. That is the sizzle. It is not the steak.
- Is basically jargon free.

The goal of the book is to show you how to transform your business into e-business without repeating the mistakes of the past. It is also a book to help you in an e-business startup. This book is the result of over 35 major e-business efforts as well as consulting and support for many more implementations and expansions of e-business. The approach has been employed with over 50 organizations in over 30 countries, in which there were a variety of political, technological, cultural, and business environments. The methods work because they are common sense, have shown results, and have been employed in many different situations.

E-BUSINESS REQUIRES A RAPID
BUT ORGANIZED APPROACH

E-business is going to be a fact of life for most firms for a simple reason. It represents the next step in the evolution of the organization and business processes as people apply more technology and automation to their work. As such, it opens up new opportunities as well as risks. If you just plunge into e-business, statistics show that you are likely to fail. If you hold back and proceed slowly, trying to get it right, you will miss opportunities and fall behind. You must attack e-business in an organized but rapid way.

THEME: FOCUS ON KEY TRANSACTIONS NOT PROCESSES

E-business implementation is more restricted in scope in terms of process depth, but is wider in scope than reengineering and other methods because you address more processes. Key to e-business is the transformation of major business transactions. But this is different from reengineering, continuous improvement, or other similar methods. These focus on changing an entire process. But you all know that almost all business processes are burdened by exceptions, workarounds, and the dreaded world of shadow systems. A shadow system is a manual or automated system that a business department creates to suit its needs. Departments have developed shadow manual systems for hundreds of years. When you attempt to change the process, you have to address all of these. In e-business you work to identify only key common transactions and create new transactions. You leave many of the exceptions and shadow systems behind in the dust. You don't have time to change the entire process. If you did, departments would create new ones. After all, that is what happened many times after ERP systems were installed.

What happens to these exceptions? As the mainstream transactions move into greater automation, there is more pressure later to eliminate the exceptions. This can be done later in a natural way without massive analysis up front. It is not within the scope of the transformation into e-business unless the exceptions are part of the future e-business transactions.

E-BUSINESS IS BUSINESS ORIENTED

E-business does involve implementing new systems and technology, which is a minor but important part of the puzzle. E-business impacts the technology, processes, organization, and management of the organization. These statements have strong implications for carrying out a successful e-business effort.

- Politics is an important part of e-business implementation. You cannot ignore it or sweep it under the rug. It is there because e-business has such far-ranging impacts. E-business alters the power structure of departments and the entire organization.
- The culture of the society, organization, and environment is an important factor in e-business because you are dealing with customers, suppliers, and employees.
- Information technology (IT) has a major role that goes beyond systems work. IT is the only group that spans the organization and addresses the technology. IT must have a central role in e-business implementation.

E-BUSINESS IS MAGIC

By magic we mean that e-business has pervasive and long-lasting positive effects. Here are some magic elements of e-business:

- E-business tends to be self-enforcing. If you screw up, either customers or suppliers will start screaming. You will have to act. How many methods and processes do you know with this characteristic? Not many.
- Done right, e-business forces a company to look within its soul and really determine what its business goals are. E-business success depends on the support of many different employees. Thus, a critical success factor is collaboration among employees.
- E-business continues to change the organization and business processes after it goes live. Why? Because the employees, customers, and suppliers begin to have a role in business direction.
- E-business provides the basis for measurement internally and externally.
- E-business is positive and fun. E-business is not downsizing or reengineering, which tend to be depressing because they result in layoffs. The good people leave and the gnomes and trolls stay. Instead, e-business implementation can get people excited. Roles change, but you probably won't lose good people.
- Perhaps the greatest magic of all is that when you implement e-business, you have the opportunity to improve the lives of employees and service level to customers and to strengthen relationships with suppliers.

In short there are few things like e-business that have come along in the past 40 years in computer and communications. E-business is really the next step in evolution of the application of systems beyond online systems.

THE GOAL OF THIS BOOK

The goal of this book is to show how to improve your business through the implementation and expansion of e-business. Over the next decade, e-business is likely to be the most positive approach to implementing improvements in business. In the end your business can be transformed into a more positive, dynamic, and responsive organization with highly motivated employees.

THE APPROACH

The approach in the book follows these guidelines:

- You not only must have a vision and objectives for e-business, but also must have an e-business strategy that relates how e-business and regular business will fit together.
- Many issues and opportunities must be addressed and resolved before you can implement e-business. You cannot get to e-business in one step. Therefore, we employ the use of Quick Hits, which are intermediate steps with positive benefits for the short term.
- E-business is a program and so must be managed differently than a one-time project.
- Implementing and managing e-business involve addressing many political, cultural, and social issues. If you treat e-business as an IT project, you are likely to fail, as many have, because e-business is a program and IT plays a key but not dominant role in e-business. IT provides critical support and coordination.

KEY FEATURES OF THE BOOK

Here are some of the major features of this book:

- How to transform your enterprise into e-business without destroying and disrupting your business.
- How to develop your down-to-earth e-business vision, objectives, and strategies.
- How to align business, e-business, and IT for success.
- How to employ collaborative methods and empowerment for e-business success.
- How to determine your e-business readiness.
- How to achieve political and cultural goals through e-business.

- How to define and implement Quick Hit process improvements that lead to e-business.
- Over 100 specific guidelines for e-business transformation.
- How to overcome resistance to e-business.
- How to develop a usable e-business implementation strategy.
- How to direct and manage outsourcing and ASPs.
- How to measure business processes, business involvement, and vendor work.
- Down-to-earth writing style.
- How to avoid failure in e-business implementation.
- Examples drawn from different industries and agencies.
- Covers business-to-business, business-to-consumer, and intranets.
- Addresses the needs of startup firms.
- Specific suggestions that you can use after each chapter.

ACKNOWLEDGMENTS

We express our appreciation to the many organizations, managers, employees, vendors, and students who provided us with the settings and feedback.

About the Authors

Bennet P. Lientz is Professor of Information Systems at the Anderson Graduate School of Management, University of California, Los Angeles (UCLA). Dr. Lientz was previously Associate Professor of Engineering at the University of Southern California and department manager at System Development Corporation, where he was one of the project leaders involved in the development of ARPANET, the precursor of the Internet. He managed administrative systems at UCLA and has managed over 70 projects and served as a consultant to companies and government agencies since the late 1970s.

Dr. Lientz has taught information technology, project management, e-business, and strategic planning for the past 20 years. He has delivered seminars related to these topics to more than 4000 people in Asia, Latin America, Europe, Australia, and North America. He is the author of more than 25 books and 70 articles in information systems, planning, project management, process improvement, and e-business. He has been involved in over 40 e-business projects in 15 industries.

Kathryn P. Rey is president and founder of The Consulting Edge, Inc., which was established in 1984. The firm specializes in e-business, information technology, project management, and financial consulting.

Ms. Rea has managed more than 65 major technology-related projects internationally. She has advised on and carried out projects in government, energy, banking and finance, distribution, trading, retailing, transportation, mining, manufacturing, and utilities. She has successfully directed multinational projects in China, North and South America, Southeast Asia, Europe, and Australia. She has conducted more than 120 seminars around the world. She is the author of 8 books and more than 20 articles in various areas of information systems and analysis. She has been an e-business project leader on 10 projects and has been involved in several startup e-business companies.

Part I

E-Business Strategy

Chapter 1

Introduction

E-business can be defined as the use of automation and communications to carry out business transactions without manual or labor-intensive activities. E-commerce consists of the transactions that support e-business. Figure 1.1 gives an overall picture of e-business. On either end you see the customer and supplier. As interfaces you see boxes for Web sites and the system interfaces. Most of the attention in books and articles tends to be focused here. However, the benefits are not here. These areas are the enablers of e-business. The core of e-business is shown in the middle. Here you see customer and supplier information, business processes, technology and systems, goods and services, and organization and infrastructure. It is here where you either make money or lose your shirt in e-business. Surrounding this we have management and measurement. Measurement is crucial because you want to take advantage of the information that e-business provides.

Let's use Figure 1.1 to explore e-business.

- *Customer and supplier information.* E-business can give you billions of bytes of information on how people navigate your Web site. This is nice in academic books and journals, but it is not the real world. If you gather these data, you have to ask if it is worth it. How will you analyze it? What decisions will you base on all of these raw data? Experience shows that it is best to gather sales, workflow, and other tangible information. This can help you determine where you can further improve your processes. Recent research questions the effectiveness of banner ads and tracking visitor traffic in too great detail.
- *Business transactions.* It is here that e-business makes the difference. Organizations rise and fall depending on the performance of key transactions. Here is also where many e-business efforts fail. They do not address existing transac-

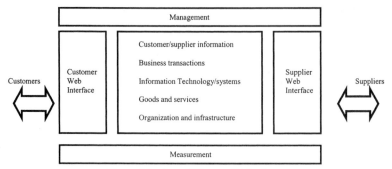

Figure 1.1   Overall Picture of E-Business

tions, but instead focus on just the e-business. How well you do in e-business depends on how you deal with both regular and e-business transactions.

• *Information technology.* Information technology (IT) is obviously a main ingredient in e-business. However, IT supports and enables e-business. IT is not e-business. When you implement e-business, you will enhance your IT infrastructure, but you are not going to replace it. Even with a startup you will be able to afford only some key components. Moreover, if someone obsesses over IT, e-business is diverted. Important areas such as marketing and logistics are neglected.

• *Goods and services.* Unique among concepts that have come along in the past 40 years, e-business supports having the organization review what goods and services it offers. Dot com failures reveal the stupidity of just throwing a bunch of products on the Web without analysis.

• *Organization and infrastructure.* Some organization change may be necessary for e-business, along with changes in business processes such as warehousing, manufacturing, and other areas.

• *Interface to the customer.* Beyond the Web site, this box includes all of the other interfaces that the customer sees with the organization. While many focus on the Web site, this technology is changing with mobile communications and Extensible Markup Language (XML).

• *Interface to the supplier.* This includes all business-to-business transactions as well as the delivery of goods and services. Problems in interfaces restricted electronic data interchange (EDI) growth for years.

• *Management.* Managing both regular and e-business is complex and different from regular business. E-business creates its own dynamics and pressures. Let's take an example. Marketing typically works on campaigns and promotions. These are discrete events. When you move into e-business, marketing becomes continuous rather than discrete.

• *Measurement.* Taking data from all of the boxes in the diagram, you want to determine trends as well as measures of service and performance. You also want measurements for the business processes, e-business, vendor performance, and other factors. A number of dot coms thought that they were doing OK, because of sales. They failed because their expenses grew out of control and their business processes became unwieldy.

Notice that we did not use the term *process* very much. Process encompasses all transactions in a given area. As you know from any job you have had, there are many exception transactions. If you attempt to improve or eliminate these in e-business, you are headed down the dreaded reengineering path. Your scope has broadened. You are now more likely to never finish the e-business transformation. E-business focuses on transactions within processes.

DEFINITIONS

Here are some basic definitions that will be employed in this and later chapters.

- *E-commerce.* This will refer to the transactions in e-business.
- *Business-to-business.* This consists of the e-business transactions that support work directly with suppliers.
- *Business-to-consumer.* These are the e-business transactions that link the firm to customers.
- *Internal e-business.* These are intranets that make communications and work electronic in a structured way (going beyond e-mail). Examples are sharing knowledge and automating communications among employees and departments.
- *Business goal.* This is an objective of the business and is typically stated in annual reports and company presentations.
- *E-business vision.* The e-business vision is a statement of where you want the organization to be after e-business is implemented.
- *E-business goal.* This is one of the goals of e-business in terms of a specific audience or perspective (e.g., customer, employee, IT). The vision provides an integrated view of e-business while the e-business goals support the vision.
- *Business model.* This is the new business model that emerges from the transactions.
- *E-business strategy.* This is a strategy and approach for achieving the goals and attaining the vision.
- *E-business implementation strategy.* This is a roadmap for how to achieve e-business in a phased approach.
- *Quick Hits.* You seldom can get to your e-business vision in one step. It takes many intervening steps. The initial ones that can be taken will be called *Quick Hits.* Quick Hits must be consistent with the e-business approach.
- *Industry assessment.* This is the data collection and analysis of information from industry, competitors, and society through the literature and the Web. This is ongoing.

- *Technology assessment.* This assessment consists of examining new products and services as well as trends related to technology for e-business. This is an ongoing activity.
- *Technology architecture.* This is the structure of hardware, software, and network components to support current and e-business work and systems.
- *Outsourcing.* Outsourcing is the process whereby you contract out specific activities related to regular and e-business.
- *Application Service Provider (ASP).* This is a firm that provides a range of services to support e-business and is a type of outsourcing vendor.
- *E-business readiness.* This is an assessment of your organization's capability to implement e-business rapidly.

E-business does not have to be performed only on the Web. The Web is now the most common means, but there are other ways to do e-business. You can employ EDI. You can establish direct links with suppliers or customers that totally bypass the Internet and Web. These alternatives are considered in this book.

BENEFITS

Benefits of anything, including e-business, are in the eyes of the beholder. So you must consider different perspectives for benefits.

- *Stakeholders.* These are the investors and owners of the enterprise. For public agencies this is the general public.
- *General management.* Management can obtain many tangible benefits from e-business, including improved measurement of the business, reduced costs, and better knowledge of customers and suppliers.
- *IT.* When IT implements a system, there are often no benefits for IT. There is only additional maintenance and support. E-business should provide benefits (such as a modern infrastructure) that reduce or stabilize support.
- *Business departments.* Business departments and the organization receive benefits from e-business in terms of reduction in clerical work and improved productivity.
- *Customers.* Customers may receive a wide range of benefits in terms of selection, choice, ease of ordering, returning, canceling, and other transactions.
- *Suppliers.* If you implement business-to-business successfully, then there should be benefits to suppliers in terms of their costs and even sales as well as productivity and efficiency.
- *Long-term company direction.* E-business benefits must support the company direction and goals. Otherwise, these goals may not be as easily obtainable.
- *Business processes.* The business processes and transactions generate the

revenue and costs for the business. This is where the key benefits of your e-business implementation must be.

When benefits are discussed, the attention will be on tangible and measurable benefits. As an example, implementing e-business using Web-based technology can result in an easier-to-use interface. This is too fuzzy. You want to translate this into reduced training, fewer errors, and less rework of transactions. Why this insistence about tangible benefits? Systems and technology have promised savings, revenue, productivity, paper savings, and many other benefits over the past 50 years. Yet, many failed to deliver. Management and people in general have grown very cynical and skeptical. If you overpromise with fuzzy benefits and then fail to deliver, there could be trouble. Look at all of the dot com startups that never made it out of the starting gate.

RISKS

Some surveys indicate that half of all e-business implementations either fail or are only partially successful. Therefore, we need to give attention to risks. Many risks will be explored in the following chapters. Here are some examples of specific risks:

- *Loss of customers.* If you drive customers to the Web, they may find a better site and leave.
- *Customer dissatisfaction.* Customers may not receive acceptable service through the Web and the normal business.
- *Supplier dissatisfaction.* Suppliers get involved with you in e-business and find the experience to be less satisfactory than was planned.
- *Reduced productivity.* Due to a faulty implementation of e-business productivity is actually reduced.
- *Employee morale decline.* Employees see e-business as a threat even after implementation.
- *Decline of IT level of support and service.* With e-business implemented, IT resources may be stretched too thin. IT then may not be able to respond to the business in a timely way.
- *Management depression.* E-business fails to deliver to the standards of the overly high management expectations set at the beginning.

TRENDS IN E-BUSINESS

While there are many technical and business trends, here are a few important ones:

- E-business is crucial to business success. It is being proved in industry after industry that you must do e-business in order to be profitable, grow, and even survive. E-business has proved to be more long-lasting than the fad of reengineering, for example.
- Technology focus is on e-business. If you consider the activities of the hardware, software, and network vendors, they are directed toward providing the tools for e-business. To them e-business is a natural extension of their products and services. In addition, new technology offers greater support for wireless and land-based communications and networking—keys to the capability to do e-business.
- E-business produces cumulative effects. E-business is long-lasting. As you implement e-business, the nature of your relationship with customers, suppliers, and employees changes. New dynamic forces are set loose that are not as easily controlled and dealt with as compared to those of the standard internal business. Dependency on business departments continues, but there is a greater dependence on IT resources.
- E-business implementation results in many successes and failures. The literature abounds with examples of both success and failure. Failure tends to be more obvious and dramatic with e-business because e-business is more visible externally.

SIX E-BUSINESS MYTHS

MYTH: E-BUSINESS IS A PROJECT

Once started, e-business is not easily stopped. The implementation is never over. Implementation of some transactions for e-business leads to more transactions and change. As business departments see the potential for e-business, they tend to embrace it and expand on it. Therefore, e-business is not a single project. Rather it is an ongoing program. This has a tremendous impact on how you organize the implementation of e-business.

MYTH: YOU CAN MANAGE AN E-BUSINESS IMPLEMENTATION AS AN IT PROJECT

It is easy to consider treating e-business as an IT project given its base in technology and systems. Yet it is so much more. In most implementations, the IT-only part of the work is less than 30% of the effort. The rest clearly lies with the business. However, there is a need for coordination and support of e-business across the organization. While this can be supported by consultants and contractors, the IT role is changed to one of coordination and project management along with the business.

MYTH: YOU HAVE TO CHANGE ENTIRE PROCESSES FOR E-BUSINESS

If you take the time to change entire processes, you will never implement e-business. E-business crosses many processes. To change them all is too major an effort and, hence, is doomed to fail. In e-business you may occasionally have to consider entire processes. However, this is more the exception. So then, where should the focus be? The attention must be directed toward specific transactions that interrelate with each other to serve customers, suppliers, and employees. This new focus makes the e-business effort feasible in a reasonable amount of time and with reasonable resources.

MYTH: UPPER MANAGEMENT INVOLVEMENT IN E-BUSINESS IS ESSENTIAL

This is a myth common to any new method. Management support and initiation of e-business are definitely critical. Otherwise, people do not see e-business in either their or the organization's self-interest. The line is drawn there. If management becomes too involved in the details, experience has shown that the implementation is slowed down and even stopped. Direction may be changed too often. Management involvement should be limited to considering critical issues that arise during e-business implementation.

MYTH: YOU CAN AFFORD TO RUSH E-BUSINESS IMPLEMENTATION BECAUSE YOU CAN FIX THINGS LATER

Many organizations rush to implement something on the Web. It is not surprising then that there are many failures. Rushing implementation can disrupt established processes and transactions. Employee morale sinks as the place falls apart. What ends up on the Web ends up only being a partial solution to customers or suppliers. While you can move expeditiously in implementation, you still must follow a planned, organized approach. Remember that e-business is a program and not a project, so that you are targeting for the long term as well as short term.

MYTH: IF YOU DESIGN E-BUSINESS RIGHT, YOUR EFFORT WILL BE SUCCESSFUL

This one is also reflected in the saying, "If you get the requirements right, your project will be successful." In e-business as in modern IT, "right" is a relative term with respect to time. Moreover, after e-business is in operation, there will be more changes generated due to outside factors in the industry, in technology, and in government regulation.

There is then no complete or total design of e-business. You implement as best you can with the time and resources available. Then you gain more knowledge and experience and carry out more changes. While this may seem frustrating, it reflects the growth and dynamics of e-business. You must realize that e-business is in some sense a moving target. The e-business program feeds on gathering and using lessons learned from experience and from outside information.

WHAT DO YOU WANT TO ACHIEVE WITH E-BUSINESS?

So overall, what are you trying to accomplish with your e-business effort? If you stop at the goals of making money and securing higher profits, then you miss the point. These are really temporary. Sustaining goals are things such as the following factors:

• Instill and sustain a collaborative culture across the organization that establishes and then fosters e-business. This pays benefits over many years. Employees and managers work more closely together.
   • Customer and supplier relationships are stronger and more satisfactory.
   • Business growth and expansion occur because of the above two factors.

BARRIERS TO E-BUSINESS

INTERNAL TECHNICAL AND TECHNOLOGY BARRIERS

Organizations have been using computer systems for many years. Many of the existing systems in use were designed and built long before the "e-" arose. This is true of on-line systems implemented less than 5-years ago. These "legacy systems" constitute a major challenge to e-business. Here are some of the reasons:

• Maintenance and support over the years have made the systems less flexible to change.

- Only a few programmers are knowledgeable about how the internal programs work.
- There are often design limitations that restrict your ability to support the full range of e-business transactions.
- Multiple legacy systems are not easily integrated with each other due to logic, data structures, and design of the software.

So what do you do? Do you try to replace these as part of e-business? Only in the most dire of circumstances. Doing this would also extend the implementation beyond what is reasonable. Instead, you will have to make an effort to understand the limitations as you proceed with the implementation. You will mostly front-end and back-end these systems with e-business software. You will also have to implement some interfaces among systems.

Limitations go beyond software. A major issue is often the network. It may be employing communications protocols or methods of talking that are not compatible with the e-business standard protocol, transmission control protocol/internet protocol (TCP/IP). In order to achieve decent performance the network may have to be seriously upgraded or even replaced.

BUSINESS RESISTANCE

Business departments and staff have been subjected to major upheaval and change due to new buzzwords. Some examples have been quality improvement, reengineering, and downsizing. In addition to disturbing work, morale has been impacted. Employees are reluctant to support another new term. Here are more details:

- Employees may perceive that management adopts a new concept after attending some seminar that promises happiness and success. The employees have been the victims; the manager moved on to new things.
- There may be management turnover. The feeling may exist that if you just play for time and delay, the manager who endorsed e-business will go on to something else or another job and you can return to normal.
- Many of the so-called improvement methods have not really touched the core processes of the business.
- Some systems efforts, such as Enterprise Resource Planning (ERP), have provided data to management, but have not benefited the processes or employees. In some cases, the result has been more work in the departments.
- Employees are reticent to adopt something that appears to be more work and of no direct benefit to them.
- Middle managers may openly support the new initiative, but then they return to their departments and tell people to do their normal work without change.

How do you approach this? A suggestion is to downplay the "e-" and focus instead on improvements in the process. Another suggestion is to avoid promising things that cannot easily be delivered. After all, you cannot promise what the people themselves must do. Don't discuss the exotic nature of e-business. Avoid the expense and time of trying to train people in e-business. They will be in essence trained when they define new transactions to support e-business. They do not need to know all of the aspects and wonders of e-business. That will lead to confusion and distrust. Another suggestion is to have them see the positive aspects of making changes that directly benefit them.

YOUR CURRENT BUSINESS PROCESSES AND POLICIES

Many business processes and policies have existed unchanged for decades. There is substantial inertia. If it works, don't try to fix it. Many processes are not measured or analyzed so that the real situation is masked from upper levels of management. Beyond this there is the factor of time. At some time in the past a new system was implemented. The department adjusted to it. As time passed, the system was found to be inflexible in handling new situations. Systems tend to lack flexibility except in limited forms—even modern systems. What does the department do in response? It creates exceptions, workarounds, and shadow systems. A shadow system is a system (manual or automated) created by a department. Most people outside of the department do not realize that these exist. Yet they are there and they do help the people carry out their work.

What do you do? If you attempt to go and fix these, you are embarking on major reengineering. Like replacing legacy systems, this is not feasible. An alternative is to focus only on specific transactions, not the entire process. This narrows the scope and reduces the tensions created by change. It is less threatening. Moreover, if you were to totally reengineer processes, who is to say that new exceptions would not be created or that the department would not revert back to the old? E-business is different in that the transactions become more automated. There is measurement. It is more difficult and visible to create new exceptions because this would require IT support.

THE EXISTING BUSINESS ORGANIZATION

Any organization has an existing power structure. People who are in place wield power because of their positions, time in their jobs, experience, and knowledge. Any new idea that includes the word "change" means that their power position is threatened. Is it any wonder that there is often widespread resistance under the table? There may also be many organization layers, making it more challenging to implement change.

What do you do? Avoid organization change to the extent possible. After e-business has been implemented, there will be time to assess the organization. Also, at the start of e-business implementation, you probably do not know the best changes to make. Focus on involving people who do the actual work in the process.

CUSTOMER AND/OR SUPPLIER PUSH BACK

Suppose that you embark on e-business without having tested the waters with customers and suppliers. You may later be faced with an "e-business white elephant." You will have implemented something that customers and suppliers will not use or work on with you.

What do you do? Collect data ahead of time. There is no law that says that 100% of suppliers or customers have to use e-business with you. If you get the 15% of suppliers that constitute 40% of the volume of work, you are successful. The same applies to customers.

CULTURE PROBLEMS

In different countries and companies there is an established unique culture. Culture permeates all aspects of work. You must be aware of this when you carry out the transformation to e-business. After applying the techniques in this book to over 50 organizations on four continents, we can see that there is evidence that the methods can be adapted to different cultures. A final guideline here is not to fight the underlying culture. The major culture change that you are trying to carry out is to improve collaboration.

COMPETING DEMANDS FOR RESOURCES

Getting management support and money for e-business is not enough. You have to compete with normal work and other work for resources. Don't ignore this and assume that resources will flow into the e-business program. One suggestion is to involve junior people who are more in tune with automation. These people are more receptive to e-business than are older employees. Use older employees when necessary to get business rules behind transactions. A benefit of this approach is that you will have less of an impact on the business department. Another idea is to ensure that you are not consuming the full-time effort of many employees. It is better to get the efforts of more people for limited time.

HIGH MANAGEMENT EXPECTATIONS

Managers have been literally besieged by the media, vendors, and consultants, who claim that e-business is absolutely wonderful. They play up the benefits and downplay the effort and time requirements. This is a difficult one to handle. Later in this chapter an approach will be presented for organizing your e-business effort. This approach tends to limit the involvement of management in the details. Under this method managers tend to focus on issues such as policy questions in implementation.

END PRODUCTS

The basic end product is successful e-business implementation. Here are examples of more detailed end products:

- Your e-business vision and objectives linked to your business goals.
- E-business transactions identified that support your business and e-business goals.
- Your e-business strategy for achieving the e-business goals.
- Plans for your business processes and transactions.
- Determination of your readiness for e-business.
- Assessment of trends and factors in the industry and technology impacting e-business.
- Your resource strategy for outsourcing and managing internal resources.
- Marketing of e-business.
- The e-business implementation strategy.
- Organization approach for change to e-business.
- Your project plan and approach.
- Quick Hit implementation.
- Implementation of e-business.
- Measurement of results of e-business.
- Expansion of e-business.

APPROACH

The approach in this book is a logical one that has been carried out in public and private organizations around the world. The components of the approach are discussed below. It is important to understand that these are not sequential steps. Wherever possible, you must make the effort to undertake these in parallel. For example, developing the e-business goals and process plans are performed while you are analyzing the business goals. If you follow a sequential approach, your e-business effort is jeopardized. Your biggest enemy is often not money—it is time. You can always approach people for money. But there is only so much time. Another challenge is competing for resources for e-business versus other work. We address this by spreading out the demands on individual people across more people.

The first set of activities focuses on planning.

- Understand your business goals. You have to understand what the basic objectives of the business are.
- Develop your transaction and process plans. This is the definition of where you want the work to go in terms of e-business and modifications to the current business.
- Determine your e-business goals and vision. These must be defined in terms of different audiences and address political and cultural concerns as well as technical and business aspects.
- Define your e-business strategy. This is the roadmap to achieve your goals.
- Analyze your e-business readiness. If you have too much work to do and too little time, then you might have to revisit the goals, vision, and strategies of e-business.
- Assess the industry and technology. Obviously, this should be performed very early. It should be continued as a program forever.
- Establish your strategy and approach for outsourcing. In today's environment it is very difficult to go it alone. Outsourcing is used in most e-business implementations.

After these are underway, you can move into implementation-related activities. Don't wait for the above work to be completed. Get going early.

- Undertake marketing. Marketing of e-business is essential. There are three aspects: marketing to employees and managers to gain support; marketing to suppliers and customers; considering the marketing organization.
- Set your organization approach. How will you organize the effort?
- Build the e-business program and project plan. This is a detailed plan for both initial and longer term implementation.
- Create your e-business implementation strategy. This is one of the most important things to do because it acts as a bridge between the planning results mentioned above and implementation.
- Implement Quick Hits. These are short-term improvements that lead to e-business.
- Implement e-business.
- Expand e-business and measure the results.

How long does it take to perform individual activities? Obviously, it varies by organization, technology, country, and other factors. However, experience has demonstrated that major factors are purpose and scope. If you are too ambitious, you risk getting nothing and disrupting the business. If you are too conservative and aim too low, you get some results, but their benefit and impact are often pathetic. To the extent possible, you will want to perform the activities in parallel. That is why the above items were not numbered steps.

QUICK HITS AND GETTING FROM HERE TO THERE

As was noted, it is almost impossible to implement e-business in one direct step. You must have intermediate changes in areas such as policies, procedures, organization, and systems. These lead you down the road to e-business. These intermediate steps have to be carefully thought out and coordinated so that the current business is not disrupted and that the Quick Hit actions are consistent with e-business. A Quick Hit is a specific tangible, tactical action that can be taken in a short amount of time with limited resources. You will be bundling a number of these and implementing them in waves. After each wave, you will measure the results and make any adjustments. A Quick Hit paves the way for e-business later.

Quick Hits can provide sufficient economic benefits to pay for the e-business implementation. As important as this is, you provide the culture change to support improvements for e-business. You in essence change behavior. People begin to believe in the e-business effort because it results in fixing many long-standing problems. Another benefit is that implementing Quick Hits can take the some of the pressure off of e-business teams to produce rapid results. Finally, we have experienced several cases where suppliers were not ready for e-business. The project was still a success due to the Quick Hits.

HOW TO ORGANIZE A WINNING E-BUSINESS EFFORT

A critical success factor in e-business implementation is collaboration. E-business crosses departments and requires many compromises and trade-offs. If people fail to get along, then this effort will fail. The following aspects of collaboration are useful:

- There is a need for employees to be involved from the start.
- Employees can define Quick Hit opportunities for improvement as well as identify issues related to e-business.
- Employees can vote on the opportunities in terms of benefits, urgency, and ease of implementation.
- Employees should, in general, continue to do their normal work. Only limited involvement is needed because much of the detailed work is performed by a core e-business team. This also puts pressure on the employees to get opportuni-

ties identified faster. In addition, they are not isolated from their department homes.

- Involve as many employees as possible. If you only involve a few people, the other employees have no idea what is going on. They may feel estranged from the work. By getting more people involved on a limited basis, you get a broader base of support for e-business.

The basic organization for the e-business implementation involves three tiers. The organization is coordinated by a core e-business team.

- Action teams and individual project teams. These are teams that consider transactions of a specific type. Examples are international, accounting, sales, and customer service. An action team should be headed up by someone who is not from the transaction area. This person will be more likely to question the ways things are being done. Otherwise, you could have a case where there is no recommended change because the chairman feels that the way it is now is fine. An e-business effort can have 10–15 action teams. To make the involvement reasonable, a single person should be required to serve on only one team.
- Steering committee. This is the committee that oversees the teams. It is composed of some managers as well as outsiders such as key customers and suppliers, and consultants.
- Executive committee. This is the management oversight committee. They deal with issues and opportunities that surface from the project teams through the steering committee.

Some comments are appropriate here. There should be some members on both the steering committee and the executive committee. This ensures continuity and provides more insight to management. The steering committee acts as a buffer to protect the project teams. After the project teams have completed their work on Quick Hits, the core team may select several people to serve on the core team. The project teams can also reappear later during the actual implementation of e-business.

The method is as follows:

- *Step 1:* Project team members identify opportunities for improvement working together and individually. The core e-business team coordinates this effort and ensures that the opportunities are consistent with e-business.
- *Step 2:* Action teams vote on the opportunities. The results and winners are passed for review to the steering committee. The steering committee votes to endorse the slate of opportunities. Changes can be made.
- *Step 3:* Project team members develop business cases for the approved opportunities. These business cases address ease of implementation, issues that need to be addressed (such as policies), benefits, and implementation. Support is provided by the core e-business team.

- *Step 4:* Business cases are reviewed by the steering committee.
- *Step 5:* The executive committee votes on the business cases and approves implementation.
- *Step 6:* Implementation of the Quick Hits occurs in waves so as not to be disruptive to the business. This is organized as more traditional projects.
- *Step 7:* Results are measured. Project teams and management celebrate and acknowledge their success.

This organization approach supports the collaboration goals expressed earlier. There is collaboration within and across teams. Project teams vote on opportunities. The method is more fully discussed in Chapter 10. The collaborative approach continues through implementation and expansion of e-business (see Chapters 13, 14, and 15).

This structure is supported by the core e-business team. The team should have multiple leaders. At any point in time one person is designated to be in charge. There are many benefits to this approach. E-business is technical and business in nature. No one person can easily do both. E-business is a program, so you want to have continuity across time. E-business is important, so you seek to have backup. E-business is political, so you want to have the flexibility of two leaders—one can be the good guy ("white hat") and one can be stern ("black hat").

Do you have to follow this approach to employ the methods in this book? No! You can do what you feel comfortable with. These ideas are meant to be suggestions.

STARTUP

Startup firms have been neglected in much of the literature. In fact, if you followed the rules in most books, you would barely have a Web site up. Our two examples are interesting in themselves and because their success has disproved many myths about e-business. Note that in each chapter there is a table that summarizes some of the key points for each example for that chapter. These tables have been collected in Appendix 5 as a reference for you. The example startup firms represent experiences from a number of different firms.

- Indo Furniture is basically a family-run business in Asia. It started as a one-person firm. The founder and his family make beds and chests as well as other furniture. Initially and for over 25 years he sold his products only to the local populace in a small and dingy storefront on the island. We ran across him and admired his work and thought that his products would do well on the Web. You will follow the family's adventure with the Internet through the chapters. Today, he does 45% of his business through exports. His firm has grown to include all of his relatives. Yet, the only automation he has is a plain paper fax machine!!

- Diamond Engineering Data is a startup founded by Chris and Mike. Chris heads up the business side and Mike handles the engineering. They thought that there would be a market for a lessons-learned data repository on the Web for engineering-related projects and work. Their business has also prospered.

These two examples reveal some basic truths about e-business startup firms:

- You have to have a good idea for a product or service that is sustainable.
- Your Web site has to attract people on a recurring basis.
- Money and technology are important, but as you will see with Indo, they are not critical.
- You have to have a detailed plan and organized approach to e-business. Both of these firms followed the methods in this book.

EXAMPLES

There are examples throughout the book. As with the startup examples these are combinations of real firms. The three major ones that are covered are listed below. Note that there is an example for each of the major areas of e-business: business-to-business, business-to-consumer, and intranets for internal use.

- Asean Construction. This is a large construction, engineering, and operations firm operating in Southeast Asia. Asean builds apartments, houses, roads, tollways, and other construction projects. Asean has felt pressure to get into e-business from the government, suppliers, and competitors. Asean has over 4000 employees and deals with over 500 suppliers from its five business units. Each business unit operates as a profit center. The main emphasis here is business-to-business with limited business-to-consumer.
- Walters Catalog. Walters is an example of a company that screwed up at almost every step of the way in their first attempt at e-business. They did better in their second effort. We will look at both as the book progresses. Walters is obviously an example of business-to-consumer. This example will be covered in the section on Approach.
- Rogers County. Howard is a local government agency. Howard has over 1500 employees and is concerned with using intranets as well as extranets to implement e-business among its employees. In addition to internal intranets, there is also a business-to-consumer push to reach the general public.

LESSONS LEARNED

Lessons learned are guidelines from experience in past e-business and other efforts. Lessons learned are critical in e-business because e-business is an ongoing program. Experience provides not only short-term guidance, but also delivers the following benefits, if properly gathered and used:

- Increases morale as people see improvements.
- Enhances the ability to do estimates of time and money.
- Supports the view of cumulative improvement.
- Provides opportunities for collaborative work.
- Gives an opportunity to provide a break from the day-to-day work in the project.

Using lessons learned requires an organized approach. Without this, supporting lessons learned is only giving lip service to an idea. Here are some guidelines:

- Gather lessons learned as you go. If you wait until the end of the work, it is too late. People have forgotten things. Others have moved onto other projects and work.
- Use team meetings to gather lessons learned. This shows the importance that management gives to them.
- When lessons learned are applied, the experience is used to extend, modify, and create new lessons learned.
- Create and maintain a lessons-learned database.
- Insist before work in a specific area is undertaken that lessons learned be reviewed and used.
- Appoint a lessons-learned coordinator. This role manages the database and coordinates changes and new entries. There is also a facilitation role. In the short term this can be performed by the core e-business team.

THE SCORE CARD

E-business implementation depends on the involvement of many people. These resources have other day-to-day responsibilities that conflict with e-business. In addition, management may remove resources for emergencies. There are also pressures to speed up the implementation. Given the diverse nature of the activities in e-business as well as these pressures, it is wise to measure your progress as you go. Measurements are proposed for both implementation and ongoing assessments. You should create these score cards as you go and employ them in reporting to management.

WHAT TO DO NEXT

It does you little good if you read something and then are provided with no direction or suggestions as to what to do to use what you have just learned and read. In these chapters, what to do next translates into specific actions that you can take without spending money. As an action item you should review your current approach to e-business. Look in the literature for tales of success and failure. You will also be gathering lessons learned. These are ongoing activities that are supportive of your success in e-business.

ORGANIZATION OF THIS BOOK

The book is structured into three parts. The first deals with developing your e-business vision, objectives, and strategy. The second addresses e-business planning. The third deals with managing implementation and expansion and growth of your e-business effort. Each chapter is organized in a parallel fashion.

- *Introduction.* This gives survey results and an overview of the chapter.
- *Purpose and Scope.* This is divided into three areas: business, technical, and political. This reflects the reality that there is often a political component to what you do in e-business.
- *End Products.* End products are also grouped into the same areas as purpose and scope.
- *Approach.* Here is where the methods appear. In general, the methods are organized into specific actions for your ease of use.
- *Startup.* Specific guidelines and examples are discussed here that pertain to a startup e-business effort.
- *Examples.* Our three example firms are discussed here.
- *Lessons Learned.* Guidelines developed from e-business implementations are included here.
- *The Score Card.* This section contains a measurement technique for you to assess how you are doing.
- *What to Do Next.* These are specific actions that you can now take.

In addition to the chapters, there are several appendices that deal with the following subjects:

- *The Magic Cross Reference.* This is a quick way to find topics without having to refer to the Index.
- *The E-Business Project Template.* A list of tasks by area is given to be used as a project planning template.
- *Web Sites.* Interesting Web sites for e-business are given here.
- *Bibliography.*
- *Tables for Examples.* In each chapter a summary table for the examples contains pertinent comments about the examples. These are captured here to use for reference purposes.

THE E-BUSINESS SOLUTIONS SERIES

The E-Business Solutions series from *Academic Press* aims to provide a comprehensive library on implementation and expansion of e-business. The following books constitute the series.

- *Breakthrough Technology Project Management,* Second Edition. This provides detailed project management guidelines for implementing e-business. There are over 200 project management guidelines.
- *Dynamic E-Business Implementation Management.* This book addresses implementation management issues in e-business. Over 150 issues are covered in a variety of areas.
- *Start Right in E-Business.* This volume gives a step-by-step approach for e-business implementation and process improvement.

Additional books are planned in outsourcing, growing, and expanding e-business, and in technical implementation.

Assess Your Business and IT Goals and Activities

INTRODUCTION

In order to figure out where to go, you have to understand where you are now. Your current business and IT goals, activities, and problems have deep impacts on what you can do in e-business. E-business success is dependent on these factors:

- The business goals, because e-business must support these.
- IT infrastructure, systems, and organization, because e-business automates selected business transactions.
- Business issues, because these may affect e-business.
- IT issues that could limit what is possible for e-business.

In addition, you want to understand the culture of the organization and both the opportunities and roadblocks that cultural factors play on e-business.

At the heart of the technical side of e-business is the automation of specific business transactions. These transactions belong to individual business processes. In this chapter, you will make a selection of which processes (process group) to consider. Later, you will narrow down your focus to specific transactions.

PURPOSE AND SCOPE

BUSINESS OBJECTIVES

One business goal is to understand some of the major issues and challenges that face your organization. If e-business can help address these issues, then you are more likely to gain management support on a sustained basis. A second business objective is to understand the business processes and business departments. What are the conditions of the business processes? If you think that you can resolve problems by moving work to electronic form, you may be sadly mistaken. The transactions and processes may get worse in terms of performance, cost, and error rates. A third objective is to assess the organization and infrastructure in terms of its ability to handle the nature of the work generated by e-business transactions. For example, changes may be needed in manufacturing planning, accounting, warehousing, and shipping/receiving. If the organization is distributed and decentralized, you could face additional problems. Each location may perform its work slightly differently. This may conflict with e-business that stresses uniformity.

POLITICAL AND CULTURAL OBJECTIVES

One objective here is to understand the existing power structure of the organization and that among departments. If you were to focus e-business efforts on weaker departments, you might find that the managers of more powerful departments become resentful and jealous. They may act to undermine the implementation. Another political factor is the laws and regulations affecting e-business in your country and region. Still another political factor is what a parent company dictates to specific large divisions.

Culture plays a role in e-business. To implement e-business quickly requires that employees and managers across the organization work together to carry out both short-term changes leading to e-business as well as e-business itself. Cultural factors may inhibit what can be done in e-business in terms of customers and suppliers as well.

TECHNICAL OBJECTIVES

E-business automation will tend to integrate existing and new e-business systems because transactions must be passed on-line among them. The condition of these systems and the availability of IT technical staff to support making enhancements to support e-business are important factors in your e-business success. Another technical objective is to assess the state of the IT infrastructure to handle e-business transactions. If, for example, the current network is very old and based on communication protocols that are not compatible with that of e-business, this will impact performance—perhaps severely. This may require large-scale investment in modernizing the IT hardware, network, and software.

SCOPE

This chapter addresses the following areas:

- Business goals and strategies
- General condition of business processes
- Structure of the business organization
- Products and services provided
- Customer and supplier relationships and characteristics
- Business infrastructure, offices, etc.
- IT strategic goals and strategies
- Current IT architecture
- Current systems
- IT staffing and resource management

END PRODUCTS

The overall goal is to select which processes you want to pursue for e-business. You will set the direction for e-business based on what is realistically possible in terms of the business and IT. More specifically, you will obtain an understanding of the following factors:

- Business goals and how they might be related to e-business.
- Business issues and how e-business might help.
- Condition and issues with business processes that impact e-business.
- Organization and culture factors—the understanding of which can make your e-business implementation easier.
- Customer and supplier relationships and constraints on e-business.
- The fit of IT goals and plans with e-business.
- The state of the IT systems and infrastructure and its impact on e-business.
- IT staffing and resource management.

APPROACH

In many books you might expect to see general text and discussion. However, one can question whether this is really usable or useful. Instead, from experience your work can be more effective if it is in the form of tables. These analysis tables provide the basis for your development of e-business goals and strategies.

The approach begins with defining elements for the tables. After this, you will create tables from these elements in Actions 1–7. How to collect the information for the tables is discussed. Not all combinations of elements are required for the tables. Your goal is to generate potential groups of processes (Action 8) and then make a selection (Action 9). You are going to be use the tables to both generate and evaluate potential processes for e-business.

ACTION 1: IDENTIFY AND ANALYZE BUSINESS GOALS

There are three elements in this Action.

• *Business goals.* These are the stated goals of management for the organization.
• *Business issues.* Management usually identifies the challenges that they face in performing and expanding the business.
• *Dimensions.* These are the dimensions used to assess the business goals and issues. The following dimensions will be used:
— Stakeholders (private companies) or the public (government agencies)
— Management
— Employees
— Customers
— Suppliers
— Organization (representing business departments)

Rather than resorting to interviews to collect data and create lists, a faster approach is to review annual reports, statements, press releases, and analysis by stock advisors. You can find a great deal of information on the Web about most companies and governmental agencies. After coming up with a first version, you can pass the tables around for review and correction. This is shorter in time because people are often better at reacting to information than generating it from scratch.

These are the relevant tables to produce:

• *Business goals versus business issues.* Business goals are listed as rows and the business issues are columns. The entry is a measure of the impact of the issue on the business goal. You might want to use a simple high, medium, or low method. The purpose of this table is to identify which business issues are important. Later, you will hope that the business processes that you select will address some of these issues and so support the business goals, for it is difficult to relate directly something tangible, such as business processes, to something fuzzy, such as business goals.
• *Business issues versus dimensions.* The entry is this table is the effect of the business issue on the specific entity. This can be either text or your estimate of high, medium, or low. This table shows you how the issues impact customers,

suppliers, and employees. It is another way to determine which issues are important.

- *Business goals versus dimensions.* Here the entry is in text form. It explains how the business goal applies to the stakeholders, customers, employees, etc. As a validation of what you have done, you can put the first two tables together (the equivalent of multiplying two matrices or tables) and check that with the text.

So what do these tables reveal? They begin to bring the fuzzy business goals down to earth to the entities and issues. Before going further, we should add a cautionary note. You will find that there are gaps and holes in the tables because you are unable to find the information. Don't be hard on yourself. It may be due to the fact that the individuals who developed the goals and other items did not follow a systematic approach. Building tables here and throughout the book is very useful because of their support for collaboration, understanding, and use in presentations and marketing of the results of the work in e-business transformation.

For Walters Catalog there are two cases. Walters 1 was their first attempt at doing e-business. It was a miserable failure due to many factors. Walters 2 was their second attempt and was more successful. In the tables of examples keep this in mind as you read Walters 1 and 2 entries. No tables were prepared nor were analyses performed in their first attempt. In Walters 2 the business goals were shown to be incomplete, as revealed in a partial table of business goals versus dimensions. This led to a refinement of the business goals. E-business implementation in fact had to fix many other errors as well. There were many business issues, so the table of business goals versus business issues became unwieldy. The list of business issues had to be cut down to only critical ones.

ACTION 2: REVIEW BUSINESS PROCESSES

In this action you will create a list of business processes. To help you get started, an initial list has been provided in Figure 2.1. Your objective in this action is to generate a reasonable list of processes that will be the potential candidates for e-business. Keep in mind that you should include not only processes for customers and suppliers, but also for employees.

Now you are prepared to create some analysis tables:

- *Business processes versus business issues.* The entry is the impact of the business issue on the business process. This is important to your e-business analysis because you want to understand some of the problems that the processes face. If you pick a process for e-business and it has many insurmountable business issues, then your e-business effort may be dying before you really get started.

Note that the list below is only a sample list of processes to get you started.

- Marketing
  Customer profiling
  Marketing planning
  Web planning
  Coordination of regular business and e-business promotions
  Internet promotions
  Sales promotions
  Relations with selected vendors in marketing channels
  Promotion programs for repeat customers
- Sales
  Sales prospecting
  Contacts and followup
  Sales commissions
- Product and Service Setup for the Web
  Web design
  Item design
  Item setup
  Item verification and validation
  System setup of items
- Manufacturing
  Manufacturing planning
  Manufacturing
  Sourcing from vendors
- Distribution and Warehousing
  Warehousing operations
  Inventory policies
  Inventory control
  Warehousing layout
  Shipping
- Order Entry
  Merchandise and services questions and inquiries
  E-mail response
  Order entry
  Order changes
  Customer credit card processing
  Purchase order processing
- Customer Service
  Customer service
  Back orders
  Returns
  Cancellations
  Refunds and credits
  Promotion point programs
  Fraud
- Information Technology
  Priorities of workload, resource allocation
  Infrastructure and architecture modernization
  Systems and network operations
  Approach for project management
  General technology issues impacting the business
- Human Resources
  How people are interviewed and screened
  Familiarization for new employees
  Training in processes
  How people learn about other departments and enter into collaboration
- Organization
  Modification to become an e-commerce organization
  Organization interfaces and overlaps
- Purchasing
  Identification of vendors
  Lining up potential vendors
  Vendor setup
  Procurement
  Bidding
  Contract negotiation
  Contract changes and extensions
- Accounting—Vendor
  Vendor payments
  Reconciliation
  Disputes
- Finance
  General ledger
  Accounting systems
  Payroll
- Management Information and Reporting
  Customer information and analysis
  Vendor information and analysis
  Product information and analysis
  Operations performance information and analysis
  Management information and analysis

Figure 2.1   Potential Business Processes for Consideration

- *Business processes versus dimensions.* This table gives you an opportunity to explain in text form how the processes are important to each of the entities at a general level. It will also help you to define process candidates for e-business in Action 8.
- *Business goals versus business processes.* The entry in the table is the extent to which the specific business process is critical to the individual business goal. This can be high, medium, or low.

Why do you need all of these? You will be developing alternative groups of business processes in Action 8 for e-business.

For Walters 1 none of this was done. There was a lack of attention to business processes. Too much attention was placed on the organization. For Walters 2 the key business processes were sales, customer service, fulfillment, accounting, and marketing.

ACTION 3: ASSESS THE ORGANIZATION AND INFRASTRUCTURE

Let's begin by identifying the elements:

- *Organization.* Here you might list critical business departments.
- *Infrastructure.* Any organization depends on its warehouses, offices, telephone system, and other facilities and infrastructure. This is a list of the major infrastructure elements relevant to e-business.

You can now create the tables using these and the elements from the previous actions.

- *Organization versus business issues.* The entry is the impact of the business issue on the business department (high, medium, or low). The table is interesting to e-business because the departments involved in the e-business may be seriously affected by the issues, then the implementation may be impacted.
- *Organization versus business processes.* An entry is the extent of involvement and ownership of a business department in a business process (high, medium, or low). E-business will deal with specific transactions that are today performed by the departments. The table tells you all of the departments that you will have to involve.
- *Infrastructure versus business issues.* The entry is the impact of the business issue on the infrastructure element (high, medium, or low). This table reveals how some elements of infrastructure may inhibit your move into e-business.
- *Infrastructure versus business processes.* The entry indicates the dependence of the business processes on the infrastructure (high, medium, or low). This table can be employed to determine what parts of the infrastructure may have to change.

While none of this was done in Walters 1, the tables were prepared for Walters 2. The table of organization versus business processes revealed excessive involvement by many departments in the same processes. There was a lack of accountability—for which the customers and vendors suffered. The infrastructure was shown to be adequate in supporting the business processes.

ACTION 4: REVIEW PRODUCTS AND SERVICES AND CUSTOMERS

E-business is based on providing products and services to consumers, giving services to employees, and obtaining goods and services from suppliers. What is possible in e-business is often constrained by the products and services that you now provide. Therefore, it is useful to consider the relationships between key products and services and the elements of the preceding actions.

After generating a list of products and services you can now prepare the following tables.

- *Products and services versus business issues.* The table entry is the impact of the business issues on the specific products and services offered by the firm. Problems can be traced to specific products or services—useful to know if they are to be offered on the Web.
- *Products and services versus business processes.* The table entry indicates which business processes support individual products and services. The table highlights which processes you might devote attention to based on the products or services to be offered on the Web.

In their first attempt at e-business, Walters Catalog realized that there were problems with specific vendors and, hence, their products. However, they did not follow up on this. The tables were developed in Walters 2 and showed that some products consumed far more cost and effort than the profits that they generated. It became clear that these products and the corresponding vendors would not be good candidates for the Web.

ACTION 5: REVIEW THE IT PLAN AND GOALS

E-business is obviously heavily dependent on IT. If IT resources are not available, then you might have to consider canceling some work to free up resources for e-business, using outsourcing or an ASP (Chapter 8), or delaying e-business implementation. Thus, it is important to examine elements of the IT strategic plan and the IT goals in order to understand how IT is aligned for e-business. The following entities are to be considered:

• *IT goals and objectives.* These are typically found in the IT strategic plan. Examples are given in Figure 2.2.

• *IT issues.* These are issues and opportunities faced by IT. Some examples appear in Figure 2.3.

• *IT key projects.* At any given point in time IT has several major projects going on. Examples are given in Figure 2.4. The word "key" is used so that you don't consider maintenance.

The lists for these can be gathered from current work in IT and from the IT strategic plan. The first set of tables concerns just the IT elements listed above. These tables help you understand what is happening in IT and IT's ability to support e-business implementation.

• *IT goals versus IT issues.* The entry is the extent to which the issue or opportunity restricts or impacts a goal (high, medium, or low). This table shows the effect of problems as well as potential.

• *IT key projects versus IT issues.* The entry is whether or not a specific issue or opportunity is being addressed by a key project (high, medium, or low). The table indicates if some of the key projects are targeting major IT issues and so, therefore, might have to be continued—even if this impacts e-business.

• *IT goals versus IT key projects.* The entry is the rating (high, medium, or low) of the extent to which the IT goal is supported by a project. This table helps to validate what you have created. You are seeing if the actual work of the projects supports the IT goals.

You can perform some analysis here before going further. If there are significant issues that are not being addressed by the projects, then future projects to

---

Specific areas of objectives for IT are given as examples. You should consider using these areas when you define your objectives for IT to ensure completeness of coverage.

• Business Processes
  Improve key business processes through automation
• Architecture and Technology
  Provide for stable, flexible, and responsive IT architecture and infrastructure
  Implement proven technologies that improve the IT architecture and support business objectives
• Systems
  Operate and support application systems for effectiveness
  Adopt new systems where there is a compelling business need
• Resource Management
  Effectively manage IT human resources across regular work, projects, and e-business
  Manage vendors and consultants to ensure effective use and knowledge transfer
  Support a collaborative environment for work
  Support projects that have a clear business need and management support

Figure 2.2 Examples of IT Objectives

- Infrastructure and architecture
  - — Some components do not integrate well, creating interface problems
  - — There are missing components
  - — The current architecture does not easily support e-business transactions
  - — The current network lacks sufficient security
- Systems
  - — Some of the systems in use are legacy systems and are old and difficult to change and maintain
  - — Vendor software does not easily support e-business
- Human resources
  - — It is difficult to retain technically good IT staff
  - — Some of the current IT staff do not want to learn new technology and methods
  - — It is difficult to hire experienced IT employees who have e-business experience
  - — The IT staffing levels are inadequate to handle current work and e-business
  - — The staff who would support e-business are required for other work of high priority
- Business units and management
  - — IT is reactive to requests from specific business units
  - — Management wants to do e-business, but lacks an understanding of e-business
  - — Business units do not get along with each other
  - — Many business units have invented shadow systems that get in the way of e-business
- Methods and tools
  - — There are missing tools that are needed
  - — There are gaps in the methods and tools currently in use
  - — Many of the methods and tools currently in use are not e-business oriented
- Vendors
  - — There are problems in vendor response to problems
  - — Given demands for vendor services, it is difficult to get good vendor staff

Figure 2.3   Examples of IT Issues

deal with these issues are likely on the horizon. This could rob resources from e-business.

The next analysis step creates tables that relate the IT elements here with business elements identified earlier. One could say that these tables show where the "rubber meets the road" in that they reveal how IT is aligned to the business. This is useful to understand politically because if there is a lack of alignment, business managers may be tempted to outsource e-business almost completely.

- Major enhancements to current application systems
- Maintenance work to keep application systems effective and efficient
- Upgrades to systems software in the architecture
- Major hardware upgrades
- Installation of new system and network management software systems
- Network upgrades
- Expansion of the network
- Support of secure Internet access

Figure 2.4   Examples of Key IT Projects

- *IT goals versus business processes.* The entry in the table is the extent to which attaining the IT goal supports and improves the business process (high, medium, or low). This table is important because it indicates how aligned IT is to the business processes—obviously important to e-business, which exists between the two.
- *IT issues versus business processes.* The entry is the impact (high, medium, or low) of the issue or opportunity in IT on a specific business process. If you were to select a process for e-business and later find out that there were major technical issues, then your ability to implement e-business in a timely manner would be reduced.
- *IT issues versus business issues.* This table serves to highlight which IT issues are important to the business in addition to the business processes. The entry is the extent to which the IT issue contributes to the severity of the business issue.
- *IT key projects versus business processes.* The entry is the rating (high, medium, or low) of support of a project for a process. If a process you are considering for e-business is being addressed by a major project, then e-business may have to wait until the project is completed. Examples of architecture elements are given in Figure 2.5. There is more discussion ahead in Chapter 7.
- *IT key projects versus products/services.* While this table may take some analysis time, it can show how IT supports the true end products of the company. The table value is the rating of contribution of the project to the specific product or service.

- Network links
- Network hardware (routers, hubs, gateways, etc.)
- Mainframe and minicomputers
- System software (operating systems, utilities)
- Software development tools
- Configuration management software
- Quality assurance and testing software
- Network management software
- Security systems
- Capacity planning software
- Web management tools
- Web utilities
- Software development utilities and libraries
- Database management software
- Statistics software
- E-mail software
- Groupware software
- Computer-aided design software
- Business software utilities
- PC and user hardware and software

Figure 2.5   Examples of Architecture Elements

Walters Catalog had never had an IT plan. There was just a list of projects and work to be done in a 6-month period. Without a plan, priorities were changed. Few projects were ever completed because resources were ripped off to do other work—a vicious cycle. In Walters 2 there was no time to generate an IT plan. Instead, the core e-business team worked on the tables directly and tried to define some planning elements.

ACTION 6: EVALUATE THE IT ARCHITECTURE AND SYSTEMS

Architecture will be the subject of Chapter 7 in more detail. Here there are two elements in this action:

- *IT architecture.* This is the structure of hardware, software, and network components. The architecture list includes major components.
- *IT systems.* This is a list of major systems supporting the business processes.

Tables of interest to e-business include the following:

- *IT architecture versus business issues.* The entry is the contribution of an architecture element to the business issue. It may indicate which architecture elements need work for the business.
- *IT architecture versus business processes.* This table indicates how the architecture supports the individual business processes (high, medium, or low).
- *IT architecture versus IT issues.* The entry is the extent of impact of an issue on an architecture element (high, medium, or low). This table reveals how the architecture elements may have problems that may impact e-business.
- *IT architecture versus key IT projects.* An entry is whether an IT project is addressing or improving an element of the architecture. This can indicate that your timing for e-business is affected if work on a critical element in the architecture is under work.
- *IT systems versus key IT projects.* Like the previous table, you can use this table to identify systems work. If a system is being worked on, then this could delay having this system involved in e-business.
- *IT systems versus business processes.* Here an entry indicates which systems support which processes (high, medium, or low). This table reveals which systems are critical to specific processes.

In Walters 1 the company decided to develop an intranet/extranet system to replace the current client-server ordering and customer service system. The development vendor and the management at Walters had a falling out. As a result there were now two systems. The intranet/extranet system could be employed only by customers. The client-server system had more features and so was used by internal staff. This was a continuing flaw in the IT architecture.

ACTION 7: ASSESS IT STAFFING AND RESOURCE ALLOCATION

Rather than tables, you will analyze the current IT staffing to determine the skills of the IT staff. The end product is to identify both strengths and weaknesses that are relevant to e-business. If there are many shortcomings, then you may be forced to outsource major activities in e-business implementation.

Resource allocation is the method of the IT organization for assigning IT staff to projects and normal work. If there is an organized and formal approach, then getting IT resources for e-business will have to adhere to these rules. If there is no formal approach, then the problem is how resources will be diverted from their other work to e-business. It is important to note that management can push or demand that e-business be implemented, but ongoing support and maintenance of critical system may practically prevent much work.

At Walters Catalog the IT group was too small. There was also high turnover. About 40% of the IT staff were contract programmers. They worked in isolation. There was a lack of quality assurance and testing. Things improved somewhat for Walters 2.

ACTION 8: DEVELOP ALTERNATIVES FOR E-BUSINESS

In this action you seek to identify candidate process groups based on different triggers or approaches. Here are some questions that you can address—leading to process groups:

- Which processes are important to customers?
- Which processes are important to suppliers?
- Which processes are important to employees?
- Which processes are important to business goals? Business issues?
- Which processes are important to the organization?
- Which processes are important to IT?
- Which processes are important to products and services?

At Walters Catalog the initial shot at e-business focused on sales. This was a disaster because the customer service department could not easily cope with the Web customers. In Walters 2 the scope was expanded to include customer service, accounting, and marketing.

ACTION 9: SET DIRECTION FOR E-BUSINESS

Here you will end up selecting specific processes for e-business. The criteria for evaluation are first defined and then the evaluation proceeds. Examples of evaluation criteria are as follows. Note here that you are likely to develop three sets of processes—one each for customers, suppliers, and employees. You can then pursue a specific group in the next chapter.

- Does the process group make sense for customers?
- Does the process group make sense for suppliers?
- Does the process group make sense for employees?
- Does the process group either help resolve or prevent business issues?
- Does the process group selected support the business objectives and goals?
- Is the process group feasible in terms of business infrastructure?
- Are the organizations involved in the processes capable and have resources to support e-business?
- Are the issues involved in the IT systems inhibiting factors on the processes?
- Does the architecture support or work to negatively impact e-business?

Note that some of these are constraints on what you can do with respect to e-business. To undertake the evaluation you can prepare a table where the criteria are rows and the columns are the alternative groups. The entry is a rating (either numeric or high, medium, or low). You can also prepare a table where the rows are the processes and the columns are the alternatives. In the table you can place an "X" if the alternative contains the specific process. This table shows the commonality among the alternatives.

There are a number of benefits and uses of these tables. First, they help in the analysis. Second, they provide the basis for presentation to business managers and employees to explain the direction of e-business.

STARTUP

Refer to Figure 2.6 for comments on the example companies.

INDO FURNITURE

This example arose out of a random visit to a furniture store in Southeast Asia. The storeowner and his family produced beds, chests, and other furniture. It was determined that the beds and chests were good candidates for products using the Web. The owner and his wife (who controlled the money) were interested, but expressed a number of concerns, including these issues:

- They did not know anything about technology or the Web. They only had a thermal paper fax machine for technology and a standard telephone.

- Infrastructure in the area was poor, so that doing any further automation was infeasible.
- They could spend a lot of time learning or being involved in e-business.
- They did not want to risk any great sum of money.

These constraints were daunting, but could still be handled. The key things that you should keep in mind are as follows:

- *Quality at a reasonable price.* They manufactured quality products for very reasonable prices.
- *Money.* The currency exchange rate was favorable.
- *Safety.* The products could safely be shipped overseas.
- *Simplicity.* The information and support for selling and servicing these were absolutely minimal.
- *Automation.* No additional automation was essential in the manufacturing facility. Automation would have to be used overseas.
- *Scalability.* They could scale up the manufacturing to a limited extent by hiring other relatives and friends.
- *E-business dreams.* There were no lofty e-business dreams and goals that could never be realized.

The basic business objectives and other factors are highlighted in Figure 2.6. It became very clear that they would need the following things to do e-business:

- Order-processing center and facilities that could transship to customers.
- Customer service center that could address customer relations.
- Shipping and trading support in moving containers of furniture to the order-processing facility.
- Overall management and coordination of e-business.

Thus, the key factors lay not in Southeast Asia, but elsewhere around the world. Setting this up was a real adventure.

DIAMOND ENGINEERING DATA

Through their experience in engineering, Chris and especially Mike had established many industry and personal contacts. Their past work experience had given them many lessons learned from engineering projects related to design, construction, manufacturing, and fabrication. Their business goals were to get at the knowledge base and how it could be employed by engineers in their everyday work. They also realized that they had to develop software wizards as well as new business processes for accounting, credit cards, knowledge updating, and customer information and service. Neither one of them had substantial IT knowledge.

			Company			
Subject	**Indo Furniture**	**Diamond Engineering**	**Asean Construction**	**Walters Catalog-1**	**Walters Catalog-2**	**Rogers County**
Business goals	Stability, low risk; low cost; minimal technology	Need to define precise benefits and use of knowledge base; establish sustainable business	Maintain relations with government; maintain competitive position; increase collaboration across diverse business units	Business goals unclear; goals are too general	Focus on integration of e-business and regular business	County government must be efficient and run with limited staff; use technology as much as possible
Business processes	Manufacturing, shipping	Knowledge base, wizards, payments, customer database	Many different processes—some cross business units	Focus on sales	Focus on customer service as well as sales	Focus on customer service delivery and operations
Organization/infrastructure	Family business, thermal paper fax	Nothing	Major data center serving business units; dispersed business infrastructure	Centralized business	Centralized business	Distributed across the county
Products and services	Western-oriented products	Knowledge base	Public work; housing; toll roads	Everything	Focus on limited products on the Web	Scheduling and operations

IT plan	All external	Nothing	Overall plan to upgrade architecture for e-business	Lack of plan	Plan that emphasizes fixing problems	Existing plan is not intranet oriented
IT architecture	Use others as remote user	None	Modern, but needs Web components	Many systems issues; frequent breaks	Limited modernization was done	Basically in place to support intranets
IT staffing	No one	One person knows IT	Regular IT group	Very limited	Very limited	Management is traditional IT; staff lack Web skills
Direction— e-business	Get basic logistics, order processing, and customer service in place	Focus on customer and on support for knowledge base	Need to pursue some e-business initiatives across business units as well as within	None	Service and fulfillment as well as sales	Focus on intranets that involve largest number of employees for maximum impact

Figure 2.6   Summary of Examples

EXAMPLES

ASEAN CONSTRUCTION

Asean has a number of semiautonomous business units. Upper management was concerned that each business unit was going their own way—being pushed and pulled by dynamics in their own marketplaces. Asean saw e-business as a way to get the business units to collaborate more and work together more closely. In addition, the country government was placing pressure on companies to enter into e-business.

With business units in housing construction and operation, highway and toll road construction and operation, trading, and building operation across five countries, it was clear that there must be a logical approach to e-business. To respond to business pressures, there would have to be e-business initiatives within each business unit. However, because this would only isolate each business unit from each other, there would also have to e-business across business units. The IT architecture was fairly modern, although some upgrading was needed to support e-business transactions. There was also an existing IT plan for supporting e-business, but this dealt only with what was required for e-business in IT.

ROGERS COUNTY

Rogers County has one major group in operations as well as in finance, accounting, and other smaller groups. It was clear to management that the benefits of e-business internally would be in operations. There were also some limited opportunities to use business-to-business in procurement and business-to-consumer for residents of the county. Employees in the county and the public in the county had embraced the Web and Internet.

The IT group had gone through substantial management change. A backward-oriented IT operations manager had been replaced by the manager of business planning. However, this new manager lacked IT knowledge and experience and listened too much to the old-line IT supervisors and programmers who felt most comfortable with legacy systems and the host minicomputers—not exactly the most friendly environment for e-business. So the leadership for e-business would largely have to come from operations.

LESSONS LEARNED

You can spend too much time on the actions in this chapter and never get anything going. Return to the purpose and scope of the chapter. You want to use the work here to highlight issues and obstacles to e-business. You can see from the actions that you are reviewing both the business and IT objectives as well as processes and architecture. You are not attempting to define detailed e-business objectives and strategies. That will come later. Here you are paving the way for change. This means that you must work in a collaborative manner to encourage managers and employees to see the shortcomings of what they have in order to implement e-business. You can also point out that e-business can serve as a vehicle to carry out other related long-needed changes.

THE SCORE CARD

How do you evaluate how you are doing in this action? Here are some questions for you to answer:

• *Are the table entries consistent?* You can combine tables so that comparisons can be made.

• *Are there major gaps and missing entries?* This can indicate other problems in business or IT planning.

• *Do you have a sufficiently broad spectrum of process groups?* It is better to have more alternatives. Work is very cheap here. Later, after you start spending money, you will regret any shortcomings here.

WHAT TO DO NEXT

Experience has shown that the best way to approach this is to create some of the tables that have been identified. This will get you more familiar with the method as well as providing you with a better understanding of your own organization. Here are some lists to create:

• Business processes
• Dimensions
• Business goals
• IT goals
• IT systems

For each table you will list only two or three items. Keep this number small. Otherwise, you might become too mired in the detail. After preparing these tables, follow the guidelines in Action 8 and create three alternative process groups for e-business—one each for customers, suppliers, and employees.

Develop Process and Transaction Plans

INTRODUCTION

Establishing process and transaction plans is critical to your e-business success. You can have all of the goals, visions, and strategies, but when you get down to work, you must deal with the details of transactions. There are specific problems that this chapter addresses.

Problem: How to Align Business, E-Business, and IT

As was seen in the previous chapter, it is very difficult to link business, e-business, and IT goals and strategies directly to each other. While there have been several theories on how this can be performed directly, these efforts meet with limited support. There is both a desire and a need to link business, e-business and IT, so the subject cannot be ignored.

Problem: How to Get Definitive Requirements

Separately, but related to this issue, is the subject of requirements for e-business and systems. Traditionally, requirements would be gathered through interviews and other means as to what department staff and managers wanted and needed. This is often tainted by politics. People often like the system that they have. They have invested a lot of time and effort in developing exceptions, workarounds, and shadow systems. A shadow system is one developed within a department to meet some needs that the systems provided by the IT organization did not produce. These can be spreadsheets or database management applications or they can be manual procedures. In one instance, we found over 35 such shadow systems in a large department. Shadow systems can be logging systems, calculation systems, or procedures that perform other functions.

Requirements have many shortcomings, including the following examples:

• Requirements reflect what people want to get away from in their current environment. They don't reflect often what the long-term goal is for the work and methods.
• Employees may not be aware of what options are available so their requirements tend to be incremental.
• Employees may feel threatened in terms of their jobs. If they get a new system, it may put them out of work. This is not unrealistic in eras of reengineering and downsizing.
• People often change their minds as the project proceeds. This reflects not having true requirements and direction.

To deal with potential problems, the traditional approach has been for users to sign off on requirements. The mistaken belief is that by signing off there is commitment and certainty. However, there often arise proper additional needs that have to be addressed. It's no wonder that "scope creep" and "requirements changes" appear consistently in the systems literature going back to the 1960s. Because of these factors, requirements are often incomplete, incorrect, and political.

Approach: Focus on Key Processes and Transactions

An approach that we and others have employed for years has been to consider processes and transactions as the bridge between business on the one hand and e-business and IT on the other. Here is the approach in general:

• Identify key business processes and transactions for the business and, hence, for e-business and IT.
• Assess your current transactions and business processes to determine problems and issues. These are not requirements, but instead are problems and issues and their impacts on the business.
• Develop long-term plans for business processes and transactions in terms of e-business. Where do you want the business to go? How would you like to see the work performed in the long-term? Answering these questions is done with the backdrop of what is reasonable in terms of technology and systems.

• Now compare the current and long-term transactions and processes. You can now derive the benefits of moving to something new. You will also address the question of what happens to the current processes, if anything.

• Also, through a comparison, define what is needed to get you there. These are the requirements. They include systems, infrastructure, procedures, policies, and even organization.

• Analysis can be performed to determine the impact of transforming the selected transactions into e-business on the other transactions.

IMPACT AND BENEFITS OF THE APPROACH

If we were to apply this approach to the entire set of transactions for a business process, it would take too long. By the time we finished, the situation would have changed. Yet, for e-business it is reasonable and appropriate. Why? Because in e-business you are not implementing an entire process change. Instead, you are going to be making a few selected transactions electronic. This is a natural evolution in systems and technology that continually attempts to streamline transactions. In e-business you are not going to even touch exceptions and odd transactions unless they are critical. What happens to these transactions? They are left alone. Experience in real-world e-business implementation shows that after implementation, there is substantial internal pressure in the business to deal with these. They are now much more obvious because the volume of transactions has been automated.

This approach has several benefits to management, employees, and IT. Here is a list of these from past projects:

• The problems and their impact on the business become evident. There is greater support for e-business.

• With a process and transaction plan in place, business managers and employees have a clearer idea of where they want to go.

• There tend to be fewer changes in requirements later because the plan was developed at the transaction level.

• Everyone gains a common vision of what the process and transactions should be. It is very important to note that this is a shared vision across the organization and not within IT or user departments.

• Internal politics still exist, but are in the context of the plan.

• There is less user resistance to change because the users realize the problems and limitations with the way that they currently do their work.

• Employees in business departments feel less threatened. They still have the remaining work that will not be touched by e-business.

- The impact of what is to be implemented in e-business on the remainder of the business can be determined.
- With the new, future processes and transactions defined, you pave the way for culture change.

These are definite benefits to all parties. Yet, there is one major benefit that deserves special attention. Organizations have developed in the past plans for the enterprise, departments, and IT. However, it is in the actual transactions and work that profits are made, sales are generated, and costs are controlled. You can define wonderful plans, but if they don't improve the work, you still lose! You can make the case that the process and transaction plans are the most important of all and that all other plans should be derived from the process and transaction plans.

PURPOSE AND SCOPE

BUSINESS OBJECTIVES

The business objective is to define the new e-business transactions and thereby to determine the benefits of e-business. The organization must also be assured that e-business will not tear up the revenue base of the firm. Thus, there are both positive as well as defensive objectives.

POLITICAL AND CULTURAL OBJECTIVES

The political goal is to address concerns by staff and managers who might perceive e-business as a threat to both their jobs and power positions. If you don't resolve potential resistance now at the start, experience reveals that the situation will likely grow worse. Cooperation will be less than enthusiastic—even with top management endorsement and support. You have to gain support for e-business across the organization.

E-business impacts the culture of the organization. In many cases, the current culture does not support efficiency and effectiveness. There are often cultural barriers among and within business departments. Doing the work presented in this chapter paves the way for a new culture. It, however, must be reinforced during the entire implementation.

TECHNICAL OBJECTIVES

IT has always desired and pushed for stable requirements. This desire is even more pressing for e-business. There have been many failures that can be traced back to a lack of effort early in the implementation to define requirements and gain consensus on this. Remember that you must not only identify requirements, but also gain widespread and persistent support.

SCOPE

The scope of process and transaction planning is to consider almost all business processes that may be involved in e-business. Thus, you cannot stop at sales for business-to-consumer e-business; you need to examine customer service, fulfillment, returns, accounting and other transactions. Haven't you ordered something on the Web only to find that when you had a problem or questions, you had to follow traditional manual methods? This results in dissatisfied customers and lost profits due to higher costs. This scope would be impossible to use unless you add the constraint that you will be looking for critical transactions.

END PRODUCTS

The technical end products of the work are as follows:

- Identification of key business processes.
- Determination of which transactions among these processes are critical for e-business.
- Definition of benefits to the business and employees as well as suppliers and customers.
- Establishment of requirements for both systems and business work.

If this were a standard book, then you would stop here. Unfortunately, you must also obtain the following political and cultural end products:

- Realization by business staff of the shortcomings and problems with the way that they do their work. Otherwise, they will likely resist change. Remember that the first step in addiction rehabilitation is to acknowledge that you have a problem.
- Support and commitment for e-business as manifested through involvement in the specific actions of this chapter.
- Acceptance (enthusiastic acceptance, you hope) of the new transactions for e-business and the minimum modifications to current transactions that link to the e-business work.
- Establishment of the work process collaboratively to implement e-business. As you saw in the first chapter, e-business is not an IT project. It is a joint project across many departments that goes on and on—it is a program.

APPROACH

ACTION 1: DETERMINE THE CRITICAL TRANSACTIONS FOR THE SELECTED PROCESSES

In the previous chapter, you selected a group of processes for e-business. Which transactions in these processes are important for e-business? For example, for insurance you might consider applications, address change, payments, and inquiries critical. You probably don't want to have cancellations on the Web and make it easier for business to be lost. Even this definition is too broad, because an insurance company might have many different insurance products. You should focus on one or two. Here are some basic guidelines:

• Specify a limited number of products. This is true for retailing as well as services. Putting up thousands of items on the Web site can just lead to confusion, difficult navigation of the site, and slow performance.

• Consider the most common and frequent transactions. Drop any idea of unusual and uncommon ones. There is no time.

• Take into account the characteristics of the products and services. If some items such as clothing are being considered, you might want to give them a second thought because people want to touch and try on the clothes.

How do you go about this work? Go down to where people are performing the transactions today. Find out what are the most frequent and common transactions? As you are doing this, pick up information on the problems that they encounter in performing the tasks. For Walters 1 the critical transactions were restricted to sales. Walters 2 included the following services:

• Sales
• Customer service
• Customer information and tracking
• Management information
• Marketing campaigns and promotions
• Cancellations
• Back orders
• Order tracking
• Credit card processing
• Credit card reconciliation
• Vendor relations

ACTION 2: ANALYZE THE CURRENT TRANSACTIONS AND DEFINE INTERRELATIONSHIPS, ISSUES, AND IMPACTS

Here you analyze the current transactions that were selected in terms of how they are currently performed. You can use the data collected and prepare some simple tables. Figure 3.1 can be used for analyzing a single transaction. To prepare this table, you first identify the steps in the transaction and enter these in rows. An example for sales for Walters 2 has been given to help you visualize this. In this table you proceed to identify who and what is done for each step in the transaction. This should not be new. It is playscript and is over 2500 years old. Include both manual and automated steps.

The fourth column in the table is for you to indicate issues and problems that people face in performing the step. Why collect this information at the step level? Because you will be building requirements and benefits at the detailed level and then moving up. This not only provides more supportable analysis, but also will help you win people over politically. Some guidelines for this action are as follows:

- Break up complex transactions into smaller ones.
- Have people review these as you go. Don't circulate the tables at the end. It will be too rushed and the employees may think that you are putting on too much pressure.

Transaction: Complete the Sale of Merchandise			
Step	**Who**	**What**	**Issues**
1	Customer	Identifies products for ordering	Need better product information
2	Sales	Answers questions on products	Too much training is required; supervisors are contacted frequently
3	Customer	Places order	Some confusion on shipping and discounts exists
4	Customer	Provides credit card information	
5	System	Processes order	
6	Sales	Provides customer with confirmation and shipping information	Exacting delivery dates are not accurate
7	Accounting	Reconciles the credit card transactions	Very labor intensive, manual process

Figure 3.1 Table for Assessing Current Transactions

- Take as much elapsed time as you can. Iterate the tables as much as you can. This will increase familiarity and support. Elapsed time gives people more time to think about the information and analysis.

Next, you can roll up the transactions into a summary table. An example is given in Figure 3.2 for Walters 2. The example lists the following components as columns. However, you can always add more.

- *Issues.* Here you highlight the issues.
- *Impacts of the issues on the business* (error rate, rework, poor customer service, etc.).
- *Volume.* This is the volume of transactions in a given time period. It helps validate that you are considering the major transactions.
- *Frequency.* Here you can indicate when the transactions occur and whether they bunch up.
- *Time required.* This is the response time in doing a specific transaction. An average is used often.

If you have many issues, you can move from a table to a list approach.

In addition to the summary, you want to consider how transactions interrelate with each other. The table in Figure 3.3 can be used. The transactions are listed in both rows and columns. The entry in row I and column J is the effect of I inputting

Transactions	Issues	Impact	Volume	Frequency	Time required
Provide information	Too much variation among products	Lost sales	High	High	Several minutes
Sales	Manual steps, lack of information	Lost sales	Medium–high	High	Can range up to 20 minutes
Cancellations	Fail to get reasons	Lost sales	Moderate	About 10% of sales	5 minutes
Returns	Tracking and processing refunds are problems	Customer dissatisfaction	Low	Several each hour	10 minutes or more
Back orders	Difficult to track	Lost sales	Low	Low	High

Figure 3.2 Summary Analysis of Current Transactions

Transaction/ transaction	Provide information	Sales	Cancellations	Returns	Back orders
Provide information	—	Natural lead in; more cross-sell needed	Leads to cancellations later due to bad information	Leads to returns later	No information provided on status
Sales	More information needed	—	Treatment of customer can lead to cancellation	Need more information to reduce	Too many sales and partial orders are back ordered
Cancellations	Lack of correct information	—	—	Can have cancellation and then return if shipped	Can have cancellation too late
Returns	Lack of correct information	Sales needs to handle customers better to reduce returns	Fuzzy area here sometimes	—	N/A
Back orders	Need more information	Does not know item back ordered	Back orders tend to generate more cancellations	Back orders tend to generate more returns	—

Figure 3.3   Interrelationships among Transactions

into J. The (J,I)th entry is the reverse. This table is useful because it helps identify how transactions cross departments. The entries in Figure 3.3 are for Walters 2.

ACTION 3: DEFINE THE NEW TRANSACTIONS AND BUSINESS MODEL AND HOW THEY WILL WORK IN TERMS OF E-BUSINESS

Working with the same employees as you proceed with the previous action, you will be defining new transactions as to how the situation can be improved. The automation of this new transaction will serve as the basis for e-business. Use the table in Figure 3.4 for recording your analysis. The same Walters 2 example is being used here. In the table you will enter each step. These steps may not correspond to the current ones exactly. Some may be eliminated or combined. After the "who" and "what," you enter the difference between the old and the new transaction steps along with any comments. You can also start to identify requirements in terms of procedure, policy, system, or other change needed. Benefits can also be listed. Guidelines for requirements and benefits are discussed in the Lessons Learned section later in this chapter. Next, you can roll up the analysis into the table in Figure 3.5 (for Walters 2). Here summarize the differences, requirements, and benefits. Add any comments. In terms of analysis you can now combine or jointly consider Figures 3.2 and 3.5. This helps to give people an overall picture. From this table you can create an overall summary of requirements and benefits.

Carrying out any analysis method takes more effort the first time. So you should do one sample transaction and then you can increase your speed. The benefit of the approach is that you have a vehicle for communicating with people without using the dreaded "e-." It is more common sense. This saves a great deal of time. Another useful table is that of Figure 3.6. This corresponds to Figure 3.3 and defines how the new transactions will interrelate with each other. The definition of the entry is the same as that of Figure 3.3. The situation for Walters 2 is summarized here. Note that in Figure 3.6 some entries are not changed by e-business. This is because the scope of e-business did not touch the return and back order processes. With the transactions defined, you can now generate a new business model for the company. This approach has the benefit that the business model is based on definite transactions.

ACTION 4: ANALYZE THE CROSS-IMPACT BETWEEN THE NEW TRANSACTIONS AND REMAINING WORK

One of the reasons e-business implementation is complex is that you will be leaving behind other transactions that you did not consider. To be successful, you

New Transaction: Complete the Sale of Merchandise

Step	Who	What	Difference	Requirements	Benefits	Comments
1	Customer	Uses Web to select products	More information is provided	More product information; good search engine	Reduced labor	Getting the product information is not trivial
2	Customer	Places order	Automated	Need to have shipping and taxation tables	Reduced labor	Substantial effort for foreign sales
3	System	Processes order	Credit card interface	On-line credit card interfaces	Reduced time	May need a new credit card vendor
4	System	Provides confirmation	Automated	Must provide this to client-server system	None	Interfaces needed

Figure 3.4 New Transaction Definition

Transaction	Differences	Requirements	Benefits	Comments
Provide information	More information	More product information/ verification	Fewer problems	May be difficult to do for a lot of items
Sales	Automated	Automation of business rules	Automation	—
Cancellations	Automated	Need order access and status	Automation	Don't want to make this too easy
Returns	Unchanged	—	—	Problems more visible
Back orders	Unchanged	—	—	Problems more visible

Figure 3.5 New Transaction Summary

have to perform some analysis to determine if there are any required changes needed. However, you are not going to replace these transactions. Here again is yet another table. Figure 3.7 lists the e-business transactions as rows and the other transactions as columns for Walters 2. The entry is the cross impact of the two transactions for the specific row and column. Impacts can go both ways. For example, if you were to put order status on the Web as a transaction, then customer service support would have to answer questions if the person did not like the order date. Similarly, the system used in customer service should have the same date as that on the Web. Note also that you may have the same transaction performed in the automated and semiautomated manner.

Transaction/ transaction	Provide information	Sales	Cancellations	Returns	Back orders
Provide information	—	Automated			
Sales	Better information	—			
Cancellations	Reduced		—		
Returns	Reduced			—	Still problem
Back orders	Still problem	Still problem	Still problem	Still problem	—

Figure 3.6 Interrelationships among New Transactions

Other Transactions		
E-business transactions	**Accounting**	**Marketing**
Sales	More credit card labor for checking	More marketing information provided that must be analyzed
Order status	N/A	N/A
Cancellations	Must be integrated into adjustments and credits	Need to have feedback into marketing

Figure 3.7   Relationship between E-Business and Other Transactions

ACTION 5: MAP THE BUSINESS, E-BUSINESS, AND IT GOALS THROUGH THE TRANSACTIONS AND PROCESSES

Well, you are making progress. As you proceed, you evaluate your progress with a reality check. You can take the business and IT goals of Chapter 2 along with the e-business goals and vision of the next chapter and create some additional tables. Remember that you are doing the work in these early chapters in parallel. This helps you to assess whether you have selected the right transactions. Here are some useful tables. Note that we recognize that it is impossible to quantify the entry fully. Most of the time you will be putting in comments. Tables related to e-business goals and the vision will be discussed in the next chapter.

• *Current transactions selected versus business goals* (Figure 3.8). The entry is the impact of the issue on the business goal. This table shows the need for improvement. The entries are for Walters 2. There are three business goals here for Walters—revenue, profitability, and service.
• *Future transactions versus business goals* (Figure 3.9). The entry is the benefit of the transaction to support the business goal. This table should be similar to the first one. If there are major differences, then they should be analyzed.

What do these tables do to help your e-business effort? They provide information to management to show that the project is on the right path. For the employees, they show how the vision and objectives for e-business are related to their work. For IT, requirements are reinforced.

ACTION 6: IDENTIFY QUICK HIT OPPORTUNITIES

You have worked hard to create a picture of where you are now and where you want to go. Unfortunately, in e-business, you cannot go there in one step. This is

Current transactions	Business Goals		
	Increased sales	**Increased profitability**	**Improved customer service**
Product information	Lost sales through incomplete and bad data	More labor effort due to bad data	Dissatisfied customers
Sales	Labor intensive; dropped calls	High cost of sales	Dissatisfied customers
Cancellations	Reduced sales	Lower profits	Dissatisfied customers
Returns	Reduced sales	Lower profits	Dissatisfied customers
Back orders	Cancelled orders	Lower profits	Dissatisfied customers

Figure 3.8   Current Transactions versus Business Goals

a common mistake for dot com startups as well as for established major companies. Here are some examples of things that get in the way:

• There can be many transactions that work just fine now, but which do not scale up for e-business volume. These may have to be automated first.

• The organization may be decentralized. Transactions may be performed inconsistently at different locations. E-business tends to centralize activities and control. You'll need intermediate steps of consolidation first.

• Some exceptions and parts of transactions may have to be eliminated to pave the way for e-business.

The guideline here is to define intermediate steps to take to pave the way for e-business. You will come up with more Quick Hits later as you form the action teams. Note that Chapter 10 addresses this organizational approach in more detail.

In Walters 1 there were no initial Quick Hits. In Walters 2 action teams identified over 200 Quick Hits that could lead to e-business. Some of these had to be carried out, because e-business would bring in more transactions and sales, making any manual efforts in accounting and other areas very expensive and even infeasible in e-business.

New transactions	Business Goals		
	Increased sales	**Increased profitability**	**Improved customer service**
Product information	Firmer sales	Indirect	Better relationships through better information
Sales	Faster, automated sales	Lower cost of sales	Improved
Cancellations	Reduced cancellations through better data	Reduced cancellations	Improved
Returns	N/A	N/A	N/A
Back orders	N/A	N/A	N/A

Figure 3.9 Future Transactions versus Business Goals

ACTION 7: DEVELOP COSTS AND BENEFITS

You can use the data collected to generate tangible benefits and impacts. Revenue estimates would normally be generated by marketing and reviewed by finance. In terms of costs, there could be the following elements:

- Hardware upgrades and new servers and workstations.
- System software and operating systems.
- Network cabling.
- Communications hardware (firewalls, routers, hubs, and gateways).
- Software applications.
- Software customization.
- Outsourcing costs for consulting, use of an application service provider.
- Testing environment hardware and software.
- Additional staff.
- Training for existing staff.
- Software for e-business.
- Software development tools.
- Infrastructure upgrades and changes (warehouses, offices, etc.).
- Security software.

For Walters 1 there was no cost and benefit analysis. Implementation just proceeded. For Walters 2 benefits of opportunities were quantified and then verified by finance.

Action 8: Document, Present, and Market the Results of the Analysis

You should document the tables as you go. These can be presented to management after their review by the employees. You want this lower level support. The review also verifies accuracy and completeness. Presentations should be informal. When presenting the tables, it is best to bring along a business employee who can give examples, validate the table, and indicate the problems and issues and their impacts. These people are far more credible than you are. They do the work everyday.

For documentation begin with the tables. Attach exhibits in the form of examples. You can also attach additional notes. If you keep to the tables, it will be easier to use, reuse, and update tables later. Remember that e-business is a program. The tables can help you define additional changes later as well as validate that the benefits were achieved. This method has benefits later when you both document and present the results formally. People will be more familiar with the results. There will be faster acceptance. What are you shooting for in terms of action by management, supervisors, and employees? The next steps are to continue planning for e-business, but also to identify the details of Quick Hits. For the Quick Hits you will follow these steps:

- Each opportunity should be reviewed by the members of the respective action team.
- The action team members then vote on the opportunities.
- The approved opportunities go to the steering committee for review and voting.
- The approved opportunities are now documented in terms of preparing a business case.
- The business cases are prepared and voted on by the action teams.
- Additional summary analysis is performed. Beyond summary tables, you can prepare a graph of business cases in terms of ease of implementation and benefits. An example appears in Figure 3.10. Here you go after opportunities that are in the upper right quadrant of the chart.
- The business cases are presented to the steering committee.
- The approved business cases are then submitted for approval to the executive committee.
- After executive committee approval, implementation starts as a series of projects. This is in parallel to e-business.

The outline of both the opportunities and the business cases are given in Figure 3.11. Note that as a result of doing these tasks, individual opportunities may be combined, dropped, or changed. Benefits are validated. Here are some benefits of these steps:

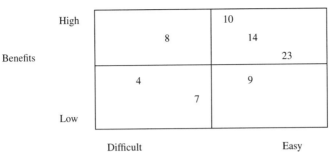

In this diagram, opportunities 10, 14, and 23 are good ones to go after. You would probably drop opportunities 4 and 7; 8 is a possibility because it has high benefits; 9 would be dropped due to limited time and because it has limited benefits.

Figure 3.10 Graph of Opportunities (Implementation versus Benefits)

- Through voting and participation employees are more committed to the effort.
- The benefits of Quick Hits can exceed the cost of e-business implementation.
- The work of the action teams is evident to management, so there is more appreciation.
- The Quick Hits provide people with support to keep the implementation going.
- The culture of change is reinforced.

- Identification number of the opportunity
- Title
- Description
- Status—tracks the status of the opportunity as it moves toward implementation
- Type—business procedure, policy, IT, etc.
- Date created
- Created by
- Impact, if not implemented—gets at the benefits in a negative way
- Benefits, if implemented
- Ease of implementation
- Implementation issues
- Actions needed for implementation
- Comments

Figure 3.11 Outline of the Quick Hit Opportunity and Business Case Writeup

STARTUP

Refer to Figure 3.12 for comments on the examples.

INDO FURNITURE

For Indo Furniture the initial business work was to establish the company for e-business and obtain funding. Firms that provided order processing and customer service had to be interviewed and reviewed to determine the ones that had compatible software. The final solution was as follows:

- Headquarters of the firm was based on a Pacific Ocean nation for taxation reasons.
- Order processing was done in the NAFTA free-trade zone in Mexico.
- Customer service was to be done in Ireland at a call center.
- The basic servers were located on the Isle of Man.
- Software development was performed in the United States and India.

As you can see, this is really an international project. The Internet and somewhat standardized software made this technically possible. Management of the "system" and processes could be done remotely. There would eventually have to be two people involved: one for direction and management and one for troubleshooting. The family in Asia was insulated from problems and the technology. Their major internal investment was to replace the thermal paper fax machine with a plain paper high-capacity fax machine! Then they could receive orders from Mexico and customer questions and problems from Ireland.

DIAMOND ENGINEERING DATA

Beyond building the business case, Chris had to create a prototype for review by investors. In addition, Mike had to start creating the knowledge base. This division of responsibility was key to a successful working team. Four specific areas had to be addressed:

- How to price the service.
- How the knowledge-based system would work using wizards.
- How to establish a list of potential customers and prospects.
- What specific services and packages were needed (accounting, credit card, etc.).

	Company					
Subject	Indo Furniture	Diamond Engineering	Asean Construction	Walters Catalog-1	Walters Catalog-2	Rogers County
Cross-impact of transactions	Ordering and customer service at different locations need to be addressed	The knowledge-base transactions need to be integrated	Transactions such as purchasing have to be made consistent across business units	Lack of coordination	Integration from ordering to customer service	New intranet systems must be useful across operations
Mapping goals into processes	Ordering, payments, shipping, returns are key	Knowledge-base transactions are of greatest importance	Purchasing across business units; b-c within units	Not done	Ordering, customer service, accounting, marketing	Sharing knowledge, forms automation
Quick Hits	Set up company; arrange for ordering and service	Set up company; build knowledge base	Streamline purchasing; centralize purchasing for many items	Not done	Pursue the key opportunities	Forms automation
Costs and benefits	Obvious	Obvious	Collaboration; some reduced costs in labor	Not done	Increased sales; reduced cost of sales	Reduced labor; improved productivity
Presentation	Business plan to get limited funding	Business plan to get limited funding	Collaboration among business unit managers	Not done	Get support at the lower levels	Get support within operations

Figure 3.12 Summary of Examples

EXAMPLES

ASEAN CONSTRUCTION

Asean had to form a number of teams. One group considered purchasing across all of the business units. This group had to identify the types of products and services that were common to all of the business units. In addition, the team had to identify a number of Quick Hits that could be implemented to prepare for e-business. A list of vendors used along with their terms and contracts was also generated.

A second group of teams focused within each business unit on e-business opportunities. Primarily this focus was on either business-to-government e-business or business-to-consumer e-business. For toll road operations, the focus was on business-to-consumer to sell electronic tags, for example. The costs of implementation were basically known from what IT had done in e-business planning. The benefits of collaboration were immediately felt as managers sought better contract terms with different vendors. The presentation of the work was directed not at management, but at employees. The idea was to involve employees in the planning and implementation of e-business. In the engineering area, one thrust of e-business was to establish a lessons-learned database based on past engineering projects. This, obviously, had to involve all of the engineers.

ROGERS COUNTY

Rogers County had two points of focus. The first was internal within operations. Here the attention was based on automating forms for employees and providing guidelines and lessons learned for employees. The second was to provide the public with more information and specific checklists for people in dealing with the county. The costs were based mainly on IT and on training for employees. The benefits were in releasing employees from routine clerical work to do more productive analysis and customer service work.

LESSONS LEARNED

Here are some lessons learned in specific areas:

• *Requirements.* In e-business, requirements go beyond system requirements. They include the following factors:
— Procedure changes required
— Policy modifications

— Facility changes
— Infrastructure
— Changes to current systems
— Requirements for new systems
— Staffing and training changes

Let's give an example. Suppose that you have two groups that handle different customer service calls based on the type of transaction. Suppose also that they both use the same client-server system. For e-business, all of the employees will have to be trained in the use of Web browsers and other software. Because routine parts of jobs will disappear, job descriptions will need to be updated. You may wish to standardize customer service and have only one call center—facilities and infrastructure work. The PCs that the employees use may have to be upgraded and new operating systems installed to support access to the Web and the client-server system simultaneously. Thus, a seemingly simple start leads you to many requirements.

• *Benefits.* The focus has been on tangible benefits. Now marketing and other groups can make projections for revenue. Here attention will be directed toward other benefits. Here are some:

— Less clerical work due to customers, employees, or suppliers doing transactions on-line. For people who do this full-time, they can be reallocated. For individuals who do this part-time, they have more time to spend on other transactions.
— Faster transaction time. This leads to reduced labor and effort in doing the transactions.
— Reduced errors. This translates into savings in rework and fixing errors.
— Providing the customer or supplier with more information. This can result in more sales, but also in reduced time to handle transactions.

• *New business processes.* When you embark on e-business, you will frequently have to design new transactions and processes. Let's consider some examples. For Asean Construction, this meant that they had to allow for taking credit card transactions. They had never done this before. In addition to establishing automated interfaces for verification and processing, processes have to set up for dealing with disputes and for reconciliation of the credit card transactions and the bank deposits from the bank. In other cases, you will be collecting more information about customers—information that you did not have before. Staff members have to be assigned and trained to perform analysis. A reporting process is needed along with structured feedback to marketing. In business-to-business you find that departments can be put directly in touch with vendors without going through purchasing after contracts are negotiated. Procedures and policies are necessary to ensure that there are proper controls. Otherwise, the company is exposed to potential vendor problems.

THE SCORE CARD

In this chapter the process plans were developed. This assists in measuring where the processes and transactions are today and sets the groundwork for future measurements after the Quick Hits have been implemented and after e-business is in live operation. Here are some measurements for your score card:

- Number of people involved in the process and work. This is often where the costs lie.
- Turnover of departmental staff. In situations where the work is tedious, there can be high turnover.
- Number of full-time equivalent staff involved in lower level work that will be automated. This is difficult to estimate, but useful. You can sample transactions and then extrapolate.
- Number of errors made. Here you may resort to sampling as well.
- Rework time. This is the time that it takes to fix errors.
- Search and locate time. This is the time it takes to find out the status of a particular transaction. In e-business this is automated so that tracking is much easier.
- Facilities overhead. E-business may reduce facility requirements.
- Volume and severity of customer, supplier, and employee complaints.
- IT staff support required.
- Total cost of the process.
- Total revenue and revenue by type.

What you would do is to gather this information as you are analyzing the current transactions. You perform similar analysis later as well. Keep this list handy!

WHAT TO DO NEXT

In order to prepare yourself, one way is to select one transaction with which you are familiar and follow through the actions that have been presented. This will give you a feel for what it will be like on a larger scale. It will also show you the importance of spending the time up front to identify a select few number of transactions.

Define Your E-Business Vision and Objectives

INTRODUCTION

At this point you have examined the business goals and issues. In the last chapter you developed process plans for how the business processes can go toward e-business. Repeated mention has been given to the need for a parallel effort. In the ideal world you would define your e-business vision and objectives prior to analyzing processes. However, in the real world you seek to pursue a parallel approach. In addition, the information that you collect from the work in the previous chapter is very useful in defining the vision and goals.

What is an e-business vision? A vision is a statement that an organization makes about where it wants to end up with respect to e-business. The vision should address the needs of various constituents. Anyone not mentioned may be assumed to be left out. The vision describes the environment after you have implemented e-business successfully. E-business objectives are goals that support attaining the vision of e-business. For example, suppose the vision includes a phrase for "flexible business processes to adapt to changing needs." Then a reasonable e-business objective is to "implement scalable systems that can be modified to address the requirements of the business." You will want to develop e-business objectives for a variety of areas and then relate these to the elements of the vision. You will also pursue linking up these two elements to the business, process, and IT elements presented earlier.

While we are doing definitions, let's consider e-business strategies. An e-business strategy is a statement of how to achieve the e-business objectives in general terms. An e-business strategy might be "to integrate e-business and regular business to obtain a more effective business process." E-business strategies are the subject of the next chapter. Moving ahead, you will be forming action teams

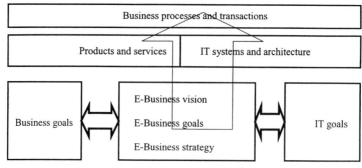

Figure 4.1   Elements of E-Business

to determine opportunities for both Quick Hits and e-business as well as defining what has to be done with respect to IT. The result of this work consists of action items (Quick Hits) and projects (business and IT) that support e-business objectives and strategies that drive toward realizing the e-business vision.

With all of these words it is useful to have a diagram. Consider Figure 4.1. This simple-minded figure is an attempt to show how e-business represents the glue along with the business processes between the business and IT. You can also see that the business, e-business, and IT all support the business processes and transactions. You may want to develop your own diagram to show this. If you produce a good diagram, please feel free to share it with the authors!

Why does all of this work? Why spend the time to develop visions and objectives, because they are not real work? Well, to some extent we agree. It may, in fact, be better to have no vision or stated objectives than to have something that causes confusion and stirs mistrust. All kidding aside, there are some real benefits to having the vision and objectives for e-business—many of these relate more to the process of developing these things, rather than to the end products.

- Having a vision provides an anchor for uniting analysis and implementation around a core theme for e-business. Without the e-business vision, people could plunge in and pursue anything ad hoc. Because there is no vision, everything and anything goes. Thus, the vision can help restrain some parts of the organization from going off of the deep end in the e-business swimming pool. The e-business vision explains what the company is transforming into.
- The e-business vision without the objectives is merely a target. There is nothing to relate the work and strategies to—hence, the need for the objectives for e-business.
- The method for developing the vision and objectives for e-business must be achieved through collaboration at all levels. Often, companies hire a consultant or public relations firm to do it. There is little internal participation. It is no won-

der that the vision and objectives are short-lived. One humorous example was a company that had paid a consultant to define the vision. This was then put up on the wall in letters that were stuck on the wall. No one paid attention. As time went by, the glue failed and the letters started to fall on the ground. The employees collected the letters and after some time had enough letters to put up their own vision. They did!

• The vision and objectives for e-business are useful externally in annual reports, presentations to stock analysts, etc. The statements can help to keep a CEO in their job if they are followed up by specific actions.

PURPOSE AND SCOPE

BUSINESS OBJECTIVES

The business objective seems so simple—just get the vision and objectives defined. Ah, don't we all wish it were so easy? The key is that the various parties (see the dimensions in Chapter 2) must buy into these. But how can they support something that is so general? That is why you will be creating tables that relate the planning, process, and IT entities defined to date. A second purpose is to provide focus for e-business across the organization. Each department should understand where e-business is going. There is a danger here. If there is a major gap in time between when the vision and goals for e-business are presented and work is actually done for e-business, departments will lose faith and begin work on their own in response to their specific business pressures. Can you really blame them for doing this?

POLITICAL AND CULTURAL OBJECTIVES

The political goal is to obtain a unified approach to e-business. The cultural goal is to begin to instill a collaborative, knowledge-sharing environment that can continue throughout e-business implementation and beyond. Thus, it is a unique opportunity that will probably only surface once. You will take advantage of this initial collaboration to establish the action teams and implement e-business. The important thing here is to instill a pattern of behavior that is self-sustaining for the most part.

TECHNICAL OBJECTIVES

When the e-business vision and objectives are formulated, it becomes very clear that e-business is not an IT project only. IT, however, has a major role to play. E-business depends on technology and the business processes being automated. The only organization that understands the technology and systems and spans the organization is IT. In short, whether you like it or not, IT is one of the few games in town. However, many IT groups have worked in a reactive mode to tactical requests from business units. The expanded role of IT is to play more of a coordination role. How do you start? By having IT be involved in the development of the vision and objectives of e-business.

SCOPE

The scope of the development of the e-business vision and objectives includes the following components:

- Knowledge of the business issues and objectives.
- Familiarity with the business processes as well as products and services delivered through the processes.
- IT goals, issues, and key projects.

The e-business vision and objectives are developed against a backdrop of the above factors.

END PRODUCTS

The stated end products are the completed and approved e-business vision and objectives. This is obvious and in some sense trivial. What is more important is your hidden agenda of end products. Here are some key milestones:

• There is greater collaboration and understanding between the business managers and IT.

• Managers and employees understand how the e-business vision and the objectives relate to their work.

• There is widespread understanding and acceptance of the e-business vision and goals. People buy into e-business transformation.

APPROACH

The actions are listed in numerical order. However, this is not to say that they are to be performed sequentially. You will want to proceed in parallel with the actions. In particular, you should develop some of the tables in Action 6 as you go. These tables help validate your definition of e-business vision and objectives and their evaluation.

ACTION 1: SET THE STAGE FOR DEVELOPING THE E-BUSINESS VISION AND OBJECTIVES

One does not just plunge in and develop a vision. There are some useful things that can be accomplished before defining alternative elements for the vision and objectives for e-business.

- Review the vision statement of the business.
- Collect information on e-business visions and objectives from other companies. Try to get their exact words.
- Consult the literature to review stories of success. What were the goals of the company involved?
- Review the literature and ads of consultants and software firms. What are they promising?

How do you get this information? On the Web. Another source can be annual reports or press statements. This has proven to be effective for initial data shopping.

What do you do with the information you have collected? For the vision make a list of the vision elements you uncovered by placing them in tables under the dimensions of the e-business vision, namely:

- Stakeholders
- Management
- Organization
- Employees
- IT
- Customers
- Suppliers

You can use these lists to generate candidates for the e-business vision in the next action.

For e-business objectives you might group the ideas that you have collected into the following performance categories:

- Revenue
- Costs
- Performance (scalability, volume, response time, etc.)
- Flexibility (including the ability to do new marketing, provide new products and services)
- Information (customer and supplier information)
- Reliability and stability
- Quality of services provided

Feel free to add or change this list. However, note that you do not want to create too many objectives because this can make the effort unmanageable.

As part of the preparation, you should develop criteria for evaluating both the e-business vision and objectives. Here are some ideas for each.

- E-business vision
  - *Clarity.* Does the vision element clearly define what the situation will be like for that audience?
  - *Consistency.* Are the elements of the e-business vision consistent with each other?
  - *Understandability.* Can a low-level employee comprehend what the vision element means?
  - *Flexibility.* Does the vision element provide for sufficient flexibility to adapt to change so that it does not have to change?
- E-business objectives
  - *Concrete.* Is each objective specific and measurable?
  - *Consistency.* Are the individual e-business objectives consistent with each other?
  - *Attainability.* Are the e-business goals really feasible in terms of resources, time, and money?
  - *Flexibility.* Are the specific e-business goals sufficiently flexible so that they don't need to be modified over time?

What if the company lacks statements about vision and objectives? Don't drop this action. Instead, develop a "strawman" of these and have people review them. The more opportunities that you can find to get people involved, the better.

ACTION 2: DEVELOP ALTERNATIVE E-BUSINESS VISIONS

You want to follow an organized approach for generating alternative e-business visions. You don't want to just write down some alternatives for each of the dimensions. Your credibility will be diminished if pursue this course. To be organized, a specific alternative should be triggered by an overall theme. Here are some examples:

- *Conservative approach.* Here you adopt a conservative idea of where you want to end up in each dimension. Figure 4.2 gives examples for this trigger.
- *Aggressive approach.* You want to implement e-business so that it radically changes your business (see Figure 4.3).
- *IT approach.* The vision for e-business is based on maximizing the IT effort and work (see Figure 4.4).
- *Business issue approach.* You want to employ e-business as a means to resolve basic business issues (see Figure 4.5).

Dimension	Approach
Stakeholders	E-business augments revenue and reduces costs
Management	Improved management decisions
Organization	More effective departments
Employees	More productive employees
IT	In-depth support for e-business
Customers	Ability to have alternative channels
Suppliers	Combination of regular and e-business

Figure 4.2 Conservative E-Business Vision Alternative

- *Short-term focus.* You just want to get e-business established in a basic mode (to get the monkey off of your back) (see Figure 4.6).
- *Product and service approach.* You want to improve and extend the range of products and services offered through e-business (see Figure 4.7).
- *Customer approach.* The entire vision is customer centered (see Figure 4.8).

These are just examples. Another source of potential vision statements is to pull from the lists obtained in the first action. While these may not be consistent, they at least have been employed by someone else. An example for Walters Catalog (Walter 2) is given in Figure 4.9. Note that for individual alternatives, there are many similarities. Also, note the fuzzy terms that are employed—consistent with a vision statement. The exact vision statement would be developed from the rows of the table that is selected.

Dimension	Approach
Stakeholders	Greater profitability through new e-business
Management	Ability to manage diversified e-business
Organization	Leverage to support new e-business opportunities
Employees	Motivated employees supporting e-business
IT	Refocus on e-business
Customers	Focus on attracting and retaining new customer segments as well as building relationships with current customers
Suppliers	Reduced cost through e-business

Figure 4.3 Aggressive E-Business Vision Alternative Stakeholders

Dimension	Approach
Stakeholders	Increased profitability through increased sales and lower cost per sale
Management	Effective resource management to support e-business
Organization	Streamlined organization using automation
Employees	Concentration on more productive tasks
IT	Coordination of e-business
Customers	Effective full services on the Web
Suppliers	Efficient automated vendor relationships

Figure 4.4   IT E-Business Vision Alternative

Dimension	Approach
Stakeholders	Improved profitability through greater effectiveness
Management	Business issues are reduced and are minor
Organization	Stable and productive organization
Employees	More efficient employees
IT	Increased automation through e-business
Customers	Improved levels of customer service
Suppliers	Enhanced relationships with key suppliers

Figure 4.5   Business Issues E-Business Vision Alternative

Dimension	Approach
Stakeholders	Greater share value; profitability
Management	Positioning to exploit e-business expansion
Organization	Continued and stable operations
Employees	Involvement in both regular and e-business
IT	Support of both e-business and regular business
Customers	Expansion of customer relationships
Suppliers	Greater efficiency in supplier relations

Figure 4.6   Short-Term Focus E-Business Vision Alternative

Dimension	Approach
Stakeholders	Increased sales and profitability
Management	Capability to manage a wider range of business
Organization	Ability to provide and support a range of products and services
Employees	Support a wider range of products and services
IT	Flexibility to handle many different types of products and services
Customers	Wider customer base
Suppliers	Supplier relationships based on economies of scale

Figure 4.7   Products and Services E-Business Vision Alternative

Dimension	Approach
Stakeholders	Greater profitability through improved customer relationships
Management	Planning and execution based on customers
Organization	Customer focus
Employees	Customer focused attitude
IT	Ability to provide for marketing, service, and other functions for customer service
Customers	Increased customer base; customer loyalty
Suppliers	Support for customer demands

Figure 4.8   Customer E-Business Vision Alternative

Dimension	Approach
Stakeholders	Long-term profitability
Management	Improved information; greater involvement
Organization	Collaborative, energetic work environment
Employees	Team focus; high morale
IT	Stability; scalability
Customers	High quality, one-on-one experience; long-term relationships
Suppliers	Wide array of goods and services

Figure 4.9   Walters Catalog E-Business Vision

ACTION 3: SETTLE ON THE VISION FOR E-BUSINESS

You now can evaluate the alternatives from Action 2. Create a new table in which the rows are the criteria for evaluation and the column headings are the alternative e-business vision triggers (see Figure 4.10). The entry is the rating of the alternative for the specific criterion. Note that this is subjective and obviously dependent on the specific company involved. In order to get the rating, you might want to have several managers vote on what they think. Another approach is to develop the table and then have them revise it in a meeting.

A collaborative method will result in drilling down to the specific elements of the vision alternative. At this level you can propose new questions to support the evaluation. These turn to the benefits if the vision element is achieved. The discussion helps to ensure that you have a tangible e-business vision. Here are some examples of the benefits:

- Contribution to revenue.
- Reduction in costs.
- Addition of new customers.
- More effective and efficient supply chain.
- Organization streamlining.
- Increase in business process effectiveness and efficiency.

When you present the selected vision, here are some guidelines:

- Present the runners-up in the competition.
- Show the list of triggers that were employed.
- Indicate how input from managers and employees impacted the evaluation.
- Reveal each part of the e-business vision for each audience before showing the entire e-business vision statement. This gives the audience a detailed understanding.

Triggers for E-Business			
Evaluation Criteria			
Concrete			
Consistency			
Attainability			
Flexibility			

Figure 4.10   Evaluation of E-Business Vision Alternatives

ACTION 4: DETERMINE ALTERNATIVE E-BUSINESS OBJECTIVES

A technique similar to that of Action 2 can be followed here. You might want to use different categories for objectives. Examples:

- Business process related
- IT related
- Policy related
- Customer related
- Supplier related
- Employee related
- Information related

Some examples of e-business objectives are given in Figure 4.11.

- Revenue
  - More items per sales
  - Increased profitability per transaction
- Costs
  - Lower cost per order
  - Reduced staffing costs in supporting processes
- Performance
  - Scalability to support higher volumes of transactions and workload
  - Efficient business processes
  - High-performance response time in working with customers and suppliers
- Flexibility
  - Ability to develop and implement new marketing programs and promotions
  - Be able to respond to customer and market demands for new products and services
  - Capability to offer new and innovative ways to deal with customers and suppliers
- Information
  - In-depth knowledge about individual customers
  - Improved supplier information to forge more effective and efficient relationships
- Reliability and stability
  - High reliability of both IT and processes
  - Capability to track all transactions for improved service
  - Stable IT environment
  - Stable staffing and human resources
- Quality of services provided
  - Improved customer information about products and services
  - Increased levels of customer support
  - More accurate information
  - Ability to provide individual services to specific customers

Figure 4.11   Examples of E-Business Objectives

Alternative E-Business Objectives			
Dimension			
Stakeholders			
Management			
Organization			
Employees			
IT			
Customers			
Suppliers			

Figure 4.12   E-Business Vision versus Alternative E-Business Objectives

ACTION 5: ESTABLISH THE E-BUSINESS OBJECTIVES

You have already generated the e-business vision. Therefore, it makes sense to use the vision as an evaluation tool. In Figure 4.12 you have a table of the e-business vision elements versus alternative e-business objectives. The table entry is the extent to which the specific alternative supports the realization of the vision element. Now turn to the evaluation criteria that you defined in Action 1. Use these as the rows of a table. The columns are again the alternatives. The table entries consist of the ratings of the alternatives according to the criteria on a scale of 1–5 (1, low; 5, high) or high, medium, or low. Use the same collaborative approach as followed in the e-business vision development. Another suggestion is that the development of the e-business goals should follow closely behind that of the e-business vision. You want to "strike while the iron is hot." The objectives of e-business for Walters Catalog (Walter 2) are given in Figure 4.13.

- Revenue—Increased revenue from the Web (xx% of total sales)
- Cost—Lower cost of operation per sale and order; reduced cost of purchased goods and services
- Performance—Scalability to support much higher volumes of sales and goods and services with excellent response time
- Flexibility—Ability to offer a much greater volume of goods and services
- Information—In-depth information about customers and suppliers and their behavior; increased information about products and services offered
- Reliability and stability—Continuous support for both e-business and regular business
- Quality of services provided—High quality customer service based on improved software, greater customer information, and increased product and service knowledge

Figure 4.13   E-Business Objectives for Walters Catalog

ACTION 6: EVALUATE WHERE YOU ARE

With the e-business vision and objectives defined it is now time to relate these to the factors covered in the previous two chapters. This action has the following benefits:

- You further validate the vision and objectives by relating them to business and IT factors.
- A complete, integrated picture is formed that supports the development of the e-business strategy.
- This is another instance where you can improve collaboration.

A series of tables will be presented. For each, the development and use of the table are discussed. How should these tables be developed? You don't want to sit down with people with a blank piece of paper. Instead, you should take a stab at each table and then review it with them—one table at a time. After you have reviewed several tables, go back and look at all of the tables that you prepared. Make adjustments for consistency. Note that most rows and columns have only a handful of entries. This makes the effort more manageable. If there is time pressure, then you might have to be more selective.

- E-business vision versus e-business goals:
How to develop the table. The rows are the elements of the vision and the columns are the e-business goals. The entry is the extent to which the objective supports the attainment of the vision element. There are two options. One is to employ a numerical or high–low rating and the other is text. The numerical rating is preferred at the start because that is more likely to generate feedback and reaction. Then in the final form the text can be supplied as footnotes.
How to use the table. This table further supports the alignment of the objectives to the vision. It indicates which objectives are the most critical. Because the vision is often vague, this table can move the attention to the e-business objectives that are more tangible. Even with all of the analysis, you still might find problems. You could have, for example, a situation where attaining all of the objectives still does not yield the vision element. You are missing an objective.
- E-business vision versus business goals:
How to develop the table. The vision elements are the rows and the business goals are the columns. E-business should obviously support the business and, hence, the business goals. The table entry is the extent to which attaining the vision element supports each goal. You have the same options as in the preceding table.
How to use the table. It is critical to demonstrate how e-business supports the business goals through the vision. If you find that a business goal is not adequately supported, then you might have to expand the vision. Another situation

occurs if there is a business goal that is not relevant to any vision element at all. What do you do then? You may want to examine the business goal with management. The reason is that e-business permeates the business processes. Consult the previous table of business goals versus business processes.

- E-business vision versus business processes:

  How to develop the table. The columns are the key business processes. The entry is the extent to which the e-business vision element is related to the business process.

  How to use the table. If there is a column with no support, then attaining the vision will not impact the process. This may be serious because it says that attaining perfection in e-business still does not impact a process. You could also encounter a vision element that affects almost all business processes. In that case, the vision element is, perhaps, too general.

- E-business vision versus business issues:

  How to develop the table. The columns are the business issues identified in Chapter 2. The entry is the extent to which the vision element takes care of the specific business issue.

  How to use the table. Of critical importance is the support of the business goals. However, this table is interesting in that you see more tangibly the benefits of e-business in the degree to which basic business issues are addressed. If there is a business issue not addressed by any vision element, then this may be an issue that goes beyond e-business. It shows the limits of e-business. If there is a vision element that resolves no business issue, then you may want to consider restating or reforming this element.

- E-business vision versus products and services:

  How to develop the table. From Chapter 2 you can enter the major products or services that the organization provides. The table entry is the extent of the contribution of the vision element to the product or service.

  How to use the table. This table is important in revealing how e-business contributes to the production, distribution, marketing, or support of the products and services. If there is a row with little contribution, then the e-business goal must relate to the enterprise overall. If there is a product or service that is untouched by any e-business goal, then you better hope that the product or service is not critical. Otherwise, you should revisit the goal and revise it.

The remainder of the tables involves the e-business goals. This is logical because the previous tables map the e-business vision to the business and to the e-business goals.

- E-business goals versus business goals:

  How to develop the table. The business goals are entered as columns. The table entry is the degree to which the specific e-business goal supports the business goal.

How to use the table. This table is significant because it reveals the alignment of e-business to the business. It should show management that e-business is critical to the business. If there is an e-business goal that does not support any business goal strongly, then you should question and change that e-business goal. If, on the other hand, there is a business goal that is not supported by any e-business goal, then you may want to revisit the scope of the e-business effort. In general, the wider the scope, the greater the benefit and impact.

- E-business goals versus business issues:

How to develop the table. Business issues are the column headings. Entries are the impacts of attaining the e-business goal on resolving the business issue.

How to use the table. This is a secondary, but interesting table. It reveals additional benefits of pursuing e-business. A row in which an e-business goal has little impact tends to indicate that the goal may be technical in nature. If there is a column in which the business issue is not seriously addressed by any goal, then that may mean that the business issue does not involve a business process.

- E-business goals versus business processes:

How to develop the table. The key business processes are the columns. The entry in the table consists of the impact of the e-business goal on the business process.

How to use the table. This table is important because it shows the benefits of e-business on the individual business processes. If there is a process that is untouched by the e-business goals, then that may mean that the scope of the e-business implementation is not very broad. If there is a goal that improves no process in a major way, then the goal probably pertains to IT support or to organization.

- E-business goals versus products and services:

How to develop the table. Products and services are the columns. Entries are the contribution that the e-business goals make to the products and services (production, marketing, support, etc.).

How to use the table. The table shows the relevance to the basic goods and services that the firm provides. In the case of e-business there may be additional services that are added later. Then you should return to this table and update it. If there is a row (e-business goal) that has little impact on the products and services, then it probably means that this goal applies to the infrastructure or organization and not directly to the products and services. If a product or service is unaffected by the e-business goals, it may not be prone to improvement through e-business.

- E-business goals versus organization units:

How to develop the table. In the column headings go the major organizations within the enterprise. The entry in the table is the degree to which the attainment e-business goal will require involvement of that unit.

How to use the table. This table will assist you in determining who should be involved in e-business implementation. If a department is heavily involved in many e-business goals, then this may serve to indicate that substantial resources may have to come from that department. If there is a row with little business unit involvement, then you want to revisit the e-business goal. Almost all e-business goals involve several departments. If there is a column (business unit) that is not related to any goal, then they may not be involved much in the implementation.

The rest of the tables relate e-business goals to elements of IT. You will want to have business managers involved in developing and reviewing these tables along with IT managers. This will give a greater appreciation for the work that lies ahead in IT to support e-business implementation.

- E-business goals versus IT goals:
  How to develop the table. The IT goals are the column headings. The entry is the degree to which attaining the IT goal will contribute to achieving the individual e-business goal.
  How to use the table. The table is central to the alignment of IT to e-business. If you find that one IT goal applies to many e-business goals, then it is clearly going to be a high priority in the IT work. If, on the other hand, an e-business goal has no strong dependence on any IT objective, then this may indicate that the e-business goal is organizational or political and not technical in nature. A third case is when you find an IT goal that does not support any e-business goal. Then the IT goal is probably internal to IT.
- E-business goals versus IT issues:
  How to develop the table. The columns are the major IT issues. The table entry is the degree to which the specific IT issue inhibits the attainment of the specific e-business goal.
  How to use the table. This table shows potential problems that you are going to face in implementing e-business with respect to IT. An IT issue impacts the systems, architecture, or resources of IT. If there is an issue that crops up frequently in the e-business goals as being important, then addressing this issue should be a central part of the IT work and e-business implementation. It can also happen that a goal is not related in a significant manner to any IT issue. This may mean that the goal can be achieved without major IT effort. Instead, business effort is required.
- E-business goals versus IT architecture:
  How to develop the table. The columns are the elements of the IT architecture. The entry is the extent to which an individual e-business goal is dependent upon that element of the architecture.
  How to use the table. It is often hard to justify architecture upgrading. The existing architecture may have provided many years of useful service and support. If you find that a number of goals depend on one architecture component, then you support the argument for modernization of this part of the IT architec-

ture. If there is an architecture component that contributes to no goal, then one has to wonder if there is something wrong with the analysis or the goal because the business processes depend on all of the enterprise architecture components.

- E-business goals versus IT systems:

How to develop the table. The column headings are the critical IT systems identified in Chapter 2. The entry is the degree to which attaining the specific e-business goal depends upon the specific system.

How to use the table. There are several cases to consider here. It is possible that a business goal will not have any dependence. This means that the objective may require new systems and technology. This is politically valuable because it will support the new e-business systems. Later, when you have identified these new systems, they can be added as columns to the table and additional entries can be made. Another situation is that you may face is to have one system be critical to many e-business goals. This may indicate the need for major work on the system, or even that replacement should be considered.

ACTION 7: MARKET THE E-BUSINESS VISION AND OBJECTIVES

During the work in the first six actions, you received input from management. You must now turn your marketing attention to the employees and their managers and supervisors. This can seem to be a daunting assignment. How do you bring general statements down to earth so that they can be understood by everyone? The key lesson learned here is to employ the tables generated in Action 6. This relates both the e-business vision and objectives to the business processes, IT, and the organization. You may want to develop some specific examples involving a department to show an even more direct link to the department work.

STARTUP

Refer to Figure 4.14 for a summary of the examples. The tables reveal the approach taken in each situation.

INDO FURNITURE

For Indo Furniture the vision of e-business was centered on the following conditions:

- An improved working environment and culture that supported having the family work together more closely.

Subject	Company					
	Indo Furniture	Diamond Engineering	Asean Construction	Walters Catalog-1	Walters Catalog-2	Rogers County
Alternative e-business visions	Revenue, culture, business alternative visions developed	Knowledge, business, and customer alternative visions developed	Developed at both the company and business unit levels	Not formally done	Comprehensive vision elements defined	Alternatives provided to many employees; voting
Settle vision	Revenue and culture vision	Provide growing and most useful knowledge	Reconcile different visions	Developed during a planning session	Many planning sessions concurrent with e-business objectives	Vision developed through consensus
Alternative e-business objectives	Extensive list generated	Developed list of e-business objectives	Developed lists for both company and business units	Not formally done	Developed for each vision alternative	Developed in a collaborative way
E-business objectives	Selected through mapping to vision	Selected by partners	Selection through voting	Not formally done; no clear e-business objectives	One set linked to vision	Developed with management and selected employees

Figure 4.14 Summary of Examples

- Satisfaction of customer requirements for delivery, cost, and quality.
- Capability to control costs so as to provide early positive cash flow from e-business.

The e-business objectives were as follows:

- Profitability by concentration on a few products and a limited overseas market.
- Cost controls for manufacturing, distribution, IT, and support.
- Ability to fill customer demands in an acceptable time period.
- Reliable service and processes.

DIAMOND ENGINEERING DATA

The e-business vision included the following elements:

- Generate profits within 1 year.
- Build the knowledge base in a cost-effective manner.
- Avoid building a large staff. Keep the organization small.
- Employ state-of-the-art technology and systems.
- Provide value added information to ensure repeat visits by customers.
- Encourage engineers to participate in supplying lessons learned.

The e-business objectives included these elements:

- Create a positive cash flow early.
- Provide high-performance software, hardware, and network systems.
- Flexibility to add new functions and features with experience.
- Gather more information for engineering work and on customers and their needs.
- Provide reliable, accurate, and usable information; support feedback from customers for the knowledge base.

EXAMPLES

ASEAN CONSTRUCTION

Asean Construction had a dual focus for their e-business efforts. On the one hand, they wanted to have a company e-business focus. On the other hand, they wanted to ensure that the individual business units had e-business visions and objectives that were consistent with the corporate vision and objectives, respectively. The e-business vision elements were:

- Align the e-business effort with the goals of the government in e-business.
- Reduce costs selectively through e-business.
- Achieve greater synergy and collaboration among employees across the company.
- Provide standardized IT systems and architecture across the company to support e-business.
- Support e-business among customers and suppliers in a collaborative manner.

Components of the e-business objectives overall were:

- Implement e-business initiatives that were consistent with government policy and directives.
- Implement e-business in such a way so as to minimize any disruption to the business.
- Leverage e-business efforts across the company.
- Implement compatible and standardized systems and technology.

ROGERS COUNTY

The operations area of Rogers County is composed of many diverse departments. Identifying specific visions and objectives for e-business for each department was infeasible. So the approach was to employ collaboration to gain consensus. The actual e-business vision and objectives are consistent with the other examples. The approach included the following processes:

- A list of vision elements was developed and presented to employees for their review. No mention of the word "vision" was made. Instead, they were given a list describing where they might want to end up with e-business in place.
- Employees then met with the core e-business team to go over the list. Valuable input was gained through feedback so that some elements were modified.
- Employees then voted in groups on specific elements of the vision.
- An overall vision statement was prepared and circulated for review.
- In order to save time, the e-business objectives were developed by the core e-business team, the steering committee, and selected employees who expressed interest in e-business.

LESSONS LEARNED

In generating ideas for both the vision and objectives of e-business seek out individuals at different levels in the organization to review what you are doing and provide input. Managers at upper levels, supervisors, and employees will all provide different perspectives. You might want to prepare the following tables:

Vision element	Management view	Supervisor view	Employee view

E-business objective	Management view	Supervisor view	Employee view

The table entries provide different meanings and interpretations to the specific vision element and objective of e-business.

THE SCORE CARD

This chapter produced the e-business vision and objectives. In order to evaluate how you did, you might answer the following questions:

- To what extent did the vision and objectives change as you worked with other people? You hope that there were significant changes—revealing that there was substantial input.
- Are there some concerns about e-business that surfaced during this work? These should be noted and addressed later in implementation work.
- Did the scope of e-business change? People often start out in considering e-business with too narrow or broad a scope. By preparing the tables in Action 6, you can adjust the scope appropriately.

WHAT TO DO NEXT

One thing to do is to use the Walters Catalog example and write down a potential vision and several e-business goals. Test your ability to generate and refine the tables. While you are doing this, attempt to combine tables so that you build up your capabilities to validate consistency.

Chapter 5

Build Your E-Business Strategy

INTRODUCTION

While the e-business vision and objectives are important, they do not tell the story of how e-business is to be implemented. Of all of the chapters so far, it can be argued that this one is the most important. The e-business strategy determines what happens from here on out. If you pick the wrong strategy, you could doom your e-business effort.

What is the e-business strategy? It is a roadmap for the implementation of e-business. The e-business strategy determines whether e-business will be part of the enterprise or a separate entity. In this chapter, you will be considering four alternative e-business strategies:

- *Overlay.* E-business is placed on top of the regular business.
- *Separation.* E-business is established as a separate entity.
- *Replacement.* E-business replaces the normal business transactions.
- *Integration.* E-business and regular business transactions are coordinated and linked.

To understand that these are the basic strategies possible in terms of positioning e-business and regular business, look at the series of figures in Figure 5.1. This rather simple-minded view shows that these are four possible combinations of relating e-business and regular business. While separation and replacement e-business strategies are clear, it is useful to discuss the differences between the overlay and integration e-business strategies. In overlay, you leave the current business processes and transactions unchanged. You attempt to implement e-business with as little disruption as possible next to the regular business processes. As problems arise in this arrangement, you have to make adjustments. The integration

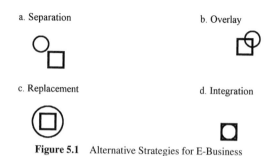

a. Separation

b. Overlay

c. Replacement

d. Integration

Figure 5.1 Alternative Strategies for E-Business

e-business strategy is a more comprehensive view—taking more time, yielding potentially greater benefits, but also entailing risk.

Another remark is appropriate here. When each of these alternative e-business strategies is discussed, you will see all of these have disadvantages. There is no perfect strategy. This is one of the reasons that while your e-business vision and goals may remain constant, the e-business strategy is changed over time based on experience. The work ahead is not only to select which of these is best, but also to determine how these alternatives relate to all of your work in the previous three chapters. This is not a one-time effort. Here are two basic lessons learned that we pull out of the text and highlight:

As you gain experience, you revisit the e-business strategies and may adopt a different strategy from time to time.
For different parts of e-business (business-to-business, business-to-consumer, and intranets with employees), you may adopt different e-business strategies.

For example, Wal-Mart started with an overlay approach by setting up a business-to-consumer Web site. After some time, they decided to move to a separation e-business strategy. Meanwhile, for business-to-business they adopted an integration e-business strategy. A major bank started out with separation and found that the Web "bank" could not attract the customers due to lack of brand identification. They then moved to an overlay e-business strategy.

There are many other cases where e-business strategy change occurred. This is a reasonable and natural thing. After all, if you keep the e-business vision and objectives steady, there has to be some element that is flexible to change due to your gaining experience in e-business. In fact, if a firm does not reconsider and reevaluate its e-business strategy, it risks failure. What if an organization fails to consider an e-business strategy? Suppose, for example, that they want to just get going in e-business. They don't have time for the development of a strategy. There is then no consensus among management. The tangible and specific actions that are undertaken for e-business implementation are not supported by an overall structure. The situation appears to some to be chaotic. Moreover, the direction of e-business is more frequently subject to changes in direction because management did not think through the e-business strategy at the start.

PURPOSE AND SCOPE

BUSINESS OBJECTIVES

The business objective is to select a specific e-business strategy for each of business-to-business, business-to-consumer, and intranets. After these strategies have been set, you will proceed with the e-business implementation planning. The e-business strategy is very important because it is the first time in your e-business effort that you consider the "*how*" instead of the "*what.*" A related business objective is to ensure that your choice of e-business strategy is validated. Why is this so important? Because after this you will start spending more money and setting a direction from which change is more complex and difficult.

POLITICAL AND CULTURAL OBJECTIVES

The political goal of this effort is to gain support for the selected e-business strategy. This is not trivial. If you pick the e-business strategy of separation, then you will be setting up an entire new business. If you select the integration strategy, then you will be getting into more detail in the regular business and making more changes there.

The cultural objective is to begin to define how to establish a business culture that is supportive of the e-business strategy. For example, if you select separation, then you are linked more to a startup company. If you pick integration, then you are concerned with achieving a high level of collaboration. For the overlay e-business strategy the detailed coordination effort is reduced, but there is more management effort because you have to monitor for any conflicts between the regular and e-business processes.

TECHNICAL OBJECTIVES

The technical objective here is to obtain a clear direction. In some cases, management wavered back and forth in terms of two e-business strategies. As a result, IT could basically do nothing for several months. The delay was costly in money, effort, and damage to the regular business. Don't you see that changing objectives has no real immediate impact on a business, but altering the strategy impacts the immediate work of people?

SCOPE

The scope of the work to define, evaluate, and select the e-business strategy extends over all of the analysis performed to date as well as the schedule and budget. Where you place emphasis in the scope is very important. Here are some examples:

- If you place a priority on time, then you probably don't want to consider the integration alternative e-business strategy.
- If you want to save money, then the separation e-business strategy is out of bounds.

The scope will be part of the trade-offs in determining which e-business strategy to pursue.

END PRODUCTS

The direct end product is the e-business strategy. The political end product is widespread acceptance of this strategy so that it is stable. The cultural end product is a start on preparing for a new business culture that is supportive of the e-business strategy. Another important end product is the analysis method and information that you amass when you conduct the evaluation and selection of the e-business strategy. You want to keep this handy when you later review the e-business strategy to see if it should be changed.

APPROACH

E-BUSINESS STRATEGY ALTERNATIVE—OVERLAY

Definition of the E-Business Strategy

In the overlay e-business strategy you are attempting to implement e-business as fast as possible. You may want to test out e-business before making a major commitment. You may be concerned about the cost of e-business. Your firm may want to dabble in e-business. Another reason to pursue this is that you are not prepared to change the current business processes. In the overlay strategy, you will implement e-business transactions side-by-side with the standard business work. There is a minimum of planning as to how e-business and the regular business will fit together.

Impacts on the Business

Let's start by considering marketing and sales. Suppose that you are implementing business-to-consumer e-business and that you are going to sell products on the Web. Marketing assigns one person to support e-business. This person looks at other Web sites as starting points to develop interesting promotions. Unfortunately, no one told customer service or other areas about what was going. The promotion hits and people call in with questions. Confusion results. Chaos is a possibility.

Take marketing out of the picture and assume that people view products on the Web site. Naturally, they have questions about colors, sizes, texture, appearance, etc. of the goods. They contact the customer service representatives. If the customer service representatives do not have Web access, they have no clue about the questions. If they have Web access, this represents an additional and, perhaps, negative impact on overall response time. Customer service standards for call answering decline.

In these two examples, e-business transactions start to intrude on the standard business work of departments—affecting service quality and performance. In an overlay approach, you would address each problem as it arose—rather than working it all out in advance. In defense of this strategy, the point may be that the business feels that this is a test and that things will be worked out more systematically later. However, it can happen that "later" comes earlier.

Impacts on IT

For IT implementing e-business is a substantial undertaking. You do not just buy a package and plug it in. There are many interfaces to establish and integration steps to perform. This is not restricted to legacy systems; it also encompasses the various software tools and packages that you acquire from multiple vendors to support e-business. There is also a new emphasis on testing and quality assurance. You can argue that this is the same effort regardless of the e-business strategy, but there are major differences.

- The overlay e-business strategy places substantial time pressure on business departments to rush the implementation. This carries over to the IT department.
- With the overlay e-business strategy there is typically a lack of overall planning. People didn't think things through. This has a major effect on IT. New requirements and situations are arising as you implement. Many of these involve systems and technology. IT is placed in a full reactive mode of operation.

Thus, to an IT department the overlay strategy has major disadvantages.

Examples

Many companies who do not consider developing an e-business strategy fall into this category by default. Most of the companies that you read about have followed this strategy. It begins with a basic Web site and then expands into e-business transactions. For companies that are not really serious about e-business, this is sufficient.

Another pattern is the evolution from the overlay e-business strategy to one of the other strategies. A company begins with doing electronic data interchange (EDI) with several suppliers. EDI is essentially a batch transfer of information. You bundle up your transactions to the selected suppliers and send them either to the suppliers or to an EDI network provider. Then you download the batch of transactions from the suppliers and process them on your systems. With e-business you move into an on-line mode with the overlay e-business strategy. As this grows, then there is increased pressure on getting the business processes straightened out.

The overlay e-business strategy was the one employed initially (Walter 1). It created many problems because there was a lack of planning and thought in the first e-business implementation, which ultimately failed. In the overlay approach you have to constantly monitor what is going on and detect any potential problems and conflicts between the regular business and e-business. These added up one at a time in marketing, finance, sales, customer service, and IT and were not addressed consistently—leading to confusion and contradiction.

Benefits

There are a number of benefits to the overlay e-business strategy.

- It gets a company going faster into e-business on a limited scale.
- Management may be pressured for speed and expediency—characteristics suited to the overlay strategy.
- The company may not be familiar with e-business or may lack resources to pursue a more aggressive e-business strategy.

Potential Problems

The overlay e-business strategy has drawbacks, including the following difficulties:

- Implementing the strategy can be disruptive to the regular business—where the company gets its revenue and provides customer service.
- As e-business grows in different departments, then there are conflicts and problems that arise individually between the regular business transactions and

e-business. Promotions, production scheduling, supplier relations, customer service, accounting, and other areas can be impacted—one at a time.

• Resolving the problems one at a time can drain management and employee time.

Comments on Implementation of the Strategy

Implementation of the overlay e-business strategy typically involves the following concerns:

• People are rushing to implement and tend to ignore potential problems. These would slow them down.
• Core e-business leaders must be very watchful for potential conflicts and problems between e-business and regular business.
• Problems that arise have to be thoroughly analyzed for ramifications.

E-BUSINESS STRATEGY ALTERNATIVE—SEPARATION

Definition of the E-Business Strategy

Under the separation e-business strategy, a company establishes an entity separate from the regular company. The entity is often likely to have a different title, individual branding, and its own staffing that can be drawn from the existing company or externally. The separation e-business strategy is the one for startup firms. Existing companies can draw from their experience and expertise as well as on some staff in supporting the core e-business transactions. This is a major problem with startup firms because they often lack experience in nontechnical and business areas.

There are degrees of separation. You can be totally separated or you can provide some degree of support from a source company to the new e-business firm. Here are some examples:

• Sharing of warehousing, fulfillment, and returns.
• Support for customer service.
• Sharing of marketing and product management.
• Sharing of IT resources, systems, and other resources.

Impacts on the Business

In some cases, separation has almost resulted in chaos to the business. Without careful planning employees may bail out of the existing firm. They may see no future for themselves in the old "brick and mortar" business. Another problem is to establish the new business and to determine both the fit and separation of the new and existing business. In the long-term the separated new company may have to establish its own infrastructure and business. It is easy to ignore this and to focus on the short-term. However, you do this at your peril. It is clear that e-business is a long-term program and not a short-term project.

Impacts on IT

The separation e-business strategy can have substantial impact on IT. Here are some of the issues:

- Priority conflicts between the new and existing company.
- Demands for rapid deployment of e-business technology to support the new business entity.
- Additional IT work to support the separation.

Examples

Banks and insurance companies have often followed this approach. The idea is that a bank can create a new bank that offers a limited number of products on the Web. Some retailers also follow the separation e-business strategy.

Benefits

One advantage of the separation strategy is that you can implement e-business without all of the baggage of the current organization and its processes. Just think of workarounds, shadow systems, and exceptions that do not have to be considered. Another benefit is that the current business can continue on its own way. In fact, suppose the new company develops its own branding separate from the existing organization. Then the existing organization could pursue e-business on its own.

Potential Problems

The basic problem here is that the separation e-business strategy may have been selected for the wrong reasons. If it was selected to protect the existing organization, then that has several potential impacts:

- The managers of the organization may think that they can avoid e-business. After all, the business may long have been profitable. E-business is inevitable, so the organization lives in a dream world.
- Changes and streamlining to the business processes do not occur. Inefficiencies continue.

- The new organization lacks the infrastructure or support organization that the existing organization takes for granted.

Comments on Implementation of the Strategy

Of all of the four e-business strategies, this is perhaps the most difficult to pull off, but on the surface it seems, paradoxically, to be the easiest. Unless you get outsiders involved who have been involved in startups, you may end up making mistakes. Why? Because the managers came from a midsize or larger company where there were so many of the business processes in place.

E-BUSINESS STRATEGY ALTERNATIVE—REPLACEMENT

Definition of the E-Business Strategy

The replacement e-business strategy is to implement e-business so that some existing transactions are made electronic. When you sit back and think about e-business, you begin to see that a long-term goal of e-business is in fact to accomplish this. The motivation for this strategy occurs when there is a sincere belief in e-business and that the partners (customers, suppliers, or employees) are ready for it. In the replacement e-business strategy the existing transactions are either eliminated or automated into e-business. This means that exceptions, workarounds, and shadow systems have to be addressed.

Impacts on the Business

There are a number of business impacts. Let's examine each area. Internally, staff members are no longer performing and supporting the mechanical part of the transaction. Instead, they may move into customer service and other activities. Management is freed up and provided with a greater volume of information. Another potential business impact is that there is new pressure on expanding e-business once its benefits have been seen.

Externally, there are also business impacts. For employees, they may perform more functions through an intranet. For customers, they may find that they must either do business electronically or go somewhere else. For suppliers, they could find the same situation.

Impacts on IT

For IT the scope of the systems effort is much more than that required for either the overlay or the integration e-business strategy. More business transactions must be automated. More requirements have to be met. Because of the dependence on e-business there must be a sturdier, more reliable, and more available IT infrastructure in place. The elapsed time for implementation will also take longer due to this expanded scope. There may be more unpleasant surprises than for other strategies because you are sometimes turning over a number of old rocks (processes) in departments that have been untouched for years.

Examples

For intranets, many companies have moved to automate payroll, benefits, and other human resource activities. In some firms, the only way you can carry out certain transactions—address changes, changes in deductions for taxes, etc.—is through an intranet. The human resource department moves away from these routine transactions into handling exceptions and special situations.

Some companies and government agencies literally almost force suppliers to do e-business with them. This is accomplished through negative incentives. Let's take an example so that you can see how it works. A supplier wins a contract valued at 100. However, the supplier does not do e-business. Rather than pay 100 to the supplier, the company will only pay 95. The difference is the cost of the manual labor to support the traditional transaction. The supplier is forced to either not do business with the organization or to accept the 95.

Benefits

The benefits of the replacement e-business strategy are that you achieve efficiencies and effectiveness that realize your e-business goals. You streamline the business processes affected. Employees can be reassigned to more productive work.

Potential Problems

Here are some potential problems with the replacement e-business strategy:

• How do you create incentives (either in a positive or negative way) for your business partners to adopt e-business?
• What if you begin to implement this strategy and find that you cannot reasonably achieve full replacement? What is your fallback position?
• What do you do with the many exceptions, workarounds, and shadow systems? Moreover, how do you prevent new ones from surfacing?

Another business issue involves flexibility. Suppose that you have succeeded in implementing the strategy. Changes arise due to business and other conditions. What do you do? How do you respond? Do you attempt to modify the software for e-business? Or, do you create new processes?

Comments on Implementation of the Strategy

Implementing the replacement e-business strategy takes longer than organizations think. You must bring the employees, customers, and/or suppliers along in the implementation. Because of their numbers and because you don't control them, this may take much longer than you think. Another remark is that pursuing this strategy is much closer to substantial reengineering and IT change. There is potentially more risk and negative impact on the business.

E-Business Strategy Alternative—Integration

Definition of the E-Business Strategy

The integration e-business strategy implements e-business by changing the appropriate internal business processes as well as implementing e-business. For example, in business-to-consumer e-business you might change the customer service department to support Web customers. Changes have to be made carefully in following this strategy as you have to think through potential changes to the existing business processes and define the new e-business transactions. In some regards, the integration e-business strategy represents the middle ground. You are not plunging into e-business, like the overlay strategy. Also, you are not pursuing the more radical e-business strategies of replacement and separation.

Impacts on the Business

The impact on the business is substantial. You will have to involve more employees in the implementation of e-business. You will have to have stronger e-business project managers. Issues that arise have to be addressed in both the traditional and e-business settings.

Impacts on IT

For IT the integration e-business strategy involves a more organized approach than the overlay strategy. That is positive. Requirements tend to be defined more carefully. There is less rework and change. On the flip side IT will likely have to make modifications to more systems and implement more interfaces among systems. For example, in customer service, the system may have to be modified to support access to the items that are offered on the Web. To achieve operational efficiency, this may require a new integrated front end for customer service representatives.

Examples

If you consider Wal-Mart you can see in their business-to-business e-business work that they have pursued the integration e-business strategy—with great success. Other firms in retailing have attempted pieces of this strategy. However, they have also received fewer benefits.

For Indo Furniture it was essential that e-business not disturb the current furniture manufacturing business. Orders and customer issues had to be handled as if they were from local customers to the extent possible. This attention to detail in planning was a critical success factor for the family business.

Benefits

The benefit of this to the business processes is that they become more carefully designed. For management, while implementation may take longer, there is more control and direction possible. Employees get to see the potential of e-business and their positive roles in e-business.

Potential Problems

The following are potential problems in the implementation e-business strategy.

- This strategy takes more effort to implement.
- Continuing efforts are necessary to coordinate between the standard business and e-business. After all, the integration must be preserved.
- The business may be under severe time pressure to implement e-business. As management sees how much effort is involved in integration, they begin to have second thoughts about the strategy.

Comments on Implementation of the Strategy

Management and the employees must be made aware of the effort that will be required to carry out e-business under this strategy. Planning is essential. Examples of potential changes should be given at the start so that there is a better understanding of what is required for implementation. It is essential to have an issues database to track and resolve issues that arise in processes, IT, policies, and the organization.

EVALUATE ALTERNATIVE E-BUSINESS STRATEGIES

You can proceed first by taking the e-business strategy alternatives and placing them in analysis tables along with the factors developed in earlier chapters. Even if you can eliminate some of the alternative strategies, this step is useful because it relates the strategy that you select to the previous work and results obtained.

Business-Related Evaluation Tables

• *E-business strategies versus e-business vision elements.* The table entry is the extent to which the e-business strategy supports the element of the e-business. For example, the separation strategy would not support a vision element of collaboration within the company because the implementation is carried out externally. The table reveals how the different strategies fulfill the e-business vision.

• *E-business strategies versus e-business objectives.* This is an important table because a strategy is a key to achieving an objective. The entry is the degree to which the strategy supports the objective.

• *E-business strategies versus business processes.* The entry is an indicator of the impact of the strategy on the business processes. This may not be as great as you think because a strategy is fuzzy and a process is very precise. You may have to get into the implementation in order to get closer to this. The table reveals which processes are most relevant to the specific strategies.

• *E-business strategies versus business issues.* Of lesser interest is whether the e-business strategy will help resolve business issues. The entry is the potential benefit in resolving the business issue.

• *E-business strategies versus organization units.* This table indicates which departments would be involved in e-business implementation if you followed a specific strategy for e-business. This is politically useful to show business departments to encourage their involvement.

• *E-business strategies versus products and services.* There may be different impacts of the alternative e-business strategies on the products and services of the company depending on which strategy is chosen. For example, in the separation strategy you would probably offer fewer or different products than with other strategies.

• *E-business strategies versus infrastructure.* This table reveals the impact of e-business strategies on the infrastructure elements. This table indicates the degree of dependence on certain infrastructure elements.

These tables can assist you in eliminating strategies as well as justifying your e-business strategy choice.

IT-Related Evaluation Tables

• *E-business strategies versus IT objectives.* In general, the e-business strategy has a significant impact on IT. It is, after all, more concrete than the more vague objectives. This table and others should probably be done in a text format

in which text appears in the table. The text entry is a summary of the impact of
the strategy on the IT objectives.

• *E-business strategies versus IT issues.* This and the later tables follow in
a way similar to that above. Here you would enter new IT issues that emerge due
to the specific e-business strategy.

• *E-business strategies versus systems.* This table reveals the impact of the
alternative strategies on the key systems. This table helps to explain the extent
of work and impact. In integration there tends to be a deeper impact than overlay.
Replacement may entail major changes. Separation could mean little impact if
the systems were not to be employed.

• *E-business strategies versus IT architecture.* This table is similar to the previous one except that the focus is on the hardware, network, and software. It indicates the need for specific architecture components.

• *E-business strategies versus IT key projects.* The entry is the extent of
impact of the strategy on a specific project. This is an important table in that
it reveals negative impacts on the key projects for IT.

Trade-offs among Alternative E-Business Strategies

What you might consider is to develop a spider chart or radar chart that includes the following eight dimensions. A general chart is shown in Figure 5.2.

• Cost.
• Risk to the business processes.
• Impact on the organization and employees.
• Impact on customers and suppliers.
• Products and services.
• Elapsed time to implement e-business.

Figure 5.2   Sample Trade-offs for the E-Business Alternative Strategies

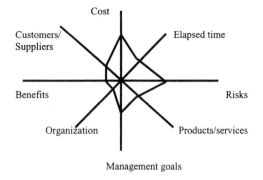

Figure 5.3   The Overlay E-Business Alternative Strategy for Walters Catalog

- Potential benefits in terms of revenue or cost savings.
- Support of long-term objectives.

Where you set a value on a specific dimension depends on your knowledge and experience. The overall purpose is to get managers involved in doing trade-offs so that they better understand the issues and benefits of each alternative. To see how this works let's return to Walters Catalog. Figures 5.3–5.6 were developed for each of the alternative e-business strategies. It is necessary to explain how the lines were generated in each figure. This was for Walters 2. The integration strategy proved to be the most beneficial. It also helped that the company had been burned with the plunge into the overlay e-business strategy.

What are the benefits of doing this work? Here are some of the ones achieved from past work:

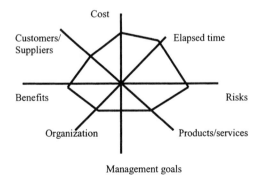

Figure 5.4   The Separation E-Business Strategy for Walters Catalog

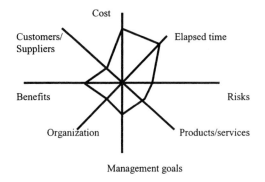

Figure 5.5   The Replacement E-Business Strategy for Walters Catalog

- You generate wider interest in the e-business implementation strategies. To many people dealing with day-to-day problems and situations, strategies often appear vague.
- The diagrams allow people to perform trade-offs in eight dimensions at one time. Of course, you can add or delete some dimensions.
- The diagrams are useful in explaining your choice of e-business strategy later.

MARKET YOUR E-BUSINESS STRATEGY

Marketing the e-business strategy begins when you start evaluating the alternative e-business strategies. This will make managers, employees, and others aware

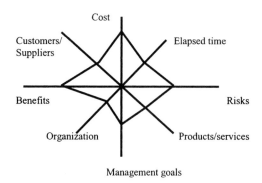

Figure 5.6   The Integration E-Business Strategy for Walters Catalog

of the seriousness and impact of the selection of the most appropriate strategy. The selection of the e-business strategy involves trade-offs that concern IT, processes, policies, organization structure, and roles, and responsibilities. As you have seen, there is no ideal strategy. Each has advantages and disadvantages.

Marketing continues past evaluation into the selection of the strategy. People must understand the implications for implementation. E-business is not just another buzzword. It is not a "walk in the park." Implementation is going to take a lot of hard, detailed work. This is a good time to get people prepared for the journey ahead.

STARTUP

Use the table in Figure 5.7 for comments on the example companies.

INDO FURNITURE

Indo settled on the integration e-business strategy by elimination. The overlay e-business strategy would be too disruptive. The regular and e-business activities had to be coordinated and integrated. The separation approach was not feasible due to the limited number of employees. It still might be a long-term strategy after e-business has been going for several years. The replacement e-business strategy was ruled out because they had to support their local market.

DIAMOND ENGINEERING DATA

For Chris and Mike the separation approach, where they started from scratch, was best. It was the only option. It is interesting to note that just thinking about the e-business strategy turned out to be a valuable addition to the business plan to get funding.

EXAMPLES

ASEAN CONSTRUCTION

The Asean organization is complex. One strategy is not suitable. In fact, there had to be individual e-business strategies for business units and corporate that then had to mesh together. The purchasing focus at the corporate level was the most appropriate. The engineering data and lessons learned could follow the overlay approach. The electronic tag e-business effort targeted on the replacement e-business strategy.

Subject	Company						
	Indo Furniture	Diamond Engineering	Asean Construction	Walters Catalog-1	Walters Catalog-2	Rogers County
Overlay strategy	Can create problems with local customers	Not appropriate	Possible in several business units	Tried this first	Rejected the second time	Possible in some areas
Separation strategy	Possible, but lack of resources	That is what a startup is in this case	Not appropriate	Never considered	Strongly considered due to the problems the first time	Not appropriate
Replacement strategy	Not really except for manufacturing	Not appropriate	Possible for parts of tollway operations	Never considered	Not appropriate	Long term possibility
Integration strategy	Capitalize on limited resources	Not appropriate	Good for corporate in purchasing	Dropped due to perceived time pressure	First time showed need for integration	Possible for b–c
Selection	Integration—easiest initially	Separation	Combination	Overlay strategy	Integration strategy	Integration for b–c; overlay for employees; eventually replacement
Impacts	Overseas orders impact business	Thinking this through helped provide focus and improve the business plan	Involve more people	Confusion during the project	More people in the business involved	Involve more people

Figure 5.7 Summary of Examples

Rogers County

As with Asean Construction, Rogers County elected to define separate e-business strategies for their internal and business-to-consumer e-business activities. The internal lessons learned, forms, and other efforts in operations adopted the overlay strategy. Because new processes were being constructed, there was limited impact. For business-to-consumer the e-business strategy was replacement for the long term to encourage the public to use the Web.

LESSONS LEARNED

Here are some lessons learned from experience:

- It is valuable to spend time here and not rush into implementation. Time allows the strategy to sink into people's minds.
- The selection of the strategy should be followed up right away with work on the implementation strategy for e-business and other activities. These are discussed in later chapters.
- Once you select an e-business strategy, you must pursue this strategy in a steadfast manner. If you show too much flexibility, some may call the strategy into question. Refer back to the e-business strategy frequently.

THE SCORE CARD

One measure of what is going on is to examine the extent to which alternative e-business strategies are seriously considered. One demonstration of this is whether the tables presented above were prepared. Another measure of the work is to assess the extent of involvement of managers and staff. This is very important because when an action is taken now, implementation is written all over it. This will require commitment of the managers and employees involved in development of the e-business strategy.

WHAT TO DO NEXT

One thing to do is to go to magazines or the Web and find articles about companies that have implemented e-business. From the articles attempt to define what their strategy for e-business was. Read through the articles to uncover benefits, surprises, and lessons learned. See how many of these can be traced back to the e-business strategy. As an exercise, make a list of the barriers that your organization might encounter in following each of the four alternative e-business strategies.

Part II

E-Business Planning

Perform Industry, Competitive, and Technology Assessments

INTRODUCTION

In this chapter you will begin to assess what is going on in e-business in your industry and with your competitors. You will not be performing in-depth benchmarking. You don't have the time. You need a method for collecting information to get started and on an ongoing basis. If e-business is going to be so much work, why spend the time doing this? If you don't, you will miss gathering and using experience from other firms. You will probably relearn what these firms went through. Another reason is to determine what your competitors are doing so that you will be better able to compete successfully.

PURPOSE AND SCOPE

BUSINESS OBJECTIVES

One business objective is to gain information on the competition as both a defensive and an offensive measure. You want to know what these firms are doing and not doing. You also want to know how they have changed in e-business and thereby gather experience from them. For the industry in general you seek to determine what methods in sales, customer service, fulfillment, supplier relations, marketing, and other areas work and fail. You may begin to identify valuable tips for designing your Web site and for deciding on which functions can be best supported through e-business.

POLITICAL AND CULTURAL OBJECTIVES

The major political and cultural objective is that you give employees an eye on the outside world. This is important because e-business is outwardly focused. Another objective is to use the data collection on the industry and competition as a tool to boost the collaboration among employees along with their awareness and knowledge of e-business. This activity helps to end isolation, the sense of uniqueness, and insularity. It also makes people want their own e-business effort to succeed.

TECHNICAL OBJECTIVES

A major technical objective is to collect sufficient information so that the requirements for e-business will be more stable. The problem that arises is that later managers will discover new and wonderful things on various Web sites and among competitors. This discovery will be followed by changes in requirements. To head this off you want to ensure that the data collection effort is broad in scope.

SCOPE

The scope of the industry and competitive assessment encompasses competitors, similar firms around the world, the industry, and information on IT systems and technology. You will be collecting information from now on. There will be no real pause after e-business implementation gets started. After implementation you must still keep up the watch because of the requirements of competition and desire to extend your e-business position.

END PRODUCTS

The major end product is detailed information about the industry, competition, and application of technology in terms of the following aspects:

- Trends in the use of technology and systems.
- Trends in the Web sites of competitors and other firms similar to yours.
- Guidelines and suggestions gathered about functions, features, and the approach of companies to e-business.

This information will provide input into the e-business requirements.

Now there are also political and social end products. First, you want employees and managers to become much more aware of what is on the Web and what other firms are doing. Second, by collecting this information, employees will begin to share information with each other. Third, you want to build up the attitude of competitiveness among employees to support your e-business implementation.

APPROACH

WHAT INFORMATION SHOULD YOU COLLECT?

If you were going to do benchmarking, then you would concentrate on economic and financial data as well as operational performance information. Here your purpose is different. The information that you gather will be employed to provide input into your e-business implementation. It will also help you to shape your e-business objectives and strategy. The information that you will collect is both objective and subjective. Objective information includes what products and services are offered, what functions are supported, the functions of the Web sites, and other characteristics. The subjective information includes what customers think about the site, your impression of whether the site is easy to use, etc. Let's now examine specific information that you should collect.

• *Competitor Web sites.* You are going to be sending employees out to view competitor Web sites. You want to have specific data collected in an organized manner. Figure 6.1 contains a form to help you. Provide this form on the network so that everyone has access to it. Also, provide an example that is completed. If you want to carry this a step further, hold a session and demonstrate your evaluation method of a site.

• *Web sites of similar firms around the world.* You are not unique. There are probably other firms around the world similar to yours that have more advanced Web sites and are doing e-business. You can use a general search engine to find these sites. Another technique is to consult industry associations for their members. Figure 6.2 provides a form of specific information that can be collected.

• *Industry information.* Here you are gathering survey information from magazines. These are typically in paper and electronic magazines that are published biweekly or monthly. Consult Appendix 3 for a list of useful Web sites. What is behind a survey? It may be the magazine itself. Or, it could be a consulting company that conducted a survey. The consulting firm may provide a summary to the magazine in the hopes of getting future business or for ordering the full survey results. Beware of this indirect marketing. Figure 6.3 contains the information that you should capture and set up in a text file or database. There are some key questions you should address when you read a survey, including these:

— What is the audience that was employed in the survey?
— If firms are surveyed that are using e-business, how long on average have they been doing it?

Date: _____   Prepared by: _____

Name of Firm: _____   Web site: _____

Time spent on site: _____

Overall impression: 1 2 3 4 5 (1-low, 5- high)

Reasons for rating: _____

_____

Functions supported: _____

Wizards/lessons learned: _____

Products/services offered: _____

Features you liked best: _____

Features you did not like: _____

Are there signs of recent updates: _____

Do they provide feedback or Frequently Asked Questions? _____

Chat room URL: _____

Selected chat room comments and concerns: _____

_____

Lessons learned from the competitor: _____

Comments: _____

_____

_____

Figure 6.1   Competitive Assessment Form for a Web Site

— Is there a standardized version of e-business? In the broadest sense, al-
   most everyone does e-business through banking.
— What is the size of the sample?
— Is there a concentration on firms of a particular size?

• *Examples of success and failure.* Magazines also have articles on successes
and failures. Not surprisingly, the ones on successes tend to be long and those on
failures tend to be short. How do these stories originate? For failures, the source
is often the writers for the magazine. Successes are more suspect. They can
come from vendors who are trying to pitch their products and services indirectly

Date: _____   Prepared by: _____

Name of Firm: _____   Web site: _____

Time spent on site: _____

Reason for selecting this site for review: _____

How the site and company relate to our firm: _____

Lessons learned:

User interface: _____

Functions: _____

Goods and services: _____

Change and evolution of site: _____

What we can learn from this site: _____

Comments: _____

_____

Figure 6.2   Information Collection from General Web Sites

through client experiences. Figure 6.4 gives a form for recording the results. You should raise the following questions when you read these articles:

— How much is the specific software product mentioned?
— Has a firm really finished implementing the software? Or, are they just now installing it?
— What results have they had? Specifically, are negative experiences mentioned?
— Are there lessons learned in the use of the technology? If not, then you might want to question whether implementation has been completed.
— What did the firm do before they implemented the software?
— Are there before-and-after measurements?

• *Examples of the application of specific technologies and systems.* There are articles that discuss a new technology or system. The article may emanate from the specific producer or vendor and may be a slightly veiled effort at marketing. Figure 6.5 gives a form for use in reviewing these articles. In reading an article, address the following questions:

Date: _____   Prepared by: _____

Magazine: _____   Web site: _____

Date of issue: _____

Title of article: _____

Purpose of survey: _____

Source of the survey: _____   Date of survey: _____

Size of the survey: _____

Survey results (Please indicate results in percentages):

Figure 6.3   Information Collection for Industry Articles

— What is the complete list of software and technologies cited in the article?
— Who is the author of the article and what previous experience have they had?
— Are there specific lessons learned cited in the article?
— What experiences are given with respect to system integration?

Date: _____   Prepared by: _____

Magazine: _____   Web site: _____

Date of issue: _____   Success or failure: _____

Business firm: _____

What they were trying to do (the project): _____

What results were achieved: _____

How long did the project last? _____

Reasons for success or failure: _____

_____

Lessons learned that we can apply to our business: _____

_____

Figure 6.4   Information Collection on Successes and Failures

Date: _____   Prepared by: _____

Magazine: _____   Web site: _____

Date of issue: _____   Author: _____

Technology products considered: _____

Business firms cited: _____

Situation that the technology addressed: _____

Benefits from the technology: _____

Lessons learned from the technology: _____

_____

_____

Figure 6.5 Information Collection for Systems and Technology Articles

It is important that you identify and collect the information in an organized way. Hopefully, many people will be participating in the data collection. You want to ensure uniformity and standardization. Otherwise, the results will be inconsistent and may not be usable later.

SOURCES OF INFORMATION

Where do you go to look for information? Here are some commercial sources of information that you would have to pay for. Using some of these services may save you considerable time. Another benefit is that you could use a service to get you started.

- Cartia.com—organizes information
- Cipher-sys.com—organizes and distributes information
- Compassware.com—distributes to sales staff
- Currentanalysis.com—news and analysis on telecom
- Delfin.com—assesses relationships between places, products, and events
- EHNC-aptex.com—reads content of customer e-mail and routes
- Knowx.com—searches public records
- Netcurrents.com—chat rooms, Web sites, bulletin boards, e-mail newsletters
- Corporateinformation.com—direct link to 350,000 profiles
- Company.sleuth.com

- Hooversonline.com
- Netmind.com
- EoMonitor—havElink.com/cat2main.htm
- Direct search—gwis2.circ.gwu.edu/~gprice/direct.htm
- Edgar-online.com
- Lexis-nexis.com
- Thomasregister.com
- Members.aol.com/kudzukat/kks__pepl.html—Kudzukat's people search

Another source of information is the Web site of a specific organization or society. Appendix 3 lists a number of these. These are free and you may be able to subscribe to get regular information. A third source of information consists of specific Web sites of firms. Try out these sites as if you were a customer. Don't be embarrassed to give a general e-mail address for additional information. In some cases, you may want to order from the site. Here are some things that you can test:

- Is the Web site easy to navigate?
- Is the Web page content accurate, complete, and consistent?
- What types of goods and services are offered on their site?
- Are there any times when the site breaks?
- What does the company do to keep the Web site active and alive?
- How do they receive company feedback?
- Do they offer wizards?
- How do they organize the information on the site?
- What is the link between the site and their brick and mortar locations?
- What incentives do they offer for frequent purchasers?
- Do they allow you to establish a customized page and content through a profile?
- If you sign up for more information, what other companies now besiege you with e-mails? This indicates if they are selling their list of contacts and customers.
- What range of functions is supported—ordering, follow-up, complaints, cancellations, amended orders, revised orders, returns, etc.?
- How do they handle payment transactions?
- What is the general appearance of the Web site?

Answering these questions gives you insight into the following data:

- How they view their Web site and its importance to the business.
- What their objectives and strategies are for e-business.
- The extent of functions provided on the site.
- The likely range of IT systems and support.
- Web design techniques employed.
- How they treat customers and follow-up with them.

You can also visit the physical stores, if they have them, to see sample prices and how they promote the Web site in the physical stores. You will want to revisit the sites at intervals of 3–4 months to see what changes have occurred in the intervening time.

Another idea that has proven valuable is to consult the chat rooms related to a site. You might find these at the site or in investment sites where people post general comments about the company. Chat rooms contain many unsubstantiated comments. Consult several chat rooms so that you can see when someone is really upset with the company. People sometimes post their experiences in dealing with the company, experiences in using the services and products of the company, and general opinions. Individuals who are really upset will continue to make contributions to the chat room.

Are there Web sites that attack the company? A number of companies have generated so much hatred and distrust in both regular business and e-business that the customers have taken the time and money to establish protest Web sites. An example is the site untied.com. This is a Web site that criticizes United Airlines. It contains not only customer complaints, but also responses to company statements. You really have to make some enemies for this to happen, given the extent of effort to set up such a site.

This is all well and good. Who has the time to do all of this information collecting? Your initial source consists of employees who use the Internet a lot. You can find these people through the action teams. Start with what they have already. Another step is to encourage more employees to surf the Web to find information. To guide these people you can provide a list of sites along with the questions that were posed above. However, we have found that an even better idea is to involve the children and relatives of employees. Children have a lot of time available. Here is an opportunity to channel it into something useful and increase their skills. Have them search the Web and chat rooms. You might consider forming a club and handing out gifts to the children. Of course, this must be done on a volunteer basis through the company. A political benefit of this action is to get the employees and their families involved in e-business.

Another source of information consists of suppliers and customers. These people are probably more aware of what is on the Web than you are. They may be doing e-business already with some of your competition. Contact them to get some hints on sites and what they like and dislike. You could also consider conducting a limited survey of your customers.

How to Organize and Use the Information

As you collect the information, you can establish and enter the data into five databases that correspond to each of the types of data that you collect. Databases are important because they give you the capability to search, sort, and summarize the information according to various criteria. Because data collection is a continuous activity, you will be using the information to respond to specific questions as well as to provide summary information. Here are some examples of questions that could be addressed by the databases:

- What is a summary of lessons learned and suggestions from the various sites?
- Overall, what are competitors doing?
- What information pertains to a specific area of e-business?
- How many of the sites use wizards?
- What new technologies have the most promise?

You will also want to generate reports and presentations from the information. A list of reports is given below along with the purpose and presentation on how to develop the reports.

- State of the competition
  — Purpose. To identify what competitors are really doing versus what they say they are doing.
  — Presentation. Indicate summary tables for specific competitors and add your own company to the table.
- Lessons learned from failure and success
  — Purpose. To apply lessons learned to your e-business.
  — Presentation. Identify specific lessons learned and how they can be used in the implementation.
- Industry profile
  — Purpose. To be able to compare industry activities with those of competitors and yourself.
  — Presentation. Develop a rating table using some of the questions posed in this chapter.
- Systems and technology product analysis
  — Purpose. To identify groups of systems and technology that offer high potential.
  — Presentation. Use charts of current and future architecture that show where the new products fit.

ORGANIZE AN ONGOING INDUSTRY INTELLIGENCE CAPABILITY

Recall that this effort is not a one-time affair. It is ongoing during and after implementation. So you will want to employ the same forms in Figures 6.1–6.5 in gathering information. Here are some guidelines for organizing the ongoing effort:

- Institute a regular reporting mechanism that provides management with an assessment of outside information every 6 months.
- Spread the work of doing the assessment across the organization.
- Develop a standardized format of presentations.
- Prepare a list of action items that can be taken based on the information presented. This step moves the intelligence past the talking and review stage.

STARTUP

Refer to Figure 6.6 for comments on the examples.

INDO FURNITURE

There were some specific targets for industry and systems surveys. The Web provided information on how other furniture firms offered their goods. Much was learned and applied to the design and development of the Web site. Mistakes were avoided. Elapsed time and cost were reduced in implementing e-business. Separately, Web sites for suppliers, regulations in various countries, and software products were scanned. Information was gleaned about specific providers of call centers and order processing. The final firms that were contracted with were found in this manner. The software products helped in the development of the Web site.

DIAMOND ENGINEERING DATA

There were two main areas of attention. One was what was offered on other sites that was involved in providing knowledge. This helped in the design and development of the Web site. Tips on marketing were also gained. The other thrust was to find sources for identifying and reaching out to various engineering groups and individual engineers. This helped not only in marketing, but also in lining up engineers who could provide knowledge on an incentive basis.

EXAMPLES

ASEAN CONSTRUCTION

Asean focused first on what other companies in other countries were doing. This was a big effort and involved many managers and employees due to the

	Company					
Subject	Indo Furniture	Diamond Engineering	Asean Construction	Walters Catalog-1	Walters Catalog-2	Rogers County
Initial industry assessment	Surveys of potential suppliers and furniture suppliers	Extensive surveys of knowledge-based services; engineering sources	Survey of similar firms in other countries	Nothing	Review of other catalog firms	Surveys of other government agencies
Ongoing industry assessment	Furniture suppliers; magazines	Ongoing search for engineering data and sources	Ongoing surveys of firms	—	Assessment of promotion and marketing	Search for new applications

Figure 6.6 Observations of Industry Assessment for Example Companies

widespread nature of the business activities of the firm. Lessons learned were gained in development of the Web site. This turned out to be ongoing. Magazines were also scanned in terms of experience and lessons learned in areas that applied to the appropriate vertical industry segments.

ROGERS COUNTY

Rogers County had its managers and employees look at sites of other government agencies to see what services they offered to their citizens. On an ongoing basis this continued, but was also expanded to search for new applications.

LESSONS LEARNED

- You are likely to receive an unbelievable number of e-mails if you subscribe to many newsletters and electronic magazines. To organize this better, find a Web site that offers free e-mail and mail folders. Send all of the e-mail to this address. Then move the messages into the folders that correspond to the areas in which you are interested. Now you can review these at your leisure and you do not disturb either your personal or business e-mail address.
- As data are collected, post the reviews on the network. Also, post a summary of what has been gathered. In that way, people will have more interest in the results.

THE SCORE CARD

Here are some questions to answer regarding your industry assessment:

- How many people are involved in doing the assessment?
- Are people picking up a sufficiently wide range of topics and information?
- Is the attitude of the employees getting more skeptical? It should, because many articles are written for success.
- What detailed tidbits of information have you gathered from chat rooms?
- Can you draw specific guidelines that would assist you in your e-business implementation?

WHAT TO DO NEXT

It is not hard to generate a list of ideas for you to pursue. One idea is to start getting and reviewing articles from e-business magazines in either paper or electronic form. When you get these, select the articles and tear them out of the magazine. Organize the articles into categories on a bookshelf. Then place the articles in the appropriate slot. Here are some examples:

- Data warehousing
- Mobile communications
- Business to consumer
- Business to business
- Intranets
- General examples of implementation
- Software development using modern methods
- Testing and quality assurance
- System integration
- Network and system security

Later, go to a topic of interest and remove about one inch's worth of articles. This will probably be equivalent to several months of articles in this area. Review these articles. This approach is useful because it concentrates your attention on a specific area. Next, write up notes in a word processing document. This forces you to read the article and not just leaf through it. These articles are often very boring, so it is a good test of your absorption if you take notes. Organize the notes into separate word processing files. Here are some examples:

- Hardware and network products
- Software products
- Surveys on e-business
- Case studies and examples of e-business implementation
- Technology relevant to e-business
- E-business concepts and methods

Chapter 7

Determine Your E-Business IT Architecture

INTRODUCTION

There are a substantial number of tasks that have to be done for your IT architecture and systems, including these activities:

- Assess your current IT systems and technology infrastructure to determine e-business readiness. What do you have and what problems are there?
- Evaluate your IT policies and procedures to determine if there are changes needed to support e-business. How do you do the work and how should it be done differently?
- Assess current IT staffing workload and skills and determine what might have to be outsourced. Who is available and what skills and support do you need?
- Review potential e-business software, hardware, and network products. What is out there that you can take advantage of?
- Develop your new e-business IT architecture and support structure. Where do you want to end up?

This chapter expands on the work you did in Chapter 2. As you can see from the list, the work involves looking into how IT assigns resources and what IT skill levels exist. These are important because you can do all that you want with hardware and the network, but if you lack the qualified staff and their time, you are in trouble.

PURPOSE AND SCOPE

BUSINESS OBJECTIVES

The business is concerned about getting e-business implemented as well as ensuring that the current systems are supported. Business managers often show little interest in architecture. Some managers may see the situation as "Since the current architecture works and has worked, why do we need to change it? Why spend money on it?" If you think about it, it is the same as with roads or water systems. Until there is a problem, no one pays attention. This is a basic issue that has to be addressed in this chapter.

POLITICAL AND CULTURAL OBJECTIVES

The political goal is to generate management support for improvements and for support of e-business. Another political goal is to obtain an understanding of how the business processes and transactions are dependent on the systems, technology, and IT staffing resources. Within IT there are also goals. A cultural goal is to instill an organized method for resource management that can support e-business implementation as well as manage outsourcing resources. Another goal is to upgrade the skills of the IT employees.

TECHNICAL OBJECTIVES

The technical objectives are clear:

- Understand the issues involved in IT systems, architecture, management, and staffing.
- Identify potential software and resources that can be employed in e-business.
- Determine approaches for resource management.
- Define a new IT architecture that supports e-business, current systems, and has sufficient flexibility and capabilities at a reasonable cost and addresses the issues in IT as much as possible.

These objectives are a tall order, but you must aim high.

SCOPE

The scope of this work includes the following elements:

- *IT organization.* Is the current IT organization suitable for e-business?
- *IT policies and procedures.* Do IT policies related to resource management and allocation have the flexibility to assign resources to e-business?
- *IT staffing.* Do IT staff members have an adequate mix of skills and experience to tackle e-business?
- *IT systems.* What is the condition of IT systems in terms of supporting e-business transactions?
- *IT methods and tools.* What IT methods and tools are in place that can sustain e-business implementation?
- *IT architecture and technology.* What changes are necessary to assist e-business in hardware, network, and systems/network software?
- *Potential e-business technologies and products.* What software tools and packages are necessary to implement e-business?

END PRODUCTS

The physical end products include the following considerations:

- Assessment of the current IT architecture, systems, and support.
- Identification of the IT issues and their impacts on the business as well as IT.
- Identification of e-business products and services for your organization.
- How the e-business fit with the architecture to produce the new IT architecture.
- How the new IT architecture and structure supports e-business, the business, and IT.
- Implications for implementation of e-business.

Beyond these milestones you also have these political goals:

- Support for changes in IT policies and staffing within IT.
- Awareness of the impact of problems in the current IT architecture and systems and their impacts on IT and the business.
- Business understanding of what is necessary with respect to IT for e-business implementation.

APPROACH

Specific actions are discussed in this section. Keep in mind that in the interests of time, you must perform some of these in parallel. For example, you can work on Actions 1–3 at the same time. After these have begun, you can work on the other actions.

ACTION 1: REVIEW YOUR CURRENT IT SYSTEMS AND ARCHITECTURE

What Is the IT Architecture?

You started this in Chapter 2. Here you will pursue it in more depth. An IT architecture consists of the structure and components of hardware, software, and network along with operations support tools. Example components were given in Chapter 2. Beyond a list of components you seek to develop an understanding of the interrelationships among the components. You should create a diagram of the architecture. Figure 7.1 lists the existing components for Walters Catalog. Figure 7.2 presents the architecture in a diagram form. Here are some comments that amplify on the architecture:

- The firewall is intended for Internet access.
- A development server is attached directly to the network and is used for development and testing.
- There are direct connections from the network to the credit card and logistics firms.
- The diagram is simplified because customer service, order entry, and other employees are shown as individual entries.

Identify Architecture Issues and Problems

There are typically many problems in the current IT architecture. A sample list of issues is given in Figure 7.3. This is not due to IT management. Don't blame

- Servers
  - UNIX-based servers for applications
  - Windows NT/2000 servers for e-mail, network support with Microsoft Back Office
  - Windows NT/2000 server for intranet and Internet applications
  - Development Windows 2000 server
- Network components
  - Firewall
  - Network routers
  - Network management server
  - Interface server to logistics vendor and credit card clearing/authorization firms
  - Limited network management software
- PC
  - Older PCs in customer service
  - Older PCs in order entry
  - PCs across the organization of various ages
  - Connection through standard Ethernet 10-mbps cards
  - Windows 98 operating system

Figure 7.1   Components of the IT Architecture of Walters Catalog

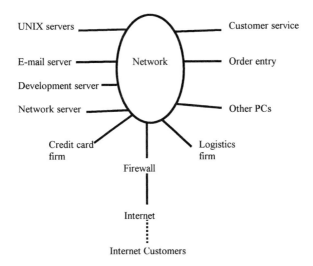

Figure 7.2   Simplified Diagram of the IT Architecture of Walters Catalog

them! While a limited number of problems can be traced to management, most of the problems are often due to the following factors:

- Age of the current hardware, network, and software. New technologies have emerged since the current architecture was installed and set up.
- Modernization was limited due to available money and resources.
- Some of the application software cannot operate on modern architecture components.
- There was no compelling reason for change.
- The IT employees were assigned to other immediate work of high priority.

Some of the specific architecture problems for Walters Catalog are listed below (see Figure 7.4).

Potential Problems	Impacts
PCs do not support many simultaneous tasks	Limited functions can be performed at the PCs
Servers do not handle backup or disaster recovery	Limited redundancy; reduced reliability
Lack of testing environment	Testing is limited
Limited network management software	Inability to do network diagnostics
Limited security	Potential for hackers

Figure 7.3   Sample Problems and Impacts Related to IT Architecture before E-Business

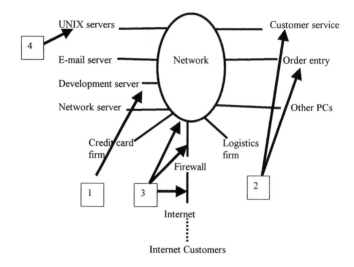

Figure 7.4   Impact of Problems for Walters Catalog

- There is a lack of a testing server and test environment (labeled 1).
- The PCs in customer service and order entry don't have the power to handle both the client-server system and the Internet system (labeled 2).
- The network capacity is limited both internally and with the Internet (labeled 3).
- Capacity of the servers needs to be increased and backup servers are needed (labeled 4).

After identifying the problems, you can graphically relate these problems to the IT architecture in a diagram. How this was done for Walters Catalog is shown in Figure 7.4.

Review IT Systems

Here you will review the application systems that might be involved in e-business. More systems than you think might be involved. A starting list is given in Figure 7.5. It is also useful to create several tables. These can be refinements of the tables presented in earlier chapters.

- *Systems versus e-business processes.* The entry is the potential role that an individual system plays in supporting the e-business processes and transactions. This table is used to highlight which systems are important.
- *Systems versus IT architecture components.* The entry is the nature and ex-

- Accounting (credit card operations)
- Credit card processing
- Inventory (linkage to Web systems)
- Payroll (commissions for Web-related vendors)
- Sales
- Marketing
- Customer service
- Order entry
- Manufacturing planning
- Finance
- Interfaces to logistics vendor
- Web application system
- Management reporting
- Customer databases and management
- Purchasing and procurement
- Contracting
- Shipping and logistics
- Security systems
- Network management systems

Figure 7.5 Application Systems Potentially Involved in E-Business

tent of dependence on the individual IT architecture parts. The table is employed to reveal the critical parts of the architecture.

Identify Systems Issues and Problems

Here you want to identify the real problems involved in the application systems. A list of potential issues is shown in Figure 7.6. Many of these relate to specific areas. Here you want to generate several tables.

• *Systems issues versus IT architecture components.* The entry indicates the dependence of the individual issue on a particular component of the architecture. This shows the root of the systems problems in the architecture components.

• *Systems issues versus IT architecture problems.* The entry is the relation-

- Application capacity—lack of ability to handle volumes of transactions.
- Poor interfaces due to systems being old and incompatible—limitations on what is possible in e-business.
- Interfaces between new software and existing system—major IT staff time may be necessary to accomplish the interfaces.
- Difficulty in having interfaces for management information—restricting management abilities to take actions in e-business.

Figure 7.6 Potential Application Systems Problems

ship between application system issues and architecture issues. This table is used to show how important the architecture issues are.

ACTION 2: APPRAISE IT STAFFING, WORKLOAD, AND SKILLS

Examine the Current Work and Backlog

The typical IT group has many current projects underway. In addition, half or more of the resources are required just to keep the application systems going and to provide ongoing user support. For each application system you can list the existing work and backlog of work for these systems. If you have a critical system for e-business and there is a lot of work going on and more waiting in the wings, then you may have a big problem in e-business implementation. For Walters 2 the IT staff was really stretched doing maintenance and providing day-to-day operations support. This would be a major issue because these individuals would be also required for e-business implementation support.

Assess the IT Staff Skills

Many IT staff members are essential to specific systems. To understand the extent of the problem, prepare the following tables:

• *IT staff versus IT architecture components.* The entry indicates the degree to which the architecture component depends on the specific staff member in IT. This table reveals dependencies that could affect your ability to change the architecture.

• *IT staff versus application systems.* The entry is the extent to which the IT staff members are critical to the operation, maintenance, and enhancement of the specific application system. The table shows the lack of flexibility and dependence of IT on critical people for the application systems.

The IT staff in Walters Catalog did not have in-depth experience in network management for the Internet. In addition, there was a shortage of IT skills in Web development. It was clear that outsourcing was required.

Review IT Policies and Practices on Resource Management

IT departments have formal or informal policies and practices in assigning people and vendor staff to application system and architecture work. As an example in some groups, work is assigned in a reactive case-by-case method. Each request may be addressed separately. This approach creates problems for e-business because e-business may require resources across IT. Dealing with this demand on an individual basis can literally tear up the IT organization. The IT department in Walters Catalog (Walters 1) did not have a formal approach for allocating resources. Each request was handled and prioritized on a case-by-case basis. This was clearly unsuitable for addressing the demands of e-business.

ACTION 3: EVALUATE POTENTIAL E-BUSINESS PRODUCTS

Find Out What Is Available

Here is a list of software products that are appropriate for e-business. This is not a complete list. However, just this initial list shows you the potential awesome effort that lies ahead.

- E-catalog software
- Ordering and market basket software
- Customer profiling software
- Cross-sell software
- Customer service software
- Order tracking
- Inventory access software
- Order processing and handling
- Accounting systems
- Credit card authorization and linkage
- Credit card processing
- Firewall for security
- Network management software
- Internet service provider
- Web development tools
- Configuration management software
- Regular network connectivity/latency pinging
- CPU loading statistics
- Network monitoring tools as sniffers
- Sniffer and network trace log analysis
- Regular storage statistic analysis
- Clickstream analysis/Web server log analyzer
- Response time analysis
- Transaction performance analysis
- Network saturation analysis

What categories are appropriate for you depends on what e-business activities you are going to implement and support. Keep in mind that you should not select individual products. Instead, you have to concentrate on groups of products that work together. Otherwise, you may have problems in integration after you purchase them.

Here is a list of criteria that are commonly employed in evaluating and selecting e-business software.

- Ease of integration
- Ease of deployment
- Personalization and customization
- Completeness of functionality
- Low total cost of ownership
- Quality of vendor support
- Vendor long-term competitive position
- Best-of-breed technology
- Low initial investment

ACTION 4: ESTABLISH AN ONGOING TECHNOLOGY ASSESSMENT

You need to undertake an ongoing approach for reviewing new technology and products. While this seems obvious, many groups do not do this due to the pressure of existing work. The approach should be undertaken by a group of individuals from IT and business departments on a rotating basis. In that way the burden does not fall on one individual.

The approach consists of the following steps. For each new technology or product, you can identify the following aspects:

- Potential benefits to e-business and IT.
- Potential barriers to implementation of the new technology or product.
- How the new technology or product would fit with the application software and IT architecture.

Walters Catalog did not have the resources to devote someone to do this work full-time. Instead, a part-time effort was launched within the IT organization.

ACTION 5: DEVELOP YOUR NEW E-BUSINESS IT ARCHITECTURE

Goals of the New IT Architecture

What are the key considerations in designing and building an e-business architecture? Here are some factors to consider.

- Reliability
- Security
- Ease of application integration
- Cost
- Adaptability of architecture
- Scalability
- Round-the-clock availability
- Speed of implementation
- Products already proven in use
- Vendor reputation

For Walters 2 the goals were scalability, capacity, and to provide capabilities for e-business expansion.

Determine the Components of the New IT Architecture

This sounds like a huge effort. It is really more reasonable than you think. After all, you are not going to tear up the architecture. You have to keep the business going. What you are going to do is to identify e-business and supporting components. You can now construct a diagram of the new architecture just as you did with the existing architecture. In this diagram you can label where each new component is placed. Here is a list of changes that are often given priority:

- Higher bandwidth
- Added servers for redundancy and capacity
- Standardized operating system and hardware
- Integrated front and back end applications
- Standardize on proven applications
- Different data storage design
- Geographical dispersion of servers/storage

Evaluate How the New IT Architecture Supports E-Business

Here you can create the following tables.

- *New architecture components versus e-business software.* The entry is the extent to which the particular e-business software depends on a specific component. This table reinforces the need for the architecture upgrade.
- *New architecture components versus IT staff.* The table entry is the ability of the person to support the architecture component. The table serves to indicate the gaps in skills that are needed for e-business.

Investigate How the New IT Architecture Supports IT Activities

Here are some relevant tables:

• *New architecture components versus existing IT architecture components.*
The table entry is the relationship of the components in the existing and new
architecture. The table shows what is to be replaced.

• *New architecture components versus application software.* The entry indicates the benefits and impact on the application software. The table is beneficial
to show the benefits to existing application software.

• *New architecture components versus IT architecture issues.* The entry is the
impact of the new architecture on the IT architecture issues. This supports the
new architecture. If there are remaining issues, then IT and the business will
have to live with these.

• *New architecture components versus systems issues.* The table entry is the
degree to which the new architecture deals with the systems issues. The table
helps to give support for changes to the architecture.

Action 6: Determine Implementation IT Projects and Action Items

This action gets to the heart of resource management. How will resources be
reprioritized to support e-business? This should be addressed in a proactive manner. The IT manager and other senior IT managers should develop a method for
IT resource allocation if one does not exist. It will do no one any good to manage
people's time in a reactive, "seat-of-the-pants" mode. This will have to be presented to management because the impact is that current IT projects may have to
be delayed. The work in the backlog may have to wait. Then you must develop a
list of projects and other action items that must be carried to implement the new
IT architecture, the e-business software, and support. You can create tables that
relate these projects and action items to the architecture, application systems, and
e-business software.

For Walters 2, the projects included these activities:

• Increase network capacity.
• Replace network cards in existing PCs.
• Replace PCs in customer service and order entry.
• Install Windows 2000 in the new PCs in customer service and order entry.
• Acquire and implement new e-business software.

- Reprioritize work and the backlog so as to free up resources for e-business work.
- Identify and contract with vendors to support network management and e-business development.
- Acquire and install more UNIX and Windows 2000 servers to increase capacity and provide backup.
- Acquire test hardware and software.
- Hire IT staff for quality assurance and testing.

ACTION 7: MARKET THE IT ARCHITECTURE

How do you market technical stuff to business management? The IT architecture is complex even for business managers who have some knowledge of IT. You want to use the tables that you have developed so far. These tables relate IT architecture to the business and application software.

The management at Walters Catalog had a limited knowledge and interest in technology and systems. The diagrams in the figures were employed to assist in communications. In addition, tables were employed along with some examples of other companies. The impact of not taking actions was emphasized as opposed to more academic benefits.

STARTUP

Consult Figure 7.7 for a table of comments on the example companies.

INDO FURNITURE

The work here was to define a minimal architecture. This was necessary because the systems and networks of the order servicing and customer service were in place. The emphasis was centered on interfaces among vendor software.

DIAMOND ENGINEERING DATA

While the hardware and network architecture were minor issues, the knowledge base and the application software were given major attention. There was also a focus on scalability and low cost. Software development also received attention.

	Company					
Subject	**Indo Furniture**	**Diamond Engineering**	**Asean Construction**	**Walters Catalog-1**	**Walters Catalog-2**	**Rogers County**
Current IT systems and architecture	None	None	In place	Accepted as is	Problems in network capacity and weak workstations	Adequate
IT staffing/ work	None; contracted	None; contracted	Retraining of some IT staff	None	Use vendors to improve internal skills	Additional staff training for IT
Ongoing technology assessment	None	None	Within IT	None	IT and core e-business team	Within IT and Operations
E-business architecture	Through the vendors	Limited	In place	No formal structure	Use the existing architecture with enhancements	Established
IT projects and action items	Integration	Focus on software development and knowledge base	Expansion of the network across the company; links to suppliers	Enhancements for security	Add hardware and network capacity	Improved security

Figure 7.7 Summary of Examples

EXAMPLES

ASEAN CONSTRUCTION

Asean had no major problems with their current architecture. The consumer-focused e-business was to grow slowly. Some retraining of the IT staff was necessary for e-business. Priorities had always been established on an annual basis. This was moved up to every 6 months and then every 3–4 months. The network had to be expanded across the company and business units. Links to suppliers had to be established.

ROGERS COUNTY

The network was adequate for e-business. Some retraining of IT staff would have to be carried out. An ongoing technology assessment function was established in the IT group. Security was identified as an IT project of high priority.

LESSONS LEARNED

A basic lesson learned is to work in parallel on these tasks. We said this before. It deserves mention again. Another guideline is to involve both IT managers and staff along with business managers who have some IT knowledge and experience.

THE SCORE CARD

How are you doing? Here are some questions to answer.

- Do you have an understanding of the problems and issues related to the IT architecture and application systems?
- Have you identified a complete list of e-business software?
- Are the e-business software packages and tools integrated?
- Does the new IT architecture support the e-business software?
- Where are the holes and gaps in the IT staffing?
- Is there a consistent and organized method for resource management?

WHAT TO DO NEXT

You can begin with the initial actions presented above. It might be useful to identify groups of e-business software. For the current application systems and IT architecture you can start developing lists of issues and shortcomings. Select several competitors or other similar firms that are involved in e-business. Identify what software they use along with their key architecture components.

Develop Your Outsourcing and ASP Approach

INTRODUCTION

BACKGROUND

Outsourcing occurs when an organization contracts with a supplier or vendor to provide specific services and support for either or both business and IT activities. Outsourcing refers to services rather than purchased products such as software. Outsourcing is considered here as a separate chapter because (1) it is so often employed in e-business and (2) it is a major cause of failure and problems in implementation and ongoing operation. Today, application service providers (ASPs) can provide many more types of services in hardware, networking, hosting, development, operations, and consulting.

Outsourcing is not new. It began in IT (then called electronic data processing or EDP) with facilities management. Companies had acquired computers, but there was a lack of trained personnel to operate them and provide support. Firms such as IBM and Computer Sciences Corporation stepped in to provide these services. Programmers and systems analysts were often provided as well. Smaller firms then could not afford their own computers. There were no microcomputers or minicomputers. This gap gave rise to service bureaus. Service bureaus provided data processing services. You might have a service bureau write programs as well as prepare data and run the programs.

When timesharing emerged in the 1970s, another opportunity for outsourcing emerged—external timesharing services. Here you paid an hourly fee and connected up to the service firm's timesharing system. With the 1980s companies expanded their internal systems staffs and brought in work that had been performed outside. The arrival of local area networks and increased complexity led firms to outsource support for these networks as well as training and other activities. Today, with the expansion of IT into more and more business activities, there are many more types of outsourcing. The Web has created even more.

What are lessons learned from this experience?

- Outsourcing of IT and business activities is growing in general.
- Outsourcing of e-business implementation work has increased.
- Given the range of activities in transforming into e-business, outsourcing becomes a necessity.
- Because outsourcing is a persistent activity and results in dependence of the organization on the outsourcer, it is imperative that you develop a strategy for outsourcing and actively manage all outsourcing relationships.

Relationships with ASPs tend to be long-lasting and extend over multiple years. This is for the practical reason that it would take too much effort and disrupt the business to make major changes in the short term.

THE ASP AND OUTSOURCER'S VIEW OF THE WORLD

How does an outsourcing firm make money? This is an important question to address if you are going to use outsourcing as an approach for business or IT work. Here are some of the major ways of making money:

- The ASP or outsourcing firm provides economies of scale in processing and support. They support many customers so that they can spread their people and other resources across their customer base.
- The ASP or outsourcer may provide cheaper or smarter resources who can do the work faster.
- Outsourcing generates additional requests for work that were not part of the original contract—adding to the revenue stream.
- The employees of outsourcing firms may use more advanced development, testing, and support tools so that their productivity is increased.
- After taking over an activity that is inefficient, they restructure the work.
- Long-term contracts provide a locked in revenue source for the firm and provide time to drive down costs.

Some specific observations on ASPs are as follows:

- There are three types of providers: general firms who provide a wide range of services, industry-specific ASPs, and niche firms that provide a specific service.
- ASPs see their value in providing solutions rather than merely infrastructure. This added value generates their revenue stream.
- Access capabilities from the client firms to the ASP are most often through

the Internet, but can also be through virtual private networks (VPNs) or wide area networks (WANs).

• The price is often determined by application management, initial application cost, implementation and integration support, and 24-hour/7-day a week operation and support.

BENEFITS OF OUTSOURCING

The benefits of outsourcing include the following conveniences:

• Reduced schedule in implementation.
• Ability to focus on the business because the outsourcing firm is doing some of the support work.
• Capability to undertake new projects such as e-business without the learning curve required when internal staff are used.
• Access to software and personnel resources that would be normally out of their reach.
• Ability to take advantage of new technology products.
• IT staff are freed up to work on critical projects.

What is important to client firms that employ outsourcing vendors? Surveys point to reliability, service level guarantees, and quality of applications and staff. Reduced cost is way down the list. You are not likely to save money.

DRAWBACKS TO OUTSOURCING

Outsourcing creates a situation where you are dependent on an outside company that you do not control. What if they fail? What if service suffers if their key employees leave? What is the impact of a management change there? What if they change their direction and decide that your line of business is not in their best long-term interests? All of these things have happened. There are other potential negative impacts from outsourcing:

• Costs are higher than expected due to unanticipated work that is required by the outsourcing staff.
• Management of the outsourcing effort may increase costs and consume more resources than estimated earlier.
• Your flexibility to change in response to new requests may be limited because the labor to do the work is not under direct control.
• Proprietary methods and data may be subject to being compromised due to external support.

- Your competitive advantage will not likely lie in software because in outsourcing you will tend to use standardized packages.
- There is a danger that what the outsourcing staff learns may be employed in work with your competitors.
- The outsourcing firm uses their own proprietary software tools, which makes it potentially more difficult to move the activities either back inside or to another firm.

So does this mean that you should outsource? No. Outsourcing may be necessary to reach your e-business goals. The main lesson learned is that you must be careful and follow an organized, comprehensive method.

PURPOSE AND SCOPE

BUSINESS OBJECTIVES

The business objectives for outsourcing include the following activities:

- Preserve the integrity, stability, and performance of the business processes. This is the key business objective. You can save money, obtain better resources, etc., but if the outsourcing firm negatively impacts system performance, which impairs the business processes, then it is all over.
- Provide for the timely and effective implementation of e-business through outsourcing support.

As you can see from this, the business does not seek very many objectives. However, these are comprehensive.

POLITICAL AND CULTURAL OBJECTIVES

Outsourcing can tear up an IT group because it creates conflicts between the contractor staff and internal employees. As an example, in some companies, a programmer quits and then returns as a contract programmer. He or she is making much more money. This is not lost on the internal employees, who feel like dummies when they see his/her better clothes and the expensive Porsche sports car in the parking lot. The political objective is that there be an organized approach to outsourcing so that bringing in the outsourcing vendors will not create political problems. These can arise because of bringing in new people who owe allegiance to an external firm. Expectations can be raised among users.

The cultural goal of outsourcing is to establish a culture in which the outsourcing staff and the employees work together. Why is this important? Because outsourcing is a program that lasts—like e-business. Hence, it is likely that the outsourcing vendor will be around for some time.

TECHNICAL OBJECTIVES

The technical objectives are to (1) develop and implement a consistent and comprehensive strategy for outsourcing, (2) manage the outsourcing work so as to support e-business, and (3) provide for stable systems and infrastructure to support both regular and e-business. Note here that outsourcing can extend to business activities as well. This means that the technical objectives are expanded to address these functions.

SCOPE

The narrow traditional scope of outsourcing has been IT. The discussion of the history of outsourcing supports this statement. However, today it is different. If, for example, a firm were to start in doing business-to-consumer without a business infrastructure, then there would be pressure to implement quickly. There would likely be pressure to outsource customer service into a commercial call center. The same comments might apply to fulfillment, shipping, and even inventory. The bottom line is that the scope for outsourcing is much broader than in the past.

END PRODUCTS

You will be developing and working toward the following end products:

- An outsourcing approach and strategy to guide the activities.
- An organized method for carrying out specific steps in outsourcing.
- Measurements taken before and during outsourcing. These are critical to the management of outsourcing.
- Management and coordination of outsourcing in a consistent manner.

APPROACH

ACTION 1: DETERMINE WHAT CAN BE OUTSOURCED

In order to carry out this action, you should consider all of the following activities that are organized the effort by area.

Hardware and Software Related

Computer Center Operation

The vendor will provide the operating staff and software to run the computer center if it remains an asset in the client's books. Alternatively, the firm will sell the center equipment and other assets to the vendor. The vendor then pays the firm cash—very attractive if a firm is having cash flow trouble because the systems continue to function. Most vendors seek to merge the computer center equipment into their own data center. This supports economies of scale of staffing and networking. If the workload can be absorbed onto an existing application system, there are even more savings because some software licenses can be terminated with the release of the firm's hardware. Operating a computer center is a generic activity and does not involve company business processes—thus making it attractive for outsourcing in e-business. This is especially true in business-to-consumer e-business where there is a need for 24/7 (24 hours a day, 7 days a week) operation and for scalability and reliability.

Some risks in outsourcing a computer center are as follows:

- What happens if the vendor goes out of business?
- What happens if there is poor performance?
- How will you oversee the computer center and ensure quality work?
- What if the vendor employs special software utilities to run your systems— raising costs and locking you in?
- How will charges be established for additional services that require hardware, software, or staffing?
- How will disaster recovery and business resumption be addressed?
- What are the service level guarantees?

Outsourcing this activity is a long-term proposition because it tends to be difficult to switch computer center due to complexity. Not only must there be compatible hardware, but also there must a network conversation, facilities work, staffing up to take over, and the establishment of the same software environment.

Overseeing the vendor requires technical personnel such as systems programmers and network professionals as well as the IT manager. On-the-spot decisions that depend on funding approval are often required. You also seek to have service-level agreements in place where there are penalties if the firm does not live up to the agreed-upon service level.

PC Hardware Installation, Maintenance, and Upgrades

This may include filling orders for PCs, installing the hardware and software, connecting PCs to networks, upgrading the operating systems, problem troubleshooting, monitoring software licenses and serial numbers, antivirus efforts, supplying replacements when there is a failure, carrying out repairs, and system upgrades and replacements. This is a natural for outsourcing, except in areas where there is no support available. PC hardware is generic. The vendor staff may work at a lower hourly rate than employees. They may have more experience in doing the work. They have more staff available in case a number of problems occur in a short period. No internal company knowledge is required to do the work because it is technology, not business, dependent.

There are some risks involved in outsourcing. One is ensuring the quality of the work. A second is to make sure that the vendor continues to provide qualified resources on an ongoing basis. A vendor could taper off on service if they have the only contract for support and have a multiyear contract.

Here are some guidelines:

- Consider giving contracts to two firms for a period of 2–3 months. Under this arrangement you reserve the right to call either one. Alternatively, you can set one up as a primary vendor and the other as a backup or alternate vendor to get a lower price from the lead vendor.
- Set standards for response time after a problem is reported, the mean time for repair, and response on upgrades and other services.
- You will almost certainly need a help desk that can log and filter calls. Otherwise, you are likely to get embroiled in disputes over service calls.

Major Hardware Support

Almost all firms outsource the maintenance of their mainframe and minicomputer hardware. Often, this work is performed by the manufacturer. There are standard maintenance contracts. However, beware that as your equipment ages, maintenance costs tend to rise significantly. This can be the major factor in deciding to replace or upgrade the hardware.

Network Related

Network Planning and Management

Network planning is crucial to e-business. There is an ongoing role in measuring the network performance, determining what steps should be taken to improve performance, and planning for upgrades, replacement, and expansion. Unless an organization is quite small, this role is performed by internal staff members. This role also includes overseeing contract work in installation and testing of cabling, new network hardware, and other network components, including the firewall, links to banks and other outside entities, and security. This activity is on the borderline between being company specific and generic. If you outsource it, you inhibit your capability to watch over other vendor work. If you keep it inside, it can represent a substantial cost.

Network Installation and Testing

You are not going to install and test a network everyday. Network installation and upgrades are performed as discrete tasks. Installation requires specialized equipment in terms of cabling tools, crimping tools, testing tools, and software. These functions are generic and not company specific, so they are suitable candidates for outsourcing.

Network Operation and Troubleshooting

There are several arguments here. One can argue that with increasing reliability of networking technology, there is a reduced need for internal staff to operate and troubleshoot the network. On the other hand, e-business is totally dependent on the network. The business becomes more dependent on e-business. This argues in favor of internal operation.

General Support

Help Desk

A help desk operation is where people respond to questions and problems. These can come from employees, suppliers, or in some cases customers. The help desk logs the problem, asks questions to determine what the problem is, routes the problem for investigation, and follows up to ensure that corrective action was taken. Should you staff the help desk with employees or with vendor staff? These positions are clearly junior level. Complex problems will have to be referred to other, more senior people. A help desk requires more than employees. There should be software to log and track calls. A database of frequently asked questions is useful. A database of profiles of potential callers and their hardware, software, and network configurations is essential.

In considering outsourcing, a major concern is quality of service. Another issue is the prediction of the workload of calls and e-mails that will reach the help desk. If you do outsource this function, you probably want to have the selected vendor restricted to this activity for division of responsibility and control. One approach is to establish the help desk with internal employees first. This will allow you to build the lessons learned and log frequently asked questions, as well as to better understand the level and expertise of staffing required. This also avoids the expensive setup costs that a vendor will pass on to you. Implement a quality measurement program in which you track the extent of user satisfaction. If you do outsource, make sure that this measurement method is accompanied by a personnel replacement approach for problem vendor employees.

IT Training

Training here includes instructions on using software tools and general methods employed in IT. It is not company specific and so is a good outsourcing target. Computer-based training (CBT) and Internet-based training can also be employed.

Application System and Other Training

Beyond IT training, there is general management and business training. Training in software packages is available for most popular software. These are natural candidates for outsourcing. Here are some pitfalls to avoid:

- The client company specifies training requirements in only a general manner. The training that is delivered, while meeting these requirements, turns out not to be satisfactory.
- The company and training firm fail to work together in developing and reviewing the training materials.
- There is no formal review after the training is given.

Management Support

Systems Planning

Many firms lack experience in developing e-business and IT strategic plans and objectives. They may have failed when they last attempted it. Thus, there is often a desire to seek outside expert assistance. Managers also may think it is useful to obtain an outside perspective. Here are some basic questions to answer when considering outside planning assistance:

- What is the planning method of the vendor? Can you live with this method? Or does it seem too complex and complicated?
- How will the internal staff learn the planning method and gain from knowledge transfer from the vendor so that they can update the plan themselves without outside help?
- Should the vendor work in a joint team approach so that much of the legwork is performed by internal staff?
- What are the planning end products? Are they fuzzy or are they specific actions that you can take? Are they general findings that require still further work?
- Can you place boundaries on the work performed so that the consultants do not run amok?

Technology Architecture and Assessment

You want to consider new technologies for e-business and develop an overall technology architecture. This requires external information, knowledge, and experience. It may include finding out what specific competitors are doing in e-business. This also applies to the industry. It is clear that many organizations lack the external expertise to undertake these tasks in a reasonable amount of time. Given that you would consider a consulting firm here, consider some of the guidelines you would use to evaluate them:

- Find out if the consulting firms being considered have any ties to specific technology providers. Do they have strategic alliances? This may bias their viewpoint.
- What knowledge and experience do they have of your specific industry? Which firms in your industry have they worked with?
- Obtain sample relevant reports from their past work.
- Identify an outline and purpose of each end product so that there is agreement at the start about what is to be done. This will avoid problems later and head off the dreaded "scope creep."

Analysis of Customer Information

Customer information will be gathered and available. Many firms lack internal capabilities to do analysis of these data. If you try to train existing employees to perform extensive statistical analysis, this can take too long. An alternative is to hire new employees—taking more time. Therefore, it is not surprising that firms employ consultants to set up the gathering, organization, and analysis of customer data.

Software Development and Maintenance

Turnkey Development and Customization

In turnkey development for e-business, a firm contracts for a complete system. Application system providers supply such services. The e-business software may be based on a package or may be composed of several packages and components. In customization, a vendor modifies and creates software to add new features, interfaces, and capabilities. The key phrase here is system integration.

Systems Analysis and Design

These are areas where it is appropriate to bring in one or a few people with specialized skills and knowledge about the new e-business tools that will be employed in the work. These individuals can serve as mentors to the internal staff. There are some potential pitfalls. First, your people are only exposed to the techniques of one or two people. Second, you could build up a dependence here if the people rely on one person too much. Another potential problem is how knowledge will be transferred to internal staff. Business departments may grow attached to these people and it may be then harder to let them grow.

Contract Programming

E-business requires different programming languages and libraries compared to traditional systems. Instead of COBOL, you have Java and Active Server Pages. Contract programmers can provide a variety of tasks. They can support new development, or they can do maintenance and enhancement to existing systems.

Contract programmers have been employed for decades. In some cases, the number of contract programmers amounts to 40% or more of the total number of programmers. Some contract programmers may be former internal IT employees. Contract programmers offer a number of advantages to companies. First, what they work on at a task level can be directly controlled. Second, their costs may be less than for internal programmers when overhead and benefits are counted. A third benefit is that management can change them out when necessary. One disadvantage is that the firm becomes dependent on the contract programmers. With their experience they can implement change to e-business software easily and quickly. There is the problem that the contract programmers may not be loyal or have no long-term interest in the system work. The firm is put at risk. You should always assume that you must have some backup approach.

System Integration

Implementing e-business often requires linking and integrating existing legacy systems, newer systems, new e-business software, and custom software. System integration firms offer substantial experience and knowledge to do this—skills that may not exist among current IT employees. If the current staff stopped their efforts in other areas and concentrated on system integration, there might still be insufficient staff to do the work. The major downside is the cost of this effort. Then there is the issue of maintaining the integration as systems that are involved are enhanced and modified.

Data Conversion and Web Content Setup

Data must be converted from existing systems to be based on servers for e-business. Data cleanup and data integration from multiple systems may be required. This is often a one-time activity that makes sense for outsourcing.

E-business requires that Web pages be designed and set up along with the content. This requires not only technical programming skills, but also desktop publishing abilities and tools. This is often an appropriate area for outsourcing. Moreover, an outside firm can supply sufficient labor to get this done according to a schedule.

Testing and Quality Assurance

Testing is absolutely crucial in business-to-consumer e-business. If you fail to test adequately, you can leave yourself open to substantial financial exposure. An example highlights this. A company advertised several promotions on its Web site. A young programmer found a way to combine the discounts to obtain the merchandise free. He ordered and received over $5000 in goods. As if this were not bad enough, he then posted how to do it in a chat room. Within 4 days over $3,500,000 in goods were ordered and shipped. Then the company woke up and shut the site down. If there had been adequate testing, this would have been prevented.

The IT staff and organization may not be set up for such extensive testing and quality assurance. Skills may be lacking, as may be the necessary test tools and methods. Outsourcing to set up the activity of quality assurance can be justified based on the potential exposure.

Software Maintenance and Enhancement

Software maintenance and enhancement of the existing applications are per-formed by the IT programmers internally. These activities require specialized knowledge of the application systems. If the system is old, then it would be diffi-cult to hire outside people to perform these activities. You have several options— none of which is desirable. If you shackle the current programmers to the current systems, you prevent them from getting involved in e-business. This can lower morale. If you outsource the maintenance and enhancement to free up the pro-grammers, then there will be a major learning curve for the outsiders to learn the internal software. This will eat up the time of the IT employees.

Software Package Related

Evaluation and Selection of Software Packages

Why go outside for this effort? Because the consulting firm may have in-depth knowledge of the software. They can provide this experience to reduce the elapsed time and to ensure that the wrong decisions are not made. The counter argument is that the internal staff needs to learn what is available and how it works.

Installation Support

Obviously, for large enterprise resource planning (ERP) systems, you will need a number of (often many) different consultants. These packages are large, complex, and integrated. Previous implementation experience is a must. However, the cost of such support can exceed the cost of the software by a factor of 10 or more! E-business systems are not as complex and are more limited. You tend to integrate software and employ tools. However, the same requirement for knowledge and skills exists.

Business Related

Call Center Operations

A call center provides customer service and order-taking support. In business-to-consumer the call center is important because it serves as the human support for customers who are ordering and using your Web site. If you have the site available on a 24/7 basis, then you may be forced to have a three-shift call center. This is not an attractive prospect given the cost and staffing issues. There are several options here. You can do the work either entirely internally or externally, or you can have a mix where the later two shifts are supported externally.

Inventory, Fulfillment, and Shipping

Suppose that you are a manufacturer with a standard warehousing and inventory operation. E-business shifts this operation to just-in-time. Rather than dismantle or radically change the current operation, you might outsource the Web inventory until the business grows sufficiently. From this list you can now identify potential outsourcing candidates. You will list more activities than you will end up outsourcing. Just thinking about these activities will help you in defining your outsourcing objectives as they relate to e-business.

Marketing Related

There are a number of marketing opportunities related to e-business. One that has been mentioned already is competitive and industry intelligence. Here are some others:

- Marketing strategies for e-business and linkage to normal business.
- Advertising design and branding. This addresses the image of the firm on the Web.
- Development of sales campaigns for the Web site.

If there are insufficient internal marketing resources or if the internal marketing department lacks skills and knowledge related to the Internet, then there may be no other viable option than to outsource. This can result in expenditures that dwarf any IT-related outsourcing. In Walters 1 the Web content and Web site development were outsourced. In Walters 2 process improvement and Web content were outsourced. Web content includes taking photographs of products and preparing these for the Web, doing graphics design, placing text for the product, and validating the content.

ACTION 2: DEFINE YOUR E-BUSINESS OUTSOURCING OBJECTIVES

A number of advantages for using outsourcing have been discussed earlier in this chapter. You can now use these to define potential objectives. Here are some candidates:

• Increase the available internal resources for implementing e-business. Here you focus outsourcing on existing internal operations, thereby freeing up employees.

• Support a faster implementation of e-business using outsourcing resources. This is useful, for example, for a startup firm in which the organization wants to devote its attention to key business factors.

• Provide for long-term support for e-business. This can be supported through major contracts with vendors to handle some components of e-business. This applies to a company that believes in the future of e-business and wants to decide on what activities will be performed by whom over a longer period.

Don't just select one of these or some other objective. Make your own list and keep all ideas in play. You will want to do trade-off analysis as you go. In Walters 1 no real objectives were defined. For Walters 2 the major objectives of outsourcing were to save time and use the expertise of the consultants.

ACTION 3: EVALUATE AND SELECT OPPORTUNITIES

Based on different objectives, you can now review the list that you developed in Action 1. You will be building different lists of outsourcing opportunities. Here are some examples for each of the objectives in Action 2:

• Increase internal resources available for e-business
  — PC support
  — Network installation and testing

— Help desk
— IT training
— Application system training
— Contract programming
— Web content
— Software maintenance and enhancement

- Support faster implementation of e-business. Here you might consider many more of the opportunities. In IT you would include software development, system integration, testing and quality assurance, Web content, and software packages. On the business side call centers, inventory-related work, and marketing are all candidates.
- Long-term support for e-business.
  — Computer center operations
  — PC support
  — Customer information evaluation
  — Contract programming
  — System integration
  — Software package support

Next, you want to develop a list of evaluation criteria for outsourcing. Here is a list to employ as a starting point:

- Potential improvement that the vendor could make in the activity in terms of performance, time, or service related to regular and e-business.
- Potential costs.
- Potential risks to the business if there are problems.
- Extent to which you are restricted due to outsourcing.
- Feasibility in doing the work without outsourcing.
- Interdependencies of the work with that of other activities.
- Special knowledge required to do the work (e.g., company or system specific).
- Barriers to outsourcing in terms of union contracts, laws, location, and other factors.
- Dependence on specific technology that few vendors are likely to be experienced in.
- Potential disruption in transitioning the work to the outsourcing vendor (includes lower morale).

For the evaluation, use the activities that you identified in the first step as rows in a table. Use the criteria defined above as columns. In the table you will enter two things in each cell. The first is the potential estimated benefit and the second is the elapsed estimated time to implement outsourcing. You can use a scale of 1–5 or low, medium, and high. These are only estimates and a starting point. With the table in hand you can seek input from key employees and managers. What is your goal here? To gather input to improve the table is one. A second is to gain consensus through collaboration. This will reduce potential problems later.

After the table has been reviewed you can now create a graph or chart. On the horizontal axis is the degree of benefit and on the vertical axis is the elapsed time. Each opportunity is then placed on the chart using the table. You may find, for example, for some opportunities that they cluster in the low-benefit and long-elapsed-time area. Drop these.

There are also the political, managerial, and operational tests for each opportunity. Here are some factors to consider:

- Politically, can the activity really be outsourced? You might outsource something that would drastically lower morale.
- Organizationally, an activity might be tightly integrated with other internal ones. Then splitting it out may be too difficult.
- The activity is doing critical work and cannot be disrupted.
- Location is a factor. If the work is being done in many places, then there is a major challenge in implementing outsourcing.
- Proprietary systems or information that cannot be released to a vendor.

You will now make the selection. This decision is not irreversible. You may to revisit this later if you encounter problems that are not visible now. Cost was the major factor in the initial e-business effort (Walters 1). The main criterion in Walters 2 was experience. Cost was a secondary criterion.

ACTION 4: PERFORM CLEANUP OF EXISTING PROCESSES

Any activity that exists internally has typically been performed for some time. Typically, there has been little effort to make it more efficient. Moreover, the activity may never have really been measured. So you don't really know what the situation is. If you rush to outsource something that has many internal problems, then you may later be faced with higher vendor costs, a reluctance by the vendor to do the work, and much longer elapsed time to establish outsourcing. The logical approach is to then clean up the activity to get it ready for outsourcing. Why don't you just clean up these things before you make the selection? There are too many potential activities for outsourcing. Also, you may delay your e-business effort.

There are a number of benefits to doing the cleanup. First, you will generate savings and efficiencies that make the activity less desirable for outsourcing. Second, you will generate measurements that can be used later to evaluate the outsourcing firm's work. Third, you will reduce the effort to transition the work to the vendor. Fourth, whoever oversees the cleanup can be the point person or project leader in the transition to the vendor and overseeing their operation of the activity. Finally, the activity is better understood, documented, and measured.

What types of things can you do to clean up things? Obviously, it depends on the specific activity. However, from past experience here is a potential list:

- Policies. You may be able to simplify or streamline policies affecting the activity. New control policies can be defined and implemented in preparation for outsourcing.
- Procedures and workflow.
- Training of staff.
- Documentation of procedures, policies, training materials, etc. This is vital for the outsourcer so that the firm can get started faster.
- Minor systems and technology. There may be some short-term actions that can help.
- Measurements of the activity.

There are constraints on doing the cleanup. There is only a limited amount of time for this (usually less than 3 months). There is no money to embark on a major effort. You cannot do reengineering. For Walters 1 there was no cleanup. For Walters 2 data had to be prepared for the Web content. Data on 15 key processes were collected for process improvement.

ACTION 5: PREPARE FOR OUTSOURCING

Didn't you just prepare the activities for outsourcing? What other preparations are necessary? Here are some things to do:

- Create a team that will evaluate and select the vendors for outsourcing. This group can also oversee the transition of the work to the vendor.
- Identify potential vendors. You can find potential vendors through internal employees, the Web, and magazines.
- Create a list of questions and factors to use to narrow the field of potential vendors.
- Collect some limited information on vendors related to their expertise and knowledge.
- Define how the evaluation process will work. Identify the steps to be taken and who will be involved.
- Prepare a checklist for vendor evaluation.

In addition, you will be developing a Request for Proposal (RFP) or Request for Quotation (RFQ) that will be distributed to vendors. The document should contain the following elements:

- Goals to be achieved through outsourcing.
- The scope of the outsourcing activity.
- Description of the activity in terms of how the activity works.
- How the activity will be measured and the current measurements.
- Any relevant staffing, facilities, IT and other resources used to perform the activity.
- Description of the requirements for outsourcing work (use lists).
- Skills and knowledge required of the outsourcing vendor.
- Transition approach that will be employed after selection and contract negotiation.
- Ongoing measurement and management control approach.
- Evaluation criteria that will be employed for the proposals.
- Method of proposal evaluation.
- Outline of the proposal in a standard format (including references, experience, etc.).
- Timetable for the evaluation, selection, and transition.

ACTION 6: EVALUATE AND SELECT THE VENDORS

Having identified the vendors you will make initial contacts and collect information. You may reduce the number of vendors to be considered further. Next, you will mail out the RFP document. Following this, you will likely hold a bidder's conference. This is an opportunity for you to present the outsourcing objectives and approach. You can supply additional information. You may want to give people a tour of the facilities. After all, within limits, the more information you can provide, the better will be their proposals. You will also answer vendor questions. Here are some examples.

- What is the term of the outsourcing work?
- How will problems be resolved?
- What are details of the transition approach?
- What changes can the vendor make in the activity?
- What is to be done with the internal staff?
- What documentation exists for the activity?

The proposals are now received. You will employ the team to conduct an initial evaluation using the checklist you developed earlier. The head of the team can then tabulate the evaluations. Meetings are held to identify the finalists. Review the proposed contracts from the vendors with the lawyers. Identify potential problems that need to be addressed later in negotiations. You will be contacting the references provided by the vendors. Here are some questions to ask the reference firms:

- How long have they had the outsourcing agreement in effect?
- What was the timeline of events from initial evaluation to today?
- What were their original goals in outsourcing?
- Did they achieve these goals? If so, how? If not, why not?
- How do they manage the outsourcing vendor?
- How do they handle additional work for the vendor?
- How do they measure vendor performance?
- How do they deal with vendor problems?
- What was the biggest surprise in outsourcing?
- How did the cost and schedule differ from that planned?
- What problems did they encounter in the transition and in operation?
- How have problems been addressed?
- What is the quality of staff provided?
- Have their staffing and management been stable? What has been the turnover?
- If they had to do it all over again, what would be done differently?
- Would they employ the same vendor for additional work?
- What benefits did they achieve from outsourcing?
- What were the challenges and lessons learned from outsourcing?

Note that in some cases you may want to visit the references. This would be very appropriate, for example, for call center operations.

Following this evaluation, a group of finalists will be identified. Each will be asked to make presentations and answer questions. To prepare for this, develop the following items:

- Define a specific agenda for the presentations. This will give uniformity to format.
- Develop a list of questions to ask the vendor. Here adapt the questions for references to generate vendor questions as a starting point.

You are now prepared to make a final selection. Two vendors should be selected. One is the primary and the other is the backup in case negotiations fall through.

Each contract negotiation is unique. However, here are some critical success factors to cover:

- *Dispute resolution process.* How will problems be handled?
- *Measurements.* How will the work of the vendor be measured?
- *Management process.* How will the vendor be managed?
- *Additional unplanned work.* How will it be addressed?
- *Transition management.* How will the transition to the vendor be addressed?

ACTION 7: ESTABLISH AND SHAKE DOWN THE VENDOR RELATIONSHIPS

Either in the final stages of contract negotiation or after the contract is signed, you and the vendor must establish a transition project plan. This should include not only tasks, milestones, and resources, but also potential issues to be handled and resolved. This will often involve human resources, vendor managers, internal business managers, IT managers, and IT staff. The act of building the project plan establishes the culture for the transition. If it goes badly, you can anticipate problems later.

After planning you will carry out the tasks. You should have a steering committee of both the vendor management and internal management to oversee and monitor the transition. Issues can also be brought to this committee.

MANAGE THE OUTSOURCING WORK

Getting the outsourcing in place is just the initial work. The real effort is to manage the outsourcing work. Failures in outsourcing can often be traced to management problems in directing the work. There should be regular management meetings with the vendor manager. If the vendor wants to change staffing, policies, and procedures, there should be a prior review with internal management. Ideally, there should be two employees who oversee the vendor. One is from IT and the other is from the business. This provides for continuity and backup as well.

STARTUP

Refer to Figure 8.1 for the examples and some comments.

INDO FURNITURE

For Indo the key was to select vendors based on the capability of their software to integrate and interface. This was critical for order processing, inventory, shipping, and customer service. Otherwise, how could customer service tell a customer when an item shipped and provide a tracking number? The objectives of outsourcing for Indo Furniture were stability and low cost. Scalability was not a factor because the furniture would be sold to dealers. Evaluation and selection were based on cost and integration. Another factor was the ability of the firms to

Subject	Company						
	Indo Furniture	Diamond Engineering	Asean Construction	Walters Catalog-1	Walters Catalog-2	Rogers County
What can be outsourced?	Virtually everything	Computer systems; Web development	Consulting; Web development	Web content	Web content; process improvement	Software packages; software development
Objectives of outsourcing	Stability; low cost	Growth; low cost	Expertise; speed up implementation	Web site development	Save time; expertise	Quality development; stability
Evaluation/ selection	Integration; cost	Stability; low cost	Experience	No real criteria except cost	Experience	Experience
Cleanup of processes	Accounting	Not applicable	Many Quick Hits	Did not occur-overlay strategy	15 key processes	Operations processes
Prepare for outsourcing	Planning	Planning; joint work	IT network	Lack of preparation	Prepare information on products	Define requirements

Figure 8.1 Summary of Examples

work together. There was no real cleanup. However, the family had to structure their accounting system to accommodate the new business. A simple PC-based system was acquired. Planning was the major focus for preparation for e-business.

DIAMOND ENGINEERING DATA

Chris and Mike had to outsource the Web development as well as computer systems and support. Even though they could do it with enough time, they both realized that if they were to do all of the other work, there would no opportunity to do both. So they went with an ASP. The objectives of their outsourcing were to provide for growth due to the anticipated expansion in use and increase in the knowledge base. Another objective was to achieve low cost. Vendor selection was based on cost and stability of the vendor. The preparation consisted of planning and joint work with the vendor. There obviously was no cleanup.

EXAMPLES

ASEAN CONSTRUCTION

Asean had substantial IT capabilities. There was no need for an ASP. However, there was a lack of internal experience in implementation of e-business and Web development. Therefore, consulting and Web development were outsourced. The objectives of the outsourcing were to speed up development and gain expertise and experience. Experience was the major criterion for vendor selection. In terms of cleanup there were many Quick Hits that had to be started as soon as the consultants were brought on board. These ranged across their major business processes. Additional preparation was to acquire and install Web software and to upgrade the network.

ROGERS COUNTY

Rogers County had an IT department and data center. Intranets were in place. So outsourcing concentrated on system development and software packages. All of the development tools and utilities for e-business had to be acquired. The major objectives of outsourcing were for quality development and stability. The maintenance of the software that was developed would later fall into the hands of the IT group. Vendor selection was based on experience. Software selection was based on compatibility with the current IT architecture. Cleanup was required in operations, where procedures and policies had to be modified to accommodate e-business. Requirements and specifications had to be drawn up in preparation for the e-business implementation.

LESSONS LEARNED

Here are some lessons learned for outsourcing:

- There is a need for an overall approach to outsourcing. Even if you are a startup with very little time for this, you can make many mistakes that can sink the startup firm.
- There is benefit in implementing a measurement method for potential outsourcing activities. It is not a bad idea to develop and use this on a regular basis.
- For all outsourcing efforts you should implement a standard management approach.
- Consider periodically the alternative of bringing the activity inside or transferring the work to another vendor.
- Create a database of issues that have been raised and are active in outsourcing. This will help you manage the activity.
- Implement a lessons-learned database. Conduct periodic meetings with internal staff and managers to collect and review these lessons learned.

THE SCORE CARD

How should you measure your outsourcing projects? Go back to your original goals and sit down and determine if these were really achieved. Another step is to use those questions for references and answer these for each activity. Consider also preparing management presentations and summaries evaluating the outsourcing.

WHAT TO DO NEXT

The best thing to do to help you gain more expertise in this area is to evaluate any current outsourcing work that is in place. Pose and answer the questions that were listed earlier for references. This will not only improve your future efforts, but it will also help to increase the effectiveness of your current outsourcing. Another step is to scan the literature for potential vendors and for experiences and surveys related to outsourcing. Vendors who have successful outsourcing projects often generate articles of success stories. Be aware of this.

Chapter 9

Perform Marketing
for E-Business

INTRODUCTION

Marketing of e-business is obviously crucial to whether you can successfully transform into e-business. However, it is more complex than just marketing to management. There are three aspects of marketing that must be addressed:

• *Marketing to employees and managers.* Even when upper management endorses e-business, this is usually not sufficient. You will get more support for e-business if employees and their supervisors support e-business.

• *Marketing to customers and suppliers.* How to market e-business to customers is a major focus of a number of books. Suppliers, however, are also important. You must gain their support and involvement. This is not automatic. Each supplier has its own agenda.

• Reviewing the marketing operations for support of e-business. Marketing is concerned about current promotions, campaigns, branding, and other aspects of marketing. E-business poses new challenges.

PURPOSE AND SCOPE

BUSINESS OBJECTIVES

The business goals are to build support for e-business from employees, customers, and suppliers. Employees will be critical to support the detailed changes to transactions and processes to handle e-business. Customers need to be approached for e-business in a creative way given the vast number of e-business efforts made to reach them. Suppliers are important in that you must market to key suppliers and then use the relationship with them to extend e-business to other suppliers.

POLITICAL AND CULTURAL OBJECTIVES

The political and cultural goals for marketing are centered on building ongoing involvement and promotion of e-business. The culture includes instilling an attitude that is pro e-business and not an "us versus them" feeling.

TECHNICAL OBJECTIVES

The technical objectives are to gain grass roots participation in e-business implementation. This participation must be sustained and not a one-shot effort. Marketing is also essential to establish and maintain involvement. This can lead to better defined requirements.

SCOPE

The scope of the marketing effort encompasses employees, supervisors, customers, and suppliers. While this is too broad for detailed work, there are more specific audiences for e-business.

• Employees and supervisors who are performing the work in processes and doing transactions that are affecting e-business.
• Key customer segments that are accepting of e-business.
• Suppliers who are using e-business or who have automation sufficient to participate in e-business.

Marketing is often viewed as positive. However, there are also negative forces at work. An increasing number of companies and government agencies are employing negative incentives to push people into e-business. Here are some examples:

• In the past decade banking institutions have instituted fees and service cutbacks to encourage customers to use ATM machines as well as electronic banking.
• Some companies reduce the money they pay to suppliers if the suppliers do not employ e-business in their transactions with the company.
• The most extreme is the position of organizations to not do business with suppliers unless the business is carried out electronically in e-business.

Thus, for many companies and individuals it is not a matter of whether to do e-business; it is a matter of when to do it.

END PRODUCTS

The end products are as follows:

• For employees, it is continuous involvement in e-business.
• For customers, it is the adoption of e-business in dealing with the organization.
• For suppliers, it is the establishment of joint efforts with the organization in implementing e-business.
• The marketing organization adapts to e-business and coordinating marketing of e-business with the regular business.

APPROACH

MARKETING OF E-BUSINESS WITHIN THE ORGANIZATION

How do you present e-business to employees? Here are some ways not to do it: (1) avoid attempting to train employees in e-business through classes or seminars; (2) have top management give big presentations at which e-business is announced. This can turn employees off. To begin exploring a more effective approach, consider what employees do everyday. They perform tasks in support of business processes. That is what they know. If you present something new, then a typical employee may feel threatened and uncertain. In their minds, the risk is due to the inability to easily draw a link between e-business and the tasks that they carry out each day. So one thing that must be done is to address the fear factor. There is a second barrier. Even if they understand e-business, they may feel that they see no need for change. After all, the process has worked for some time.

Marketing to employees for e-business often means that you have to overcome resistance. We have already examined an approach for developing the new e-business transactions and comparing these to the traditional transactions. This can reveal to the employees the benefits. However, you still have to consider potential points of resistance. Here are some potential areas of resistance and how you can counter each one:

• E-business involves too much work with little payoff. With a structured approach, no one employee is taken away from their work full time or involved for a long time. Employees will have an opportunity to suggest opportunities and fix problems that have troubled them for some time.
• What people do is unique. Each transaction may be viewed as an exception that has to be given individual attention. The answer to this is that there are standard transactions that occur frequently. There are still exceptions.
• There is no long-term benefit to e-business. It is just another one of those buzzwords, like reengineering. E-business is the next logical step in automation.

- Due to regular work people feel that there is no time to do the implementation of e-business. The approach that has been presented results in spreading the work out among many people.
- Management cannot force the use of e-business implementation. A forced approach will often fail because employees may revert back to their old methods after the heat of e-business dies down. The forced approach is not a good idea.
- With people doing their work and with many work pressures, people may feel that there are not enough resources to implement e-business. In response, e-business requires limited effort and better use of current resources. No new resources are needed.
- There is no benefit to e-business for the employees. E-business automates the mundane transactions and parts of the transactions. Employees get the opportunity to apply lessons learned from their current work.
- Implementation of e-business will slow the work down. While some employee time is required, this can be managed.
- Implementing e-business reduces flexibility. This is true in terms of structuring a few of the business transactions in a department. There are still exceptions and workarounds in the departments. The employees are still in place to handle problems.
- What's in it for me? This is a core question. Here are some benefits to an employee: e-business saves time, provides for more creative work, and there is increased productivity.

Next, we can move up to the supervisors and middle level managers. Their resistance is often based on upsetting their power and structure. They may, in response, attempt to push the employees. At Walters Catalog marketing of e-business within the organization was essential. Remember that people had been burned in the first effort. No one really wanted to step up to the next attempt. The core e-business team decided to direct their attention to improving problems that existed through the identification of opportunities for improvement and the implementation of Quick Hits. This was much more successful.

MARKETING DURING THE E-BUSINESS EFFORT

Marketing to employees must continue during the implementation of e-business. Why is this necessary? Here are some reasons:

- You must continue to reach out to more employees to increase support.
- With any reverses and problems in any substantial effort, you have to take steps to increase morale and keep the ball rolling forward.

How do you go about doing this? One method is to gather information on competitors and the industry. This outside information can be useful in showing how important e-business is. Another approach is to celebrate small successes and Quick Hits. At Walters Catalog marketing became easier with the success of the first Quick Hits. Yet, efforts were made to reach out to more employees.

THE MARKETING ORGANIZATION

The marketing organization is a major concern for to the following reasons:

• Marketing often works in a batch processing mode. There are the fall campaigns and holiday promotions, for example. E-business marketing is online. It also targets specific market segments and even individual customers.
• Marketing may never have had detailed customer information before, so that when it arrives and begins to pile up, there is a challenge to use it.

Marketing has to be brought into the e-business implementation early and must keep involved. Thus, it is important to establish a specific action team related to marketing-related activities. The marketing organization was a special challenge at Walters Catalog. Younger marketing staff saw the potential of e-business and got on board the e-business effort quickly. However, there was substantial resistance among higher level managers in marketing positions. Eventually, some new managers were brought in to assist the e-business program.

MARKETING TO CUSTOMERS

Here are some facts that emerge about e-business in business-to-consumer e-business:

• The percentage of people that feel loyalty to a site is quite low (10–15%).
• Loyal visitors tend to visit these sites more often and spend substantially more than other visitors.

The most popular types of sites are automotive, entertainment, financial services, health, search, and travel. If your business doesn't fit into one of these categories, then you might consider establishing a portal. Portals have an edge in site branding that has the following characteristics.

• Distinctiveness–uniqueness
• Appropriateness–relevance to daily life
• How the brand is regarded
• How familiar the brand is
• Perceived success of the brand
• How popular the brand is

Customer relationship management (CRM) is a growing area of popularity. The major activities of CRM are as follows:

- Customer service
- Customer data management
- E-mail response management
- E-commerce application
- Web self-service
- Marketing campaign automation
- Site activity monitoring
- Personalized sales effort
- Supply chain automation
- Real-time response automation
- Personalized marketing messages
- Cookies
- Cobrowsing
- On-line chat

Using a CRM system, you can collect the following information.

- Sales history
- Customer service requests
- Order fulfillment status
- All customer transaction
- Demographic profiles
- Web activity
- Web transactions
- Site behavior
- Competitive intelligence

CRM software has functions that support the functions and provide the information.

- Client support and services
- Data analysis and segmentation
- Sales and fulfillment
- Promotion and ad campaign monitoring
- Customized messaging

These functions and features sound very appealing. However, there are substantial hurdles in deploying CRM systems. These include:

- Integration with legacy systems
- Scattered legacy data source
- Optimizing system performance

- Cost of CRM software
- Data quality
- Cost of CRM consultants
- Quality of CRM consultants
- Ability to achieve enterprise-wide connectivity
- Lack of standards
- Employee resistance to using front office applications
- Lack of management foresight
- Organizational barriers against sharing information
- Level of service quality from customer service reps
- Round-the-clock availability
- Lack of technical expertise
- Unrealistic customer expectations
- Identification of profitable customers

Another question that arises is the financial justification for CRM systems. Here are the major factors:

- Increased customer loyalty or satisfaction
- Increased revenue
- Lower operating costs
- Increased productivity
- Higher orders per customer/repeat orders
- Increased customer interaction
- Increased number of new customers
- Segmenting higher value customers
- Increased market share
- 24/7 availability
- External connectivity
- Lower cost of promotional products/services
- Increased percentage of sales conducted electronically

Some basic points have emerged in establishing long-term customer relationships:

- Human relationships are more important than just pushing goods and services. The critical factor is to generate regular, repeat visits.
- There is a shift away from discrete transactions that are limited in time and space to relationships to ones that extend in an open-ended way over time.
- There is an emphasis on selling specialized services and providing expertise of many types.
- Companies should concentrate on the share of the customer's attention.
- A long-term goal is that of establishing almost lifetime relationships. There is a concept here of lifetime value (LTV). This balances the present value of purchases against marketing and customer service costs.

- To draw the customers, a company can take specific actions on their Web sites, including acting as agents, providing more services, information on upgrades, and new products as well as use. Being an agent here means acting more as an integrator.
- In industrial economy discrete market transactions give customers control over each decision; in the future, customers risk slowly giving up control over details; purchase of goods gives way to contracting for a range of services of which customers have limited knowledge.
- Marketing and business plans should be based on the customer rather than on production and distribution.
- Marketing tools are needed to create a more comprehensive environment for supporting personal life (hence, more return visits).

Stages in creating communities of interest include linking through awareness, getting the customer to identify with the firm's products and services, establishing relationships, and bringing customers into relationships with others who have a shared interest in the company's interest. As an example, a company that offers specialized tours might encourage interaction among customers, such as sharing experiences, photos, etc. At the heart of this, you want to concentrate on building better and more long lasting relationships with customers through both e-business and normal business channels.

At Walters Catalog there were existing customers from the first e-business effort. These were addressed in marketing as were current customers. Walters avoided providing too many discounts and incentives to customers to drive them to the Web. This would just cannibalize the customer base. Instead, more information and a wider variety of goods were offered.

MARKETING TO SUPPLIERS

This is another area of marketing that deserves your attention. You cannot just announce to suppliers that you are doing business-to-business. Here are some useful actions that you can take in this area:

- Develop profiles of suppliers and their relationships.
- Identify the small percentage of suppliers that you do a high percentage of business transactions with. This is the 5% of suppliers that generate 25% of the transactions, for example.
- Make contacts with these suppliers identified in the preceding action to determine whether they employ e-business and the degree of their e-business readiness and support of e-business.
- Make some of these suppliers members of your e-business steering committee in the implementation of e-business.

Beyond this you will want to undertake a pilot project with selected suppliers. The pilot project has a number of benefits, including:

- Nailing down the details of the business transactions through actual experience.
- Gaining experience in the use of business-to-business software.
- Identification of potential problems that exist in transactions.
- Measurement data on the benefits of e-business.
- Establishment of a closer working relationship with suppliers.
- Building links between business department managers and the vendor managers.

The suppliers in the pilot project can then be used to convince other suppliers that e-business is the way to go.

At Walters Catalog vendors were contacted to see what e-business transactions they supported. The effort in implementation then centered on those suppliers that currently used e-business. Other suppliers would be addressed later.

STARTUP

You can review Figure 9.1 for comments on the examples.

INDO FURNITURE

Indo Furniture had very few marketing issues. The attention was centered on how to line up customers and retailers. It was found that direct contact with some samples was the most appropriate approach.

DIAMOND ENGINEERING DATA

The marketing to customers and suppliers was the major focus. Customers were approached through limited advertising and direct contact. There was some advertising to get more engineers involved to submit and participate in the development of the knowledge base.

EXAMPLES

ASEAN CONSTRUCTION

Marketing to employees was done through expanding participation as the e-business grew. This effort began during the planning for e-business. For the sup-

Subject	Company					
	Indo Furniture	Diamond Engineering	Asean Construction	Walters Catalog-1	Walters Catalog-2	Rogers County
Employees	No problem	Not applicable	Joint participation in planning and implementation	As needed	Action teams, opportunities, Quick Hits	Through participation
Marketing	Limited	Limited	Limited	Not addressed	Limited organization change	Changes in thinking about promotions
Customers	Through direct contacts	Through advertising and direct contact	Advertising and incentives	Not addressed except through advertising	Through advertising	Through advertisements
Suppliers	Not applicable	Direct contact	Direct contacts	Not addressed	E-business experienced suppliers	Selected suppliers

Figure 9.1   Table of Example Companies for Marketing

pliers the approach was to find those that were large enough and sufficiently sophisticated to do e-business. This amounted to less than 50 firms. The remainder were either too small or did very little business with Asean. For the business-to-consumer areas such as electronic tag there was a promotion to encourage people to use credit and to employ the Web. This effort continued and gradually expanded.

ROGERS COUNTY

In operations the approach was to involve as many employees in the development of the vision and objectives of e-business. This continued through implementation of e-business. In the marketing area a new person was brought in with more marketing experience. For consumers, Rogers County began to do promotions and advertising. This effort continued on a limited basis with testimonials from consumers. Rogers Country does business with many suppliers. About one-fourth of these were involved in some way with e-business. So the effort here centered on these firms.

LESSONS LEARNED

A basic lesson learned is that a passive Web site does not cut it. Instead, you should concentrate on the following approaches:

• Create wizards in which you support customers to perform analysis and make decisions.
• Establish lessons learned in selecting, using, installing, diagnosing, troubleshooting, upgrading, and replacing their products and services.

These are both added-value services that are useful to provide.

THE SCORE CARD

There are a number of measurements that you can take here. These include the following:

• How many employees have been involved in the e-business implementation?
• What has been the number and type of suggestions for Quick Hits generated by employees?
• What is the overall approach with customers? Is it long-term oriented?
• How is the marketing organization involved in the implementation? Are there signs that they have adopted an e-business mentality?

- How have suppliers become involved in the e-business effort?
- Do you have a sufficient number of suppliers to start doing e-business?

WHAT TO DO NEXT

An idea here is to assess your e-business readiness in the marketing organization and among suppliers. You should undertake the survey of suppliers that was discussed earlier. For the marketing organization, you should seek out individuals in the department who have an interest in e-business. These are likely to be junior employees. For customers, you can begin to review what customer information that you have. You can also review your existing Web site to see how customer friendly it is and what services and information that you offer.

Chapter 10

Create Your Organization Approach for E-Business

INTRODUCTION

As has been said, e-business is a program and not a one-time project. As such, you want your organization approach for e-business to apply to both the short-term and long-term transformation into e-business. E-business involves the business more than it does IT. E-business has business, cultural, and political goals as well as IT goals. These statements impact how you will organize your approach to e-business implementation. At the heart of your approach is the support of the objectives in the next section.

If you organize the e-business effort along traditional lines, here are some of the potential impacts.

- A limited number of people will be involved in e-business implementation. There will be reduced commitment because the involvement is less. People will feel detached from the work.
- The focus of the implementation will tend to be exclusively on e-business. This sounds OK, but it really is not. The implementation team will miss many short-term opportunities for improvement that can lead to e-business. Management may have high expectations and want fast results. By devoting attention only to the end goal, there are likely to be few rapid results. The effort is more likely to be cancelled. Management is more likely to interfere with the implementation.
- The e-business work will probably be done in a more sequential manner. This will take longer. You need a parallel approach.
- E-business may be treated as an IT project. This has been cited in many survey of managers as a major cause for problems and failure. As a result, busi-

ness managers may not be committed to the work. It is easier for them to take the position that IT should do the implementation.

PURPOSE AND SCOPE

BUSINESS OBJECTIVES

The business purpose is to establish an organization for e-business that will support the attainment of the e-business goals. A second goal is to ensure that the current business activities are not disrupted. All you need is to have e-business implemented successfully, but the business to be torn up. This is akin to having the operation successful, but the patient dead.

POLITICAL AND CULTURAL OBJECTIVES

In organizing your e-business effort, there are a number of political and cultural objectives.

• Widespread participation and commitment to e-business. By having many employees involved, they gain an understanding of e-business and become supportive. They realize that it is not as much of a threat to their jobs. Within reasonable limits, more people means that you gain a better perspective and can carry out more parallel work.
• Implementation of a culture of cooperation among employees and departments. E-business transactions cross departments. Thus, cooperation is necessary not only in implementation, but also during day-to-day operation. The e-business implementation provides a period of time where the employees and managers can work together.
• Performance of responsibilities. Ensure that managers and employees can perform their roles without interference from each other. Management interference and micromanagement of e-business have been cited as problems.
• High morale. Through the e-business work, you want to achieve high morale and a sense of accomplishment.

TECHNICAL OBJECTIVES

You obviously want to achieve specific technical goals in the work leading up to a working e-business system and technology environment. However, this is very fuzzy. There are more tangible objectives:

• *Stable requirements.* Through widespread participation and reviewing the current processes and transactions, you are likely to have more stable requirements.

• *User acceptance.* Many systems have been implemented successfully. However, the business processes were not changed. Life continued in business departments in the same way. There were no benefits. You want to pursue an approach that leads to user acceptance without management dictates.

SCOPE

The scope of the organization includes the managers and employees and how they will approach the e-business implementation. However, the scope cannot stop here. The rest of the business still goes on. There are more projects in other areas. IT has a project slate and existing support work. You want an organization approach that is sensitive to this.

END PRODUCTS

If you review the purposes and scope, you can see that there are a number of end products. The stated end product is to implement an organization approach that supports both the initial implementation of e-business and sustains the ongoing operation and growth of e-business. Unstated end products include developing a culture of collaboration and joint work. Information is shared in such a setting as opposed to being kept within departments. Another end product is support by the employees.

APPROACH

THE E-BUSINESS ORGANIZATION

In traditional projects you just organize a team. For large projects you may have a steering committee. This approach has many problems for e-business.

• Taking a traditional approach, you tend to reinforce the organizational silos and do not support the culture.

• The two-tiered structure does not easily support the involvement of consultants or outsiders such as suppliers.

• The standard approach places management too close to the team. Upper level management may then overly interfere with the work. This has been cited among the top five causes of e-business failure.

A Three-Tiered Approach for E-Business

What is a more suitable project organization for e-business? A proven approach is three tiered. The core e-business team represents the coordination center. Here are some comments on these:

• *Lowest level.* The work is organized around action teams. An action team focuses on a set of business processes. Each action team is composed of employees from different departments. These are lower level people who do the work and know its problems and advantages. A rule is that an employee can only serve on one action team.

• *Middle level.* This is the steering committee. Members of the steering committee include some of the action team members, upper management members of the executive (highest) level, members of the core e-business team, and outsiders such as suppliers and consultants.

• *Highest level.* This is the executive committee. It is composed of upper level managers.

• *Core e-business team.* This consists of the project leaders for e-business along with key employees and consultants, if appropriate.

The core e-business team coordinates the effort of the action teams and communications and coordination across the three tiers. The approach is highlighted in Figure 10.1.

There are a number of advantages of this approach:

• Many more employees can be involved in the project because there can be a number of action teams.

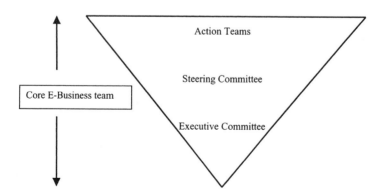

Note that this diagram is shown bottom up and not top down.

Figure 10.1   E-Business Organization Tiers

- The members of the action teams perform their normal work in addition to the action team work. Because the work of the action team is limited due to focusing on key transactions, this is reasonable. There is a political benefit here—having their normal work puts pressure on the action teams to finish their work.
- Management at the executive committee level is removed from the action teams due to the presence of the steering committee.
- Work can be performed in parallel across the action teams. This is essential to keep the elapsed time of the implementation down.

The Roles and Responsibilities of the Teams and Committees

The action teams begin to work on the implementation early. They will identify issues and opportunities that must be addressed in order to implement e-business. Some of these will become Quick Hits that will be implemented prior to e-business. Quick Hits pave the way for e-business. The steering committee reviews the selected items proposed by the action teams. They review opportunities for improvement as well as business cases. Members of the steering committee might consist of supervisors and middle level managers. The executive committee reviews the business cases approved by the steering committee for action and implementation. The executive committee also can review the results. Some managers may serve on both the steering and executive committees for continuity.

HOW THE PROCESS WORKS

The process for each action team is the same and is shown in Figure 10.2.

Step 1: Form the Action Teams and Management Committees

You first have to identify the business processes, as was done in Chapter 2. Then you can aggregate these into groups. Each group of processes constitutes an action team. Review your lists with managers to get them involved. This will show potential members of the management committees that things are serious. You already have the duties and roles of each tier. In more detail, the action teams will review the business processes assigned to them and identify opportunities for improvement. After preparing a short write-up for each of these, voting will occur. The best of these will be further analyzed. The action teams may also support implementation.

The action teams, steering committee, and executive committee are formed. Action team members are identified by management and the core e-business team.

Setup	Step 1:	Form the action teams and management committees
Teamwork	Step 2:	Identify opportunities for improvement that support e-business
Voting	Step 3:	Vote on opportunities
Review	Step 4:	Review opportunities with the steering committee
Teamwork	Step 5:	Develop business cases of approved opportunities
Voting	Step 6:	Vote on the business cases
Review	Step 7:	Conduct a management review of business cases
Setup	Step 8:	Organize the approved business cases

Figure 10.2   Collaborative Method for Opportunities

One guideline here is to use junior business department employees. This has several benefits. First, it has the least impact on the business. This will gain you allies among business managers. Second, the younger people will tend to question how things are currently performed, and are less wedded to the current procedures. In contrast, the senior business employees have their power base in the current methods. They are more resistant to change. Action team members should be from different departments. There should be four or five people on an action team. Unless there is an unusual situation no person should be required to serve on more than one action team.

Before going further, it is important to consider the individuals who will serve as the leaders of the specific action teams. Suppose that you had an action team that was addressing finance processes. It is a very bad idea to have this team headed up by someone from finance. Such a person probably thinks that the way they do their work is fine. You will not get much out of such a team. Instead of this method, select a team leader who is from another department that interfaces with the finance action team. The person might be from marketing or sales for example. Why do this? One reason is that you seek to have new, creative ideas emerge. Another reason is that you want to instill a spirit of cooperation and collaboration across departments. Thus, the major guideline is that the action team leaders must come from areas different from the processes that the action team is addressing.

At Walters Catalog in the first effort at e-business, there was no organized management approach. The project leader appointed reported to the president of the company. While empowered to get things done, the leader apparently ran into many roadblocks because people were focused on their narrow jobs. In the second round (Walters 2), the approach was initiated top down, but then moved to the lower levels of the organization. The action team method along with the two committees was employed.

Step 2: Identify Opportunities for Improvement That Support E-Business

The core e-business team explains the method to each action team. The action teams under the guidance of the core e-business team begin to identify opportunities. This starts with just a list and a one-paragraph description of the opportunity. Here are examples of opportunities:

- Issues and problems involved in the business processes that impact their ability to do work. Many of these are long-standing and have been ignored.
- Opportunities for work improvement.
- Potential policy changes.
- Workflow changes.

The core e-business team will work with individual team members to define these. This can be accomplished through direct observation of the work. Now the core e-business team is aware of e-commerce and e-business as well as the technology. They can employ this knowledge to help action team members identify how the technology could be used in their work. This has a major benefit. You do not have to train the action teams in e-business. Another benefit is that e-business is not as threatening.

The core e-business team explains to the action teams that they will understand that e-business really means changing a subset of transactions. Not everything will be altered. This will reduce fear. This also shows the major differences with reengineering. Once you have started to identify potential opportunities, the core e-business team can determine which of these can support e-business or provide short-term improvements that are consistent with e-business implementation. For each opportunity that has been determined to have potential, the action team members will now define the following parameters:

- Subject of the opportunity.
- Description of the opportunity.
- Priority and importance. Here you discuss the reasons for assigning this a high priority and giving it importance for the business and e-business.
- Impact if not addressed. If the opportunity is not dealt with, what are the impacts and effects on both the business and e-business?
- Recommended course of action. What should be done to fix this issue or pursue this opportunity?
- Expected benefits, if implemented. How will the business, employees, customers, and suppliers be benefited if the opportunity is implemented or if the issue is fixed?

You can create a form for this and place it on the network server. As these are developed, the core e-business team can enter the data into a spreadsheet. To the fields listed above you should add status. Here are some status codes:

- Created
- Written up for voting
- Approved for a business case
- Dropped
- Combined with another opportunity
- Business case completed
- Business case approved by the steering committee
- Business case approved by the executive committee
- Implemented
- Implemented and results measured

In a short time of a few weeks you will be able to generate, perhaps, several hundred opportunities. The number depends on the number of action teams as well as the business situation and e-business goals. Opportunities will often be combined and merged. Some may be dropped. During this work the action team members continue to do their normal work. This works because what they are doing is related to their everyday work. It also adds pressure to get the action team work completed.

There is a specific behavioral phenomenon that will occur during this work. Action team members who never really worked together much before will begin to address issues and opportunities more openly with each other. Each team member will see the perspective of the other members for a specific issue. There will often a move to consensus. So you see how this begins to instill your new culture. In addition, team members will often consult with other employees in their home departments. This brings more people into the e-business effort. It has a multiplier effect that is very beneficial to collaboration.

In Walters Catalog (Walters 2) over 200 opportunities were identified in a period of 6 weeks. These were evaluated and some were combined so that after weeding out ones with little benefit and high implementation effort, the number was reduced to about 55. It is interesting to note that collaboration across departments improved remarkably after the action teams began their work. Once opportunities began to surface, it seemed like there was a flood of ideas. Some ideas were good, but did not apply to e-business. These were handled separately, off-line.

Step 3: Vote on Opportunities

With the opportunities identified and tabulated, each action team can vote on the improvements. Voting will be based upon the following criteria:

- Importance of the opportunity to regular work.
- Support of and alignment to e-business (determined with core e-business team guidance).
- Potential benefits and negative impacts, if not addressed.
- Overall priority and importance.

The voting is on a scale of 1–5 with 1 being low and 5 being very high. These are subjective. The voting process is to discuss each opportunity and then to vote independently. After voting by the individual action teams, the core e-business team tabulates the results. The results are then presented back to the action team members for additional input. Action team members can then change their votes. The benefits are more collaboration and consensus. There will also be more support for implementation.

In Walters 2 each action team met with the core e-business team to discuss the opportunities and then identify additional information needed prior to voting. The person in the department where the question arose usually collected the information. After this was gathered, the action team voted.

Step 4: Review Opportunities with the Steering Committee

The voting results are circulated by the core e-business team to the members of the steering committee. The action team leaders and selected team members present their voting to the steering committee. The core e-business team does not make the presentation, because you seek to have the action team assume ownership for their opportunities and voting results.

The steering committee can take the following actions:

- Send the opportunity back for further work.
- Drop the opportunity.
- Adopt and approve the opportunity for preparation of a business case.
- Merge the opportunity with another one.
- Direct the immediate implementation of the opportunity (after all, why wait if it can be done easily without disrupting the business and if it fits with the organization?).
- Assume ownership of the opportunity to pursue it on their own (this might be true for policy issues, for example).

The core e-business team documents the results of the steering committee review.

In Walters 2 each member of the steering committee was individually briefed by the core e-business team prior to the full steering committee review meeting. This saved considerable time and effort. The steering committee provided managers with a chance to comment directly on individual opportunities. The steering committee then voted and suggested further actions on the approved opportunities.

Step 5: Develop Business Cases of Approved Opportunities

The approved opportunities return to the action teams. Each opportunity now has a business case prepared. This is a more detailed write-up of the opportunity. It includes the following parameters:

- *Area.* This identifies the action team.
- *Situation.* This is an expansion of the description in the opportunity write-up.
- *Impact* if not addressed.
- *Solution.* This is a detailed step-by-step discussion of a solution to the issue.
- *Benefit.* The business, e-business, IT, customer, supplier, and other benefits are discussed.
- *How benefits would be measured.* This provides how the benefits would be assessed.
- *Implementation.* This is a discussion of how the solution would be put in place.

There are many benefits to this step. First, the team members have to think through the solution from different perspectives. Given the team members are from different departments, this should result in a spirited discussion. The same holds for implementation. Second, the team members who do the work are determining benefits and covering implementation. This increases their commitment. It also helps to ensure that the solution and its implementation will work.

Another step to take is to have someone in finance or accounting review the benefits and certify them or raise questions. In some cases, you might even want someone from these areas to develop the benefits. This requires more resources, but it provides a separate, independent set of eyes.

At Walters Catalog (Walters 2) the employees did not have much experience in preparing business cases. As a result, the initial business cases were developed by the core e-business team with input from action team members. Then the action team members generated lists and ideas for the remainder of the business cases. The finance area reviewed the costs and benefits of the business cases. It is not appropriate to perform this review prior to this due to the number of opportunities.

Step 6: Vote on the Business Cases

Why vote again? Because you want to have people agree on the benefits and implementability of the business cases. Another reason is to provide further collaboration. In preparation for the voting the core e-business team will prepare the following items:

- A list of elements of the e-business vision. These will be rows in one table for voting.
- A list of implementation concerns. An example is given in Figure 10.3.
- Standardized voting form.

The process for voting is the same as that for opportunities. Note that the focus here is on two things: alignment to the e-business vision and implementation. Benefits are reflected in the implementation factors, but are not the main focus because they were covered in the opportunities.

- Expense to implement
- Time to implement
- Culture resistance
- Manager/staff resistance
- Technology complexity
- Effect of other projects
- Effect on other projects
- Dependence on other work
- Competition for resources
- External dependency—any other systems
- External dependency—vendor
- Ease of measuring results
- Incompatibility with organization

Figure 10.3   Implementation Factors in Voting on Business Cases

At Walters Catalog (Walters 2) the initial voting on opportunities was done on the basis of the benefits and nature of the opportunity. Specific focus is on the impact of not pursuing the opportunity. Here in this round of voting attention shifts to implementation and the ease of implementing the opportunity in the business case.

Step 7: Conduct a Management Review of Business Cases

At the end of this work, the approved business cases are ready to be grouped into waves of Quick Hits and e-business. The presentation approach for the steering committee is the same as that for opportunities. The method for the executive committee begins with the steering committee members talking to the executive committee members. Both the steering committee and the executive committee review the results. In the end, there are the following results for each business case:

- Send the business case back for further work.
- Approve the business case for implementation as a Quick Hit.
- Combine business cases.

This approach was followed in Walters 2.

Step 8: Organize the Approved Business Cases

Here the core e-business team organizes the approved business cases into waves of Quick Hits and e-business. There are waves of Quick Hits because these are interrelated and some are required before others can be carried out. E-business business cases are those that are needed for e-business, but not capable of short-term implementation. You don't want to spend much time here. You want to begin on project planning and sequencing of the business cases for implementation right after the voting on the business cases. This is because you desire to implement some of the Quick Hits right after approval by the executive committee to keep morale up and momentum going.

STARTUP

Refer to Figure 10.4 for the example companies.

INDO FURNITURE

The examples are shown in Figure 10.4. In such a small organization there is obviously no need for an exotic organizational structure. Basically, family members acted as the executive committee. The two people working in the operation side in the United States and the head of the family constituted the steering committee. This was organized informally. The team approach was based on managing issues. The main communications problem that arose was around time zones. It just is and has been always difficult to work on a global project. For all areas but the Indo factory, e-mail and some intranet groupware software were employed. Facsimile transmission was employed with the factory. Each issue was numbered and tracked for resolution.

DIAMOND ENGINEERING DATA

Chris and Mike were everything until investors were found. Then the approach changed. The investors joined the two of them in the executive committee. It was decided to involve some outside senior engineering managers and technical people on the steering committee. These people were hired as consultants. They provided a great deal of useful input on sources of people for the knowledge base as well as reviewing the software. Chris and Mike held daily meetings in person or by telephone. They employed a manual issues tracking approach for communications. Issues substituted for opportunities in what you have read.

EXAMPLES

ASEAN CONSTRUCTION

Due to the size of Asean and the distributed nature of the firm, it was obvious that the approach in this chapter had to adapt to these things. An overall executive

			Company			
Subject	**Indo Furniture**	**Diamond Engineering**	**Asean Construction**	**Walters Catalog-1**	**Walters Catalog-2**	**Rogers County**
Management approach	Remote support and management; family steering committee	Two-person approach and then investors	Same as in chapter with steering committee in each business unit	Project leader reporting to president	Action teams, steering committees, executive committees	Steering committee, action teams, informal executive committee
Team approach	Issues based	Daily meeting	Teams in business units and corporate	Ad hoc teams	As in chapter	Issues based
Issues	Communications across time zones	Maintained issues manually	Issues database	No structured approach	Overcome the past perceptions	No formal method

Figure 10.4 Organization Approach for Example Companies

committee was formed at the corporate level along with a steering committee for company-wide initiatives. At the level of the business unit, some business units that were small established just the steering committee. The two largest business units set up both an executive committee and a steering committee.

The method of defining opportunities was the same as that described above. The voting method was changed to reflect cultural characteristics. More specifically, there would be discussions of opportunities. Then the core e-business team met with individual action team members and the head of an action team. In this way consensus was achieved. The results were then reviewed in an action team meeting. An opportunities database was established as was an issues database related to specific barriers and problems for e-business. Lotus Notes groupware was employed for implementing these databases. The major issue that arose was communications across the business units and corporate. Core e-business team members handled the communications. In some cases, there had to be ad hoc meetings of management to resolve specific questions that involved business policies.

ROGERS COUNTY

At Rogers County the method described earlier in the chapter was employed, with one change. To avoid formality the executive committee was made informal. From experience in government agencies, this has always been found to be more effective than formal committees, where there is often too much political positioning. There was no formal method for dealing with issues and problems. Instead, an informal method was used with the core e-business team working with specific managers. This turned out to be quite productive. It was felt that if issues and opportunities were formally identified, it would be more difficult to make progress.

LESSONS LEARNED

You are bound to encounter either resistance or questions. Here are some that we have met:

• While the method is OK, management has never implemented employee suggestions before. Therefore, the argument goes, the effort is futile. The answer to this is that until you try it, you really cannot determine the outcome. Moreover, this method is bottom-up. It is based on grass roots effort. This is difficult to turn around.

• Many of the issues appear insurmountable. They have been around and have shown persistence for years. That is probably true. However, you want to stress that it does no harm to surface these. Also, e-business is a powerful incentive for addressing these.

• What's in it for me? This is a basic question that you must always keep in mind—even if it is not raised formally. Here is your answer. Participating in the action teams gives you a better idea of how the business works. Participation gives you the chance to be seen by management in a positive light. You will have a role in e-business. In the end you could advance your own career.

THE SCORE CARD

Is your organization approach working? Here are some things to consider:

• Are people complaining about too much work, or are they genuinely interested in the effort?
• As the method proceeds, are people getting more interested?
• What feedback do you receive as you talk with individuals informally?
• Is there substantial and growing consensus as you pursue the method?
• Is there a growing awareness of the needs of customers and suppliers?

WHAT TO DO NEXT

To prepare yourself for the approach, you can undertake the following actions:

• Select one set of processes (two or three will do).
• Walk through the method with other people.
• Discuss what potential cultural and political problems might arise.

This assists you to see both how the method will work and what potential problems you will encounter.

Establish Your Project and Program Management Approach

INTRODUCTION

You might think that you could manage the implementation of e-business like a standard project. Companies who have failed in their e-business efforts have cited this as one of the top three reasons for the failure. E-business is different for the following reasons:

• E-business is an ongoing program and not a one-time project. This has been mentioned throughout the book and it applies to project management here.

• In e-business much of the money is spent earlier in the project. However, most of the effort and risk occur at the end of the work. Why is this? Because system integration, customer/supplier/employee acceptance, quality assurance, and other critical activities happen toward the end.

• E-business success depends on parallel, nonsequential thinking. If you implement sequentially, you may never finish. That's why there is no sequencing in the chapter headings of this book.

• E-business implementation is a collaborative approach. Standard project management is hierarchical.

• In traditional project management you focus on the mathematical critical path. In e-business it is not the tasks on the longest path that give you trouble, it is the tasks that have issues and risk.

These are just some of the factors why e-business is different from traditional project management.

PURPOSE AND SCOPE

BUSINESS OBJECTIVES

The business objective is to put a project management approach in place that not only ensures the initial e-business implementation is successful, but also that the way is paved for future e-business success. Another business goal is to make the likelihood of unpleasant surprises and major problems minimal.

POLITICAL AND CULTURAL OBJECTIVES

Putting in e-business affects the power structure among departments. Some departments such as marketing often find that e-business means that they cannot operate as independently as they did before. The political goal of the e-business work is to head off and prevent or, if necessary, effectively deal with political problems so that the implementation can proceed.

E-business automates transactions across departments. Implementation requires that people in these departments as well as other employees, suppliers, and even selected customers participate in the e-business work. After e-business is operational, a critical success factor to continued success is that these people continue to work together, share information, and jointly address situations.

From the above comments it is clear that the major cultural objective for the e-business implementation is to provide an environment and project structure in which people must work together. If you organize the work in the standard way where each department is assigned tasks independently, then you will fail. People will never learn how to work together. Even if you succeed in getting e-business going within budget and schedule, you fail because when problems arise after the implementation, there is no collaboration.

TECHNICAL OBJECTIVES

Program management is management. Yet, there are technical objectives. Previously, an entire chapter was devoted to outsourcing. Outsourcing is employed by over 70% of e-business projects. Successful e-business implementation depends upon the IT organization and the vendors addressing technical issues and coordinating their technical approaches to the work.

SCOPE

The scope of a traditional project normally is very narrow. In building a bridge, it is just the bridge itself. You do not consider the organization and people involved in the construction. IT projects are broader in scope. In IT projects you consider some aspects of the business processes—but to a limited extent. In reengineering, your scope includes all aspects of the business, but not IT as much.

The scope of e-business is very different from these traditional considerations. Because e-business is political, there is both a stated scope of work and an implicit scope of work. The stated scope of work includes the following elements:

- IT systems
- IT architecture and infrastructure
- Business transactions within and across departments
- Selected business policies
- Other business transactions and processes impacted by e-business
- Vendor and contractor relations and work
- Supplier and customer relations

You can add to these the following implicit elements:

- The culture of the organization. Note the cultural objectives above.
- The business organization. The business organization will tend to change, reflecting the realities and effects of e-business.
- The role of IT. In e-business IT has to expand its role into coordination.

END PRODUCTS

Given the purpose and scope, you can identify the following stated end products:

- Enhanced IT architecture that is scalable and responsive to e-business.
- Functional e-business transactions and systems.
- Business policies and procedures that are synchronized with e-business.
- Increased customer and supplier information.

In addition to these, you have the following implicit end products:

- A changed organization culture that is more collaborative.
- Political and business pressure to address exceptions, workarounds, and shadow systems that are left over when e-business becomes operational.

- A business organization that is supportive of e-business.
- An IT organization that is more flexible and responsive to the ongoing needs of e-business.
- Improved customer and supplier relationships.

Will you attain all of these end products with your project management method? Probably not. However, if you aim too low, you will likely miss many opportunities.

APPROACH

E-Business Program Managers

Traditionally, you would appoint one person to serve as the project manager. This approach is fraught with peril. If this person becomes unavailable, then the project is in jeopardy. If the project leader gets some managers or groups angry, then recovery for a single person is very difficult at best. E-business involves the business, IT, vendors, and many other elements. It is hard to imagine that you could find and afford one person who could feel at home with all of these diverse elements. For these reasons, you should have two project leaders for e-business implementation.

There are some additional advantages to this method. E-business is a program. It will continue for a long time. Having two project managers provides continuity over time. At the end of the initial e-business implementation one of the project leaders might drop out and go on to other work. A new project leader is then appointed as a replacement. This method allows for rotation. Two project leaders can see situations, problems, and opportunities from different perspectives. This is very valuable due to the complexity of e-business. Another advantage is political. In difficult situations one person can play the good guy (or "white hat") and the other can be more strict and stern (the "black hat"). This gives you much more flexibility.

How does a multiple-project-leader approach work? Or, how do you make the approach work? A key concern is accountability. Our rule is that any given point in time one of the two can serve as the overall leader. This will shift over time. In the initial work, the business-oriented leader is the manager in charge. In the middle much of the work is technical so the IT person is in charge. Toward the end of the effort, the focus shifts back to the business so it is appropriate for the business person to be the lead manager. Who would you select for project/program leadership? One project leader might be technically oriented and come from IT. This person will have knowledge of the business processes. The second person might have a good understanding of the business and have worked in different business departments. This person will also have a good business understanding of technology and systems. What attributes should you look for to fill these positions? Start with the information above. There are two critical attributes of successful project leaders. One is the ability to solve problems. The second is the ability to communicate with managers, employees, and outsiders such as suppliers, consultants, and vendors. Not surprisingly, these are key characteristics of project leaders in general.

In Walters 1 there was one project leader who eventually just gave up. The successor did not have any overlap time with him. There was no transfer of knowledge. For Walters 2 there were two e-business leaders. The two people worked out how the work would be managed.

E-Business Team Members

In the previous chapter, the organization approach was discussed. There are four types of team members to consider.

- Members of the action teams.
- Members of the core e-business team.
- Employees who are going to be involved in the implementation of e-business after the implementation strategy (Chapter 12) has been defined.
- Consultants and contract staff who are supporting e-business.

For each you must consider (1) how they are selected, (2) how they are introduced into the e-business effort, and (3) specific situations for that type of team member. One guideline that is universal is that you should assign many of the tasks to more than one person. One person should be designated as in charge of the task. By making the tasks joint you support collaboration. You also provide for back-up in case one team member leaves. Two people will also offer a wider array of knowledge and skills to the work.

Members of the Action Teams

The core e-business team leaders can interview the managers of business departments to find people who really perform the work. You are not after support staff or managers at higher levels. You might include supervisors who are hands-on. Validate what they tell you by observing the business process in action. After you have identified someone, talk to them with the business manager. Go over the method and their role. Indicate that the work is not full time. This gives you the opportunity to answer any questions and address any concerns.

For Walters 2 managers suggested possible members who were identified to the core e-business team members. A core e-business team member then interviewed a potential action team member. Here are some of the questions that were posed:

- What activities did they work on in their departments?
- How long had they been doing their job?
- Have they held any other positions in the firm or similar positions in other companies?

Having gotten an idea of a potential action team member's range of experience, you can now make a determination as to whether the person is a "king bee" or a "queen bee." Such a person will likely have an in-depth knowledge of the business rules. As such, they are needed by the department on an almost constant basis to address problems and questions that their staff members encounter. Having them on an action team might reduce their availability to the other staff members. This is one reason for excluding them. Another reason is political. A "king bee" or "queen bee" often has substantial informal or formal power in the department. The power is formal if the person is a supervisor. If the person is not a supervisor, then their power might be diluted if some of the transactions were automated. This makes them a candidate for elimination. Such individuals may also want to include all of the exceptions of the current process in e-business.

Now you want to proceed further with questions related to their interest and ideas related to the business processes that they touch:

- What problems have they had in doing the work? What problems have others in the department encountered?
- How do they work with people in other departments on the transactions?
- What ideas do they have for fixing the problems?
- What ideas do they have for improving the work in their departments?
- If they could do two things to improve the situation, what would they do?
- If they had money for improvement, what would they do?

Here you are testing their creativity and their interest in their jobs. If they have been working in the department for some time and if they do not have any ideas, then he/she is a candidate for elimination. For action team membership you are after individuals who have some ideas of potential improvements, for it is rarely the case that a business process or department operation is perfect and not capable of being improved.

Members of the Core E-Business Team

Beyond the team leaders, there are going to be a few employees who are important. These can be either from the business or IT. They should be selected on the basis of the following criteria:

- Problem-solving ability and creativity.
- Ability to work with others.
- Steadfastness in pursuing specific objectives.

Notice that knowledge of the systems and business is not listed. These people can be action team members and members of the implementation team. In Walters 2 three people were selected based on the action team interviews. They were selected on the following criteria:

- Ability to work with other people.
- Creative ideas for improvement.
- General knowledge of the business.

E-Business Implementation Team Members

As the e-business implementation proceeds, the Quick Hits are implemented separate from, but coordinated with, e-business. E-business implementation involves systems design, programming, integration, testing, and documentation. Other work includes data conversion, Web page setup, training materials, operations procedures, and policies. You will identify the requirements as the work progresses and then get people on the team. Don't attempt to keep them on the team too long. They have other responsibilities. In Walters 2 these people were identified based on their specific roles in the business transactions that would be impacted by e-business. Some of these people were members of the core e-business team and action teams. Others were selected based on their in-depth knowledge.

Consultants and Contract Staff

In standard projects, consultants are assigned work and then go off and do it. They later show up with their end products. This is not acceptable for e-business. You want the vendor staff to participate in the project work with internal employees. This will build lessons learned and experience for the long haul. It will also provide for better tracking of work and earlier identification of issues and problems. In Walters 2 consultants were hired for a number of activities. One was in software development. Another was in process improvement.

CREATE THE E-BUSINESS PROJECT PLAN

Design the Overall Project

At the start you are faced with dividing up the large e-business effort into logical pieces. You have the following goals:

Here is a general division based on importance and risk:
- Division by action team for Quick Hits and e-business implementation
- Data conversion
- Testing and quality assurance for software
- Web data setup
- Web data verification and review
- System integration
- Marketing
- Promotions
- Customer relations
- Vendor and supplier relations

Figure 11.1   Example of Subprojects for E-Business Implementation

- Accountability for the work.
- Ensuring that areas of risk and potential problems have sufficient visibility.
- Support for a collaborative approach.

That is why you should divide the work up by risk and organize subprojects across departments. Use the action teams as the basis for the collaboration. Areas of risk include:

- Testing and quality assurance.
- Marketing.
- Data conversion and Web setup.
- Integration.
- Rollout to suppliers, customers, or employees.

The Quick Hit implementation can be done in separate projects. An example of a project structure breakdown is given in Figure 11.1.

The Use of Project Templates

In the past the project manager created the plan using a work breakdown structure (WBS). A WBS is a detailed listing of tasks that potentially may be used in the project plan. While this might have worked in the past, it is less relevant to e-business. A better approach is to use project templates. A project template consists of high-level tasks, dependencies, and general resources assigned to the tasks. General milestones are also included. The template does not include the detailed tasks. Nor does it include durations, dates, or specific resources. There are a number of benefits of using a template:

- The template provides for overall structure for e-business.
- The template supports flexibility in the detailed tasks.
- The template provides for stability. The detail can change, but the structure remains.

• Building a template provides a collaborative opportunity for people to understand and agree with the work and meaning of the tasks.

• Lessons learned can be linked to the tasks so that they can be readily identified and used later.

An example of a template is given in Appendix 2.

Figure 11.2 shows the template for Quick Hits for the individual action teams of Walters Catalog (Walters 2). Note that there were two phases of Quick Hits. Figure 11.3 gives the tasks based on this template. In Walters 1, without a template, the project leader developed a detailed plan that contained over 1500 tasks. It was very cumbersome and hard for people to follow.

Collaborative Construction of the Plan

After you have the template, you can assemble the appropriate team members and review it with them. The team members then go off and define the detailed tasks in their part of the plan. The resulting tasks are reviewed with the leaders. There is discussion on what to do and how to do it. Potential issues surface. The detailed tasks are validated.

What is an issue? It is a potential problem. It may involve resource allocation, experience, politics, technology, systems, business units, or external factors. Managing an e-business effort often boils down to managing issues. If you let an issue remain unresolved for a long time, it may later undermine the entire project. As an example, an issue might be the other responsibilities of a team member for their normal work. Another example is that the team members may not be familiar with the technology.

Phase I Quick Hits
    10100   Kickoff and initial analysis
    10200   Review of current workflow, procedures, systems, and policies
    10300   Gather, review, and present first opportunities
    10400   Implement first Quick Hits
    10500   Opportunities/missions/processes

Phase II Additional Quick Hits and Process Improvement
    30100   Business processes
    30200   Perform analysis of new business process
    30300   Management information reports
    30400   Presentation and review of new processes
    30500   Measurement prior to implementation
    30600   Implement new process
    30700   Measurement after implementation
    30800   Management presentation

Figure 11.2   Example of the Quick Hit Project Template for Walters Catalog

Phase I Quick Hits
   10100   Kickoff and initial analysis
           10110   Kickoff meeting
           10120   Initial assessment of processes
   10200   Review of current workflow, procedures, systems, and policies
           10210   Identify opportunities
           10220   Perform analysis
   10300   Gather, review, and present first opportunities
           10310   Identify short-term improvements
           10320   Review opportunities
           10330   Define evaluation method for opportunities
           10340   Strike force evaluates opportunities
           10350   Construct initial business cases
           10360   Review business cases
           10370   Present to steering committee
           10380   Present to executive committee
   10400   Implement first Quick Hits
           10410   Implementation plan
           10420   Measurement before implementation
                  10421   Determine measurement approach
                  10422   Conduct measurements
                  10423   Analyze measurement information
                  10424   Prepare measurement report
           10430   Implementation
                  10431   Organization
                  10432   Procedures/workflow
                  10433   Interfaces
                  10434   Systems and technology
                  10435   Training and staffing
                  10436   Support
           10440   Measurement after implementation
                  10441   Determine measurement approach
                  10442   Conduct measurements
                  10443   Analyze measurement information
                  10444   Prepare measurement report
   10500   Opportunities/missions/processes
           10510   Department mission
                  10511   Initial mission
                  10512   Refine mission
                  10513   Fit mission with off-site team-defined
                          general mission
           10520   Identify processes for department
                  10521   Define overall list of processes
                  10522   Define department specific processes
           10530   Opportunity, business case assessment
                  10531   Define additional opportunities
                  10532   Strike force reviews and scores
                        opportunities
                  10533   Divide opportunities into Phases I and II
                  10534   Prepare business cases
                  10535   Review business cases
           10540   Perform mission, process, business case analysis
                  10541   Map processes versus department mission
                  10542   Map processes versus company mission
                  10543   Map business cases to department mission
                  10544   Map business cases to processes
                  10545   Map business cases to company mission

Figure 11.3   Project Tasks for an Action Team for Walters Catalog

10550 Preparation and review of business cases
    10551 Prepare overall presentation to steering committee
    10552 Presentation to steering committee
    10553 Executive committee review
        10554 Approved business cases

Phase II Additional Quick Hits and Process Improvement
30100 Business processes
    30110 Identify future workflows/solutions
    30120 Determine impact of opportunities and benefits for future workflows
    30130 Compare future workflow with current workflow
    30140 Define general implementation approach
    30150 Prepare detailed business case and implementation
30200 Perform analysis of new business process
    30210 Define implementation dimensions
    30220 Determine approach for each dimension
    30230 Prepare implementation details
    30240 Perform cross-process analysis
30300 Management information reports
    30310 Identify current reports
    30320 Identify reporting and information requirements
    30330 Analyze and determine information reporting requirements
    30340 Prepare report on requirements
    30350 Determine approach for implementation
    30360 Incorporate into new process
30400 Presentation and review of new processes
    30410 Prepare business process presentation for management
    30420 Reconcile with short-term improvements
    30430 Review presentation
    30440 Presentation to steering committee
    30450 Presentation to executive committee
30500 Measurement prior to implementation
    30510 Determine measurement approach
    30520 Conduct measurements
    30530 Analyze measurement information
    30540 Prepare measurement report
30600 Implement new process
    30610 Organization
    30620 Procedures, workflow
    30630 Interfaces
    30640 Systems and technology
    30650 Training and staffing
    30660 Support
30700 Measurement after implementation
    30710 Determine measurement approach
    30720 Conduct measurements
    30730 Analyze measurement information
    30740 Prepare measurement report
30800 Management presentation
    30810 Gather lessons learned
    30820 Prepare presentation
    30830 Review presentation
    30840 Make presentation to steering committee
    30850 Make presentation to executive committee

Figure 11.3 (*Continued*)

Next, the team members define the dependencies and specific resources required for their tasks. This is then reviewed. Finally, the durations and dates are estimated by the team members. These are also reviewed. There are a number of advantages of this collaborative approach:

- By doing the defining themselves, the team members participate in project management, freeing up the e-business leaders.
- The leaders and the team members better understand the issues involved in the work.
- Through involvement, team members are more committed to the schedules and work.
- A more realistic and complete schedule results.

After this work, the e-business leaders create a baseline plan. It is often the case (is it not?) that the schedule is not acceptable. What do you do? You could go to the standard critical path and try to shorten the tasks. This, however, is artificial and often results in only a good story. A better technique is to first try to make more of the tasks performed in parallel. To do this, you and the team members may have to break up tasks. If this doesn't result in sufficient improvement, then you consider the issues behind specific tasks. By resolving these, you may be able to improve the schedule. In Walters 2 action team members defined their own detailed tasks. The same was true for implementing e-business. In Walters 1 the project leader assigned tasks to people. They often did not understand the tasks so they either did the wrong thing or did not take any action.

Issues Management

Managing issues is a critical success factor in e-business. As you identify issues, you can associate them with specific tasks. You can also place them in the issues database. From experience it is useful to consider several databases. The major issues database consists of the following data elements.

- Number or identifier of the issue.
- Title of the issue.
- Type or source of the issue.
- Priority or importance of the issue.
- Date that the issue was identified.
- Who created the issue.
- Description of the issue.
- Impact on e-business if the issue is not resolved.
- Status of the issue (open, tabled, closed, combined).
- Who the issue is assigned to.
- Date of resolution.
- Decisions made related to the issue.

- Actions taken with respect to the issue.
- Results obtained from the actions.
- Comments on the issue.

The second database is for tracking activity on a specific issue. It contains the following data elements:

- Issue identifier.
- Date of comment.
- Who made the comment.
- Action taken.
- Results achieved.
- Comments.

Both of these databases should be placed on a network for read access. The e-business leaders can coordinate the updates. In Walters 2 a formal method was employed for issues management. In Walters 1 issues were addressed as they arose. The problem was that the same issues kept resurfacing in different clothes.

MANAGE THE E-BUSINESS WORK

Determining Project Status

In the old days, people considered two major measures: percentage complete and budget versus actual. These are really trailing indicators. Moreover, they tell little about what is going on in the project. In an e-business implementation much of the money is spent toward the beginning of the work. On the other hand, much of the risk and the issues will appear toward the end of the project. An example is shown in Figure 11.4. One approach that has been employed in a number of efforts is to augment these measures with the following considerations:

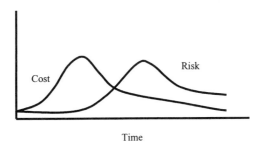

Figure 11.4 Sample Graph of Costs and Risk in an E-Business Implementation

- Age of the oldest outstanding major issue.
- Number of issues that remain to be addressed in the implementation.
- Percentage of the tasks that have issues that have been completed.

In Walters 1 the project leader held long meetings on project status. This really turned people off. While one person talked, everyone else almost went to sleep. No one ever admitted to problems in front of their peers. For Walters 2 status was obtained by having action team members update their own tasks. Meetings were reserved to discuss issues, opportunities, or lessons learned.

Issue Escalation

It is important that you define and gain acceptance of a technique for escalating issues. Issues can arise from the action teams, the implementation team, or the leaders. The first effort is to resolve the issues at this low level. If this is unsuccessful, then you move to the steering committee. If this doesn't work, you move up to the executive committee. To make sure that everyone buys into this, you should propose a specific issue to each level and talk about how the resolution method would work. This sets in place the behavior for resolving issues. Remember that it is very difficult to resolve an issue and establish an issues resolution method at the same time. In the Walters 2 case finding a solution to issues was always attempted at lower organization levels first. Then, if this did not work, it was escalated to the steering committee. It was never necessary to go to the executive committee.

Milestone Review

Milestones consist of documents, completed systems code, and many other things. How do you review these? In the perfect world you would review each one for content. Given the scope and number of activities and milestones of e-business this is impossible. You have to trust people for some milestones. You need a formal technique for reviewing milestones. Associate each milestone with the following levels of review:

- Level 0 — no review. You take someone's word for it.
- Level 1 — presence. You see the milestone.
- Level 2 — structure. You quickly review the structure of the end product for completeness.
- Level 3 — content. Here you actually review the content.

OK, which milestones get a level 3 review? Select the milestones for content review based on issues and uncertainty. How do you carry out a level 3 milestone review in the least amount of time with the best quality? Have the person or people who did the work present the milestone in a meeting. Based on the level of detail in each part, their body language, and their tone of voice you can zoom in on sections of the end product. This saves time and money. In Walters 2 the approach above was used. In Walters 1 the project leader attempted to get every milestone reviewed. Needless to say, this did not work well.

PROGRAM COORDINATION AND COMMUNICATIONS

Team Meetings

In most projects team meetings are devoted to status. People sit around a table. Each person in turn gives the status of their work. This has a number of limitations and limited value. First, no one is likely to admit to a group of their peers that they screwed up. Second, when someone is speaking, everyone else has his/her mind turned off. It is just not informative or productive.

Here is a better technique. Devote meetings to either discussing issues or lessons learned. Gather status before the meeting and summarize it at the start of the meeting. We suggest that you hold two meetings of issues and then one on lessons learned. Repeat this pattern. This ensures that you are gathering experiences as you do the e-business implementation. At the end of the meeting, the e-business leaders write up the results of the meeting. For issues the sequence is *issue, actions, decision,* and *discussion.* This gives an emphasis on actions. All action items should be followed up within 48 hours of the meeting. The issues database should be updated.

You should give attention to the frequency of meetings. Don't hold meetings at the same time each week. This is too inflexible. Instead, if there are problems, hold the meetings more frequently—several times per week. If there are no pressing issues, revert to once every 2 weeks.

Management Reporting

For management reporting we recommend a simple one-page approach for each major subproject. It includes the following elements:

- Name of the subproject.
- Purpose of the subproject in business terms.
- Scope of the subproject in business terms.
- Summary Gantt chart.
- Cumulative budget versus actual graph.
- Milestones achieved in business terms.
- Upcoming milestones in business terms.
- Outstanding major issues and their status.

This report not only gives status, but also draws attention to the unresolved issues. In Walters 1 the project leader presented formal status reports that were very detailed. The preparation of these reports consumed 20% of the project leader's time. In Walters 2 the above approach was used.

Gather and Use Lessons Learned

Lessons learned have been mentioned a number of times. A "lessons learned" is a guideline for doing specific work in e-business better in the future. Examples of lessons learned might pertain to programming, training, Web page setup, etc. Lessons learned used to be captured at the end of the project. This does not work. At the end people have left the team. Other people want to move on. There is limited memory and recall. Instead, gather lessons learned as you go. Establish the lessons learned in a database. Here are some data elements:

- Lessons learned identifier.
- Title of the lessons learned.
- Date that the lesson learned was created.
- Who created the lesson learned.
- Status of the lesson learned (active, dropped, potential).
- Tasks to which the lesson learned applies.
- Situations to which the lesson learned applies.
- Expected results from applying the lesson learned.
- Guidelines for applying the lesson learned.
- Benefits of the lesson learned.
- Comments.

When you start a given area of the e-business implementation or operation, you should review the potential lessons learned with the team. As lessons learned are applied, there is additional experience to be recorded and used to update the lessons-learned database. Here are the data elements for this:

- Identifier of the lesson learned.
- Date the comment was created.
- Who created the comment.
- Situation to which the lesson learned was applied.
- Result that was achieved.
- Recommendation for the lessons learned in the future.

Lessons learned can be linked to the tasks in the e-business template. Lessons learned were not addressed in Walters 1. In Walters 2 about 25% of the meetings dealt with lessons learned.

RESOURCE MANAGEMENT

Background

Managing IT, business unit, and vendor resources is a critical success factor for e-business. If you don't pay enough attention to this, resources may be taken away from e-business, creating delays and even a crisis. Why do problems arise? Start with IT. There can be emergency fixes and maintenance that take programming resources away from the project. Any key people you rely on may be taken away. For the business there can be marketing campaigns, year-end closing, and other activities that can interfere. Vendors may win new contracts and so want to use the staff assigned to your effort.

IT Resource Management

IT resources are generally employed in work in the following categories:

- System development.
- IT project work.
- System operation and support.
- Network and computer system support.
- Maintenance and enhancement.
- Emergency fixes.
- IT planning.
- IT project management.

You can add more categories. The list is just a sample to show you the various demands on IT staff member time that brings conflict with e-business implementation. If you take a reactive approach to IT resource allocation, you focus on operations and support related activities. These consume most of the resources. There is little left over for work in e-business or other projects.

A Proactive Approach to Managing Resources

There is a need to anticipate potential resource problems ahead of time and to adopt an approach that can deal with these for IT, business departments, and vendors. A proven method is to employ a weekly allocation of resources. What you would do is sit down with various managers each week and discuss what critical human resources are going to work on for the next week. At the meeting would be discussed the results of the previous week. A specific manager would then relate the priorities to the individual staff member. In that way they get the mes-

sage from one person. And it is a consistent message. This approach supports a
more dynamic approach to resource assignment.

DEAL WITH PROGRAM AND REQUIREMENT CHANGES

Why Changes Arise

In any project or business endeavor that consumes substantial elapsed time,
there will be changes. This is natural and should be ignored. Changes should not
be viewed as negative, but as a positive opportunity to improve the e-business
implementation and operation through change.

Types of Changes

E-business can be affected by these external factors:

• New technologies and systems that emerge. These offer opportunities for
productivity improvement. They also can divert the work of the team.
• Competition and industry events. Competitors may improve or establish
their Web sites. They may install new, more effective business processes.
• Regulation. While the Internet and Web are largely unregulated, this is
changing. There may be new laws and rules on security, privacy, taxation, customer rights, etc.

Then there are internal changes such as:

• Mergers and acquisitions.
• Pressure from shareholders and directors to accelerate or change e-business.
• Unions and organized labor pressures.
• Top management turnover.
• Changes in business processes through other systems and work.

A Method for Proactively Managing Change

How do you cope with change? You cannot ignore it. In Chapter 7 you saw that
assessments for both the industry and competition, and technology are ongoing.
These will alert you to external factors. You can use your informal project communications to find out what is going on internally. How you manage a situation
depends on the unique characteristics and situation. However, you should consider
a review of potential changes every 2–3 months. This is an organized approach
and reduces the likelihood of nasty surprises. At that time you would meet with
the steering committee to review potential changes. There are the following potential actions:

- Continue work as it is without change.
- Modify some details of the e-business implementation.
- Make major changes in the implementation.
- Defer part or all of the e-business effort.
- Kill off the implementation and resurrect it later at an appropriate time.

You must be open to all of these, including the last one. This attitude will show management that you are thinking of the bottom line and do not have a narrow project focus.

STARTUP

Consult Figure 11.5 for the example firms.

INDO FURNITURE

The major project management issues were distance, time, and language. Telephone conversations proved to be useful only if there was an immediate and urgent issue. The major method was to employ e-mail and intranet software with vendors and suppliers and fax with the Indo factory.

DIAMOND ENGINEERING DATA

Until the operation grew, things had to be kept informal. There was just no time to do more than to develop and use a template, to set up an issues database, and to set up a lessons-learned database linked to the knowledge base. As the company expanded, more employees were added. More formal project management methods and tools were introduced around the concepts of the templates, issues and lessons learned, and collaboration.

EXAMPLES

ASEAN CONSTRUCTION

For Asean two project leaders were identified in each business unit. Two people served as project leaders at the corporate level. All of the project leaders met informally to discuss issues and lessons learned. The goals were as follows:

- Share information on e-business experience.
- Share information on issues and problems.

Subject	Company						
	Indo Furniture	Diamond Engineering	Asean Construction	Walters Catalog-1	Walters Catalog-2	Rogers County
Project managers	Manager	Owners	Two people from each country	Junior person	Two project leaders	Two project leaders
Team members	Family members; technical support; consultant	Owners	Action teams and others for implementation	Lack of team member identification	Action teams and others for implementation	Many across operations and separately for consumer e-business
Planning	Use of templates	Linked to business plan	Use of templates	Overdetailed project plan	Use of templates	Use of templates
Coordination	Everything in writing for clarity	Informal	Informal	Ad hoc	Through the action teams	Through the project teams
Resource management	Informal	Informal	Through the project leaders and line management	Ad hoc	Through the project leaders and line management	Through the project leaders and line management

Figure 11.5 Project Management for Example Companies

- Allocate critical resources in IT and other areas among the e-business team efforts.

Asean developed templates for business-to-business and business-to-consumer e-business. Before any work could be done, a template was established. Lessons learned were gathered and associated with the tasks in the templates. Many issues were addressed informally in accordance with the culture of the country and organization. This informal communication method proved very useful in dealing with the more difficult problems and setting priorities.

ROGERS COUNTY

Rogers County developed two templates—one for operations and one for consumer e-business. There were also two project leaders. The method of the issues and lessons-learned databases proved so successful that it was used to collect and organize lessons learned within operations.

LESSONS LEARNED

Here we will discuss five areas of project management that augment what has been presented:

- *Standardized use of project management software.* To track e-business you will want to employ project management software, such as Microsoft Project. This and other similar software are based on a relational database. This allows you to customize the data elements of the system. There are specific items that you should customize, including:
  — Indicator of whether there are one or more issues behind a specific task. This can be handled by a flag (**yes/no**) field.
  — Indicator of whether or not the task belongs to the original template (flag field).
  — Numbers or identifiers of issues that pertain to the task (text field).
  — Numbers or identifiers of lessons learned that pertain to the task (text field).
  — Responsibility for the task (text field). This indicates what department or entity is in charge of the task.
  — Subproject that the task belongs to (text field).

As work progresses in the implementation, your team members will be adding tasks. These should be tracked for reasons of accountability. Here are some additional fields for customization:

— Who added the task (text field).
— Date that the task was created (date field).
— Reason for the creation of the task (text field).
— Requirement that gave rise to the task (text field).

• *Information sharing.* A key to a collaborative approach is to share information. Here you and the team will share the project plan, issues, and lessons learned. Consider allowing others to have read-only access to the information as well to support communications.

• *Expanding detail.* Traditional project management dictates that you develop a detailed plan. For e-business and major IT projects this results in too much work and a massive effort at maintaining the integrity of the schedule. A better approach is to define detailed tasks within the project template for a 3- to 4-month period. Leave the remainder at the template level. During project estimation if you cannot estimate a template-level task, break it down temporarily. As time progresses, you should have the team members define tasks further out in the future so that you have a rolling 3- to 4-month detailed schedule.

• *Coping with risk in the project.* Risk and risk management are terms that have been tossed around for over 50 years. Unfortunately, they are often too fuzzy and vague to have concrete meaning. Let's take a more formal approach. We will say that a task has risk if there are one or more substantial issues behind the task. Thus, risk is associated with issues. Working with this definition you can see that in order to minimize risk, you must resolve the issues. Conversely, if you solve issues, then you reduce risk.

• *Vendor management and coordination.* The schedule for the vendor work should be included in your schedule. In that way, you and the vendor will not waste time in reconciling separate schedules. Another guideline is that the vendor staff participate in meetings on issues and lessons learned, where appropriate.

THE SCORE CARD

Due to the purpose and scope of e-business and its implementation, you want to measure many critical things. Here are four score cards that should be viewed as critical success factors in your implementation and ongoing work.

THE PROCESS AND TRANSACTION SCORE CARD

Purpose

The aim of this score card is to establish agreed-on measures of the business processes and transactions prior to the start of the changes. Then you will repeat the measurement after implementing both Quick Hits and e-business. The political purpose is to gain consensus and agreement about the processes. In this way people see the problems at the start, and the benefits later with improvements.

What the Score Card Is

Here are some elements of the process score card (of course, feel free to make any changes you think are appropriate):

- Number of employees involved in the work.
- Turnover of business unit employees who are involved in the process.
- Average time it takes to carry out a transaction.
- Volume of work that is completed in a specific span of time.
- Error rate of the transactions.
- Survey concerns by employees, customers, and suppliers.
- Cost of doing the process.

We could include more, but this will get you started. If you include subjective measures, then you leave yourself open to criticism and bias.

How to Develop the Score Card

Begin in the accounting or finance area to collect the cost information. Go to human resources to obtain the headcount and turnover data. Visit the departments involved to obtain volumes and the survey information. If there is no survey information, generate a list from interviews and then review this.

How to Use the Score Card

You will be developing the score card in a collaborative manner. This will get more people involved and make them aware of the situation prior to e-business. After Quick Hits and e-business have been implemented, then the measurements provide for a useful comparison and tangible benefits.

THE E-BUSINESS IMPLEMENTATION SCORE CARD

Purpose

You want to measure the e-business effort as you go. That will be useful to present to management to gain their support. Another purpose is to show that you are serious about the e-business effort.

What the Score Card Is

Here are some of the elements that you might consider:

- Number of outstanding major unresolved issues.
- Age of the oldest outstanding major issue. This could undermine the project if it remains unresolved.
- Budget versus actual.
- Unexpected and unplanned turnover of team members.
- Percentage complete.
- Percentage complete in terms of tasks with issues. You could be 50% complete in terms of effort and only 25% complete in terms of tasks with known issues.
- Number of lessons learned generated.

How to Develop the Score Card

This score card should be developed at the start of the implementation. You will then apply it every 2 months. The core e-business leaders create the score card. Because the information is standardized, just having the score card encourages them to automate the tracking of issues and lessons learned.

How to Use the Score Card

The score card is a useful measure for the e-business team. It gives them an overall picture of what is going on. Another use is for management. Showing them the score card may head off questions and allay concerns.

THE VENDOR SCORE CARD

Purpose

E-business often involves outsourcing. The vendor work is often critical to the e-business implementation. The purpose of this score card is not to punish the vendors; it is rather a means to improve communications with vendors and get their attention.

What the Score Card Is

Here are some elements of the vendor score card:

- Number of vendor staff involved in the work.
- Turnover of vendor staff.

- Number of outstanding issues assigned to the vendor.
- Age of the oldest outstanding issue assigned to the vendor.
- Average elapsed time it takes for the vendor to resolve an issue.
- Budget versus actual for the vendor.
- Adherence to the schedule.
- Quality of work.

How to Develop the Score Card

You should define the score card elements prior to the outsourcing contract. The score card should be presented and reviewed with the vendor. At that time you and the vendor can discuss how the measurements will be undertaken and how often the score card will be created.

How to Use the Score Card

The vendor score card shows the vendor that you mean business. When taken with the other guidelines, the vendor will tend to pay more attention to your project and work versus other clients who may not be tracking their performance as closely.

THE BUSINESS UNIT SCORE CARD

Purpose

Business units are often attacked for not participating in projects that involve IT work. They are also not given credit for their involvement. The business unit score card is a useful way to measure the involvement of the business unit in a proactive and structured manner. By being aware of the score card, business unit managers may monitor the participation of their employees more closely.

What the Score Card Is

Here are the elements of the score card:

- Number of business unit staff involved in the project.
- Percentage of business unit staff that have participated in the project.
- Number of outstanding issues that the business unit is responsible for.
- Age of the oldest outstanding major issue that the business unit is responsible for.
- Average amount of time it takes for the business unit to resolve an issue.
- Quality of the business unit work.

How to Develop the Score Card

This is similar to the vendor score card. You develop it at the start of the e-business effort. As the work gets underway, you can review it with each business manager. In developing the score card values, you would develop a first version yourself. Then you would review it with the team members from the business department and the manager of the business department.

How to Use the Score Card

The business unit score card is a method to support business unit involvement. Experience has shown this to be so valuable that management in several firms has ordered that it be developed on a regular basis during both the implementation and operation of e-business. You can also develop a table where the rows are the criteria and the columns are departments. This gives a snapshot comparison. Another comparison is to create a table for each department wherein the rows are the same and the columns are snapshots of the department's score at successive times.

WHAT TO DO NEXT

To gain more insight into the project management method presented here consider reading the book, *Breakthrough Technology Project Management* (see Appendix 4 for a complete reference). The methods presented here have been employed in many projects spanning the past decade. We suggest that you consider defining the subprojects for your e-business work. For each of these define the major milestones. Then relate the subprojects to each other.

Chapter 12

Define Your E-Business Implementation Strategy

INTRODUCTION

Let's examine what you have so far. You have defined and approved business cases as discussed in the preceding two chapters. These are ready to be organized into Quick Hits and e-business. How these are phased over time is your e-business implementation strategy. The e-business implementation strategy is your roadmap to carry out your e-business transformation. You can then use the strategy to help you define the specific projects that implement the business case opportunities.

The e-business implementation strategy provides the glue between:

- E-business vision, objectives and strategy, on the one hand, and the e-business implementation, on the other.
- Definition of the specific opportunities for improvement and e-business, on the one hand, and the implementation plans on the other.

What is the e-business implementation strategy? At the heart it is a table. The columns of the table are specific phases of implementation (Quick Hit and e-business phases). There are two sets of rows. The first set consists of the areas of Quick Hit improvements and e-business implementation. The second set is composed of capabilities from the standpoint of customers, suppliers, IT, business departments, employees, management, and stakeholders (from Chapter 2) as well as overall benefits and risks. This is really what a customer, etc. can do as a result of the work in the column. The e-business implementation also supports later changes and evolution in e-business. The e-business implementation table can be reviewed and updated as you proceed. This provides support for modifications to the vision and objectives of e-business.

PURPOSE AND SCOPE

BUSINESS OBJECTIVES

One business objective is to ensure that the e-business vision and objectives are carried out in the e-business implementation. Otherwise, if you just implement improvements, you may not have them synchronized with each other. This could raise many business problems within the business processes and affect the revenue of the firm and services to customers. Another business goal is to make certain that there are tangible benefits to the parties concerned in e-business. At each phase of implementation, you want to add up the improvements for each interested party.

POLITICAL AND CULTURAL OBJECTIVES

People often don't take the general statements of e-business objectives and the vision for e-business seriously. The e-business implementation strategy shows them a roadmap for implementation. Another goal is to demonstrate that there is an organized approach that is going to yield shorter-term benefits to the employees of the organization. For the action teams this validates their work. The employees can also see how the improvements are interrelated.

TECHNICAL OBJECTIVES

Technical implementation of e-business mandates that you understand the requirements for e-business. It will take some time to make the technology infrastructure changes as well as perform systems work in integration. The Quick Hits, in essence, help you by buying time for the work. Another objective is to ensure that the requirements related to systems and technology are stable. Stability is more likely because of the interwoven nature of the improvements.

SCOPE

The scope of the e-business implementation strategy includes all of the approved business cases as well as the systems and architecture work that were identified in Chapter 7. If anything major is left out, then it is not considered to be involved in the implementation.

END PRODUCTS

The end product is the e-business implementation table. However, there are also political end products. You seek to gain widespread support and understanding for e-business. Individuals on the action teams can see the benefits of e-business. Management can also employ the table with stakeholders as well as specific groups of suppliers and customers.

APPROACH

ACTION 1: GROUP THE APPROVED OPPORTUNITIES INTO PHASES

The approved opportunities have already been grouped by the action team. For example, you have all of the finance, marketing, accounting, and customer service opportunities grouped respectively. Through the work of the action teams you have also merged and combined opportunities in some cases. This occurred where the opportunities had to be pursued together.

Prepare an Implementation Assessment of Opportunities

For each approved opportunity, write down the following information:

- *Systems and technology.* Identify the required systems and technology that must be in place to support the realization of the opportunity. For example, if the opportunity requires an upgraded network, then it would have to wait.
- *Organization.* Can the current organization support the opportunity after it is executed? Or, does it assume that there are organization changes?
- *Policies.* Here you determine any precursor policy changes before you carry out the implementation.
- *Resources required.* What human resources are needed? For example, suppose that you have a mundane change that is labor intensive (e.g., setting up Web page content for sale items). Then when you start to do the work, you find that people are committed elsewhere. Resources here also include vendor staff, customers, and suppliers.
- *Specific people* needed to undertake the work.
- Any *dependencies* with other opportunities.
- *Elapsed time* estimated for execution.

You might use the table in Figure 12.1 to tabulate this information in a spreadsheet. Note at this point that nothing is said about benefits because the attention is

Opportunity	Systems/technology	Organization	Policies	Resources	People	Dependencies	Elapsed time

Figure 12.1 Table for Execution Analysis of Approved Opportunities

on putting the opportunity into effect. There are several benefits in developing this table. One benefit is to raise the level of awareness of requirements for the approved opportunities. A major benefit is to identify specific resources required so as to identify potential resource conflicts. If current non-e-business work has high priority, this would impact your ability to implement specific opportunities. While many conflicts would occur in IT staffing, it is also true that you can have conflict among business staff. You could, for example, be in the middle of year-end closing.

For Walters 2, after the table was produced, it was clear that there would be many opportunities that affected the accounting group. This is because when the number of products is scaled up for the Web, the number of vendors increases. Many vendor accounting practices were manual due to the limited number of vendors involved in the paper catalogs. The situation became more serious when it was realized the relevant opportunities would fall on a few supervisors. In response, Walters Catalog hired temporaries to handle some of the lower level tasks in the accounting department.

Enter Opportunity Information into Project Management Software

Now you might want to enter the opportunities into project management software. You can enter the dependencies, specific people, and elapsed time. This will assist you in analyzing the schedule of opportunities. In the table, predecessor actions related to systems and technology, policies, and organization were listed. Add these as tasks to the schedule. Keep their duration to the default of 1 day temporarily. Establish the dependencies between these and the specific opportunities.

For Walters 2 doing this produced more evidence of the potential conflicts. Another step that was taken was to add more tasks for the regular, non-e-business work of the relevant departments. This supported analysis and trade-offs in allocating resources to the work.

Analyze the Sequencing of Opportunities and Regular Work

The first thing to do is to review the manpower demands over a specific period. You can do this in Microsoft Project by establishing a dual-pane view wherein the Gantt chart is on the upper pane. On the lower pane is the resource graph. This shows for a selected resource the total amount of time required in the period (such as a week) for a specific person. Use this to adjust the starting times for opportunities. A simple example shows how this can be done. In Figure 12.2 you have a simple Gantt chart. Figure 12.3 indicates the corresponding resource graph for part of the period. The resource graph reveals a resource overcommitment for Robert.

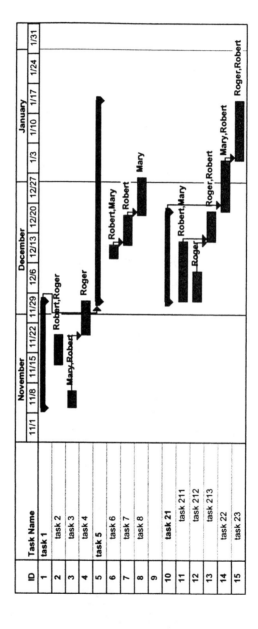

Figure 12.2 Example of a GANTT Chart with Resources

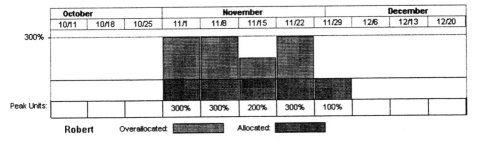

Figure 12.3 Example of a Resource Graph Showing Overcommitment

ACTION 2: IDENTIFY AND ORGANIZE THE TECHNICAL WORK

In Chapter 7 you developed a slate of changes and enhancements that had to be made to the architecture to prepare for e-business. For each of these items, enter the item as a task in the plan defined in the previous step. Enter any dependencies and the elapsed time of the task. After this has been completed, you can now replace the extra systems and technology items added in Step 1 with the items from Chapter 7. This is a valuable action because it helps to validate both the work in Chapter 7 and your understanding of the requirements for the opportunities. At this point you have an overall schedule of the implementation. However, it is not complete because some of the policy and organization predecessors have no durations. It is now time to review the work with selected managers from both the business units and IT. What are you attempting to accomplish?

- You are getting their input on any resource conflicts due to other work. Write these down and enter them in the plan later.
- You are validating your understanding of the systems and technology requirements.
- You are obtaining estimates of time for the predecessor tasks related to policies and organization.

Update the plan using the results of these meetings. There are several benefits to these meetings. These include:

- You gain a better understanding of what implementation will be like.
- Managers see that the implementation is now reaching a very serious stage. They should want to have more input.
- Through collaboration people are better understanding the scope and activities of e-business implementation.

At Walters Catalog (Walters 2) there were potential major projects in replacing the client-server system. However, this was felt to be too large an effort. Additional tasks that could be considered were upgrades to the network and hardware to increase capacity for Web customers.

ACTION 3: CREATE ALTERNATIVE E-BUSINESS IMPLEMENTATION STRATEGIES

What do you have at the end of the first two steps? You have an implementation plan, but it is composed of disjoint sets of tasks. Why is this? Because many of the sets of tasks can be performed in parallel with each other. Thus, there is a concentration of work at the beginning of implementation. There is probably too much work in the early stages to manage effectively.

It is now time to generate alternative implementation strategies. Using the project plan you will generate alternatives by placing the tasks into phases. A suggestion here is that you consider the first phase to be 1 month in duration; the second phase to be 2 months; and the third phase for beyond 2 months. In order to develop alternatives in an organized manner, use specific triggers to generate an alternative. Here are some suggestions:

• *Be aggressive with technology.* Move the systems and technology work to the front end. Because this work often requires greater elapsed time, this action will tend to reduce the overall implementation time.

• *Maximize Quick Hits.* Here you move up in time all opportunities that can be implemented without extensive predecessor work.

• *Be conservative with Quick Hits.* You want to make the Quick Hits stretch out due to impacts on the business. The argument is that they need time to absorb changes.

• *Stretch out the technology.* Here you might feel that new technologies are emerging. You also might want to get the benefits of the Quick Hits before proceeding.

You may want to combine aspects of these as well. Based on one of these triggers, you will now adjust the starting point of each set of tasks. Use the dual-pane view that was discussed earlier to look at the resource loading as you do this. After you have established the alternatives, the next action is to summarize each of these in an e-business implementation table. Enter the activity for the specific action team in the appropriate phase. Be brief but ensure that you have a complete thought. These tables are important now as tools of communications.

At Walters Catalog (Walters 2) the work yielded several alternative e-business implementation strategies. One was a very conservative strategy that minimized costs. The second was a moderate policy to implement as many products with limited costs. The third was an aggressive approach that identified what could be done with little regard for costs.

ACTION 4: EVALUATE AND SELECT THE E-BUSINESS IMPLEMENTATION STRATEGY

In the previous step you ended with the alternative e-business strategy tables being created. However, they are not complete. At the bottom of the table you want to enter the rows of the different audiences defined earlier (stakeholders, employees, IT, customers, suppliers, management, business departments). You may want to enter general benefits and risk as well. The alternative e-business strategy tables can now be prepared. For each of the new rows you will define the capabilities and overall impact in the appropriate table entry. To determine benefits for one phase read down the column. Mentally add up the capabilities and list the risks in the bottom rows.

The alternative e-business strategies are now complete. You are now prepared to review these with the managers and employees. You might want to start with the action team leaders. You will also want to make formal presentations of the results to the action teams, steering committee, and executive committee. If there are adjustments to be made, return to the original project plan and make the changes there. Then move the information forward into the e-business implementation table.

To understand this, suppose that you have four action teams (marketing, accounting, customer service, and sales) and two phases of Quick Hits. The phases are 1 and 2 months long, respectively. However, the IT work will go on for 5 months. In addition, there is a marketing campaign just being launched next month. Use the table in Figure 12.4 as a reference. In this table the nonblank entries contain specific items. Because the IT work goes on longer, it might be wise to stretch out the second phase of Quick Hits.

In Walters 2 the conservative strategy was rejected because it would not support sufficient growth of products on the Web. Correspondingly, the aggressive approach was also rejected due to limited financial resources.

ACTION 5: VALIDATE THE SELECTED E-BUSINESS IMPLEMENTATION STRATEGY

Let's use Figure 12.4 to show you what to do. You have validated the e-business implementation strategy through meetings. Now you should perform a final vali-

Area	Phase 1	Phase 2	E-Business Implementation
Marketing	X	X	X
Sales	X	X	X
Customer Service		X	X
Accounting		X	X
IT	X	X	X
Capabilities			
Management		X	X
Employees	X	X	X
Customers		X	X
Suppliers		X	X
IT			X
Stakeholders		X	X

Figure 12.4   Sample E-Business Implementation Strategy Table

dation. What happens if things change? Is the strategy flexible enough to accommodate the change? Here are some tests to conduct of your table. For each of the following changes, you will "retotal" the capabilities for each of the audiences. This will determine whether the e-business implementation strategy delivers sufficient capabilities.

• Suppose that the IT implementation slips, what is the impact? In Figure 12.4 the IT effort moves to the right. A new column might be created.
• What if the marketing organization is too busy to support marketing-related changes? You can see this by moving the marketing-related Quick Hits to the right.
• What if things are moving along well and management desires to speed up the additional Quick Hits? Then you want to shift the entries to earlier phases.
• Assume that a competitor becomes very aggressive in e-business. Management feels under pressure to speed up the overall implementation. Then the IT work will receive additional resources. What happens if you move the IT work to the left? Moving these to the left may mean that the Quick Hits also have to be accelerated.

These trade-offs can be reviewed with management. This has several benefits:

• Managers better understand the interrelationships among the rows through the analysis.

- There is a better understanding of potential changes in management direction to the implementation.

ACTION 6: DEVELOP THE DETAILED E-BUSINESS PROJECT PLAN

In the previous chapter, the general project management method was discussed. It is now time to apply it to your e-business implementation strategy. You have the implementation work divided into phases and action teams. Take the overall schedule you have and split it out so that there is one schedule for each table entry for action teams and phase. Each schedule is then the work to be done related to the specific action team for a phase. However, details, milestones, and other information are missing.

After defining the specific project plans, you are now prepared to group the small project plans into subprojects. Keep in mind the guidelines for subprojects that were presented in Chapter 11. You want to give attention to risk. Some general guidelines are as follows:

- Group the row entries for an action team if the Quick Hits do not involve risk and issues.

- Group involvement by department staff vertically for specific activities such as data conversion and testing. This gives them emphasis because they are pulled out as separate projects.

An example is given in Figure 12.5. This shows in ovals the groupings based on the table in Figure 12.4.

Area	Phase 1	Phase 2	E-Business Implementation
Marketing	X	X	X
Sales	X	X	X
Customer Service		X	X
Accounting		X	X
IT	X	X	X
Capabilities			
Management		X	X
Employees	X	X	X
Customers		X	X
Suppliers		X	X
IT			X
Stakeholders		X	X

Figure 12.5   Examples of Groupings to Form Subprojects

Now that you have subprojects, the next activity is to develop detailed project plans for each subproject. Here are some guidelines to help you.

• Number all subprojects and tasks within subprojects for each discussion and tracking.

• Develop from the work of the action teams a list of potential implementation issues and problems. Enter these in your issues database.

• Have team members now define their own detailed tasks. So this will not require too much overhead or be too onerous, keep the tasks around 1–2 weeks in length. If you go down to the extensive detail level of a few days, it becomes too much work to maintain the schedule. Figure 12.6 gives the story as a trade-off. You have two graphs in this figure. One shows that with the growing level of detail in the schedule, the effort to maintain and update the schedule increases exponentially. The second graph indicates the value. If there is no detail, there is little value. If there is too much detail, then people are overwhelmed by the detail.

• After following the guidelines of Chapter 11 in terms of collaboration, you have a first cut at the schedule. Now you can validate what you have in front of you by considering issues. Take each known issue and find the tasks that correspond to the issue. If you have an issue with no tasks, then there are missing tasks. Add these. Now work in reverse. Go down the list of tasks and uncover issues for the tasks. Each time you encounter an issue go over to the list of issues and see if it is there. If it is not, then add the issue. In this manner, you work to validate both the tasks and the issues.

• The next step is to create the milestones for the subprojects. From your milestones identify the ones that are important and have risk. You can prepare a table such as the one in Figure 12.7. The columns are as follows:

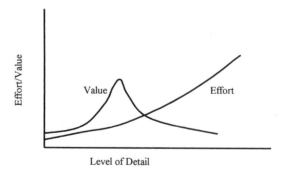

Figure 12.6 Trade-off between Level of Detail and Value

Subproject	Milestone	Risk	Importance	Level Review	Comments

Figure 12.7   Milestone Evaluation Table

— Subproject.
— Milestone.
— Risk. Are there significant issues behind the major tasks that lead up to this milestone?
— Importance. How important is the milestone to the project? If it slips, how badly is the project hurt?
— Level of review. Using the level approach to reviews of milestones in the preceding chapter determine the appropriate level of review (0–3).
— Comments. Here you can put in explanatory remarks about level 3 milestones.

This table is valuable because you are addressing how the milestone will be evaluated in advance. We aren't done with milestones yet. Return to the project plan and filter on milestones so that only the milestones are showing in the Gantt chart. Answer the following questions.

— Is there a regular stream of deliverable items or milestones? Or, are there major time gaps? If there are gaps, then you are at risk. You should return to the project plan and look for more milestones.
— Do you have milestones for each major activity in the subprojects?
— Do you have milestones to ensure that business departments and vendors are working hard on the project? If you have too few, then they might not work as hard later.

• Determine if you can easily integrate the subproject schedules into an overall master schedule. You can do this in Microsoft Project through the operation of Object Linking Embedding (OLE). This gives you an overall summary schedule that can be reviewed by team members and management.

After developing the detailed schedule you now have a complete set of end products. Let's summarize these here before starting on implementation:

• E-business vision. Where you want to be with e-business.
• E-business objectives. Your goals for implementing e-business.
• E-business strategy. The general approach for getting to the objectives reaching the vision.
• Industry and competitive information related to e-business.

- Systems and technology architecture and approach for supporting e-business.
- Outsourcing method for e-business.
- Organizational approach for implementing e-business.
- Project management methods.
- E-business implementation strategy. The roadmap for getting from the e-business objectives and strategy to the detailed plan.
- E-business project plan.

STARTUP

Refer to Figure 12.8 for comments on the specific companies.

INDO FURNITURE

Indo Furniture developed an e-business implementation strategy with the consultants. Here are the major categories of the table:

- Order processing.
- Marketing.
- Shipping and fulfillment.
- Customer service.
- Systems interfaces.
- Company setup.
- IT infrastructure and architecture setup.

As with the other examples, doing this in a collaborative way allowed the family to understand how the various e-business-related activities were related.

DIAMOND ENGINEERING DATA

For Chris and Mike the categories in the upper rows included:

- Establishment of the knowledge base.
- Software development.
- Company setup.
- Marketing to engineering firms.
- IT architecture.

Subject	Company					
	Indo Furniture	Diamond Engineering	Asean Construction	Walters Catalog-1	Walters Catalog-2	Rogers County
Group into phases	Setup; growth	Setup; growth	Within business units and coordinated with corporate	Not done	Customer service, development, marketing, order processing; Quick Hits	Software development; Quick Hits; policies and procedures
Organize technical work	Coordination with vendors	Mike did this	IT with the core e-business team	IT group	IT group with the core e-business team	IT group with operations
Alternative e-business implementation strategies	Business versus IT	Knowledge base versus software development	Quick Hits versus long term	Not done	IT versus business versus combination	Automation of clerical functions versus new applications
Selection of e-business implementation strategies	Based on need to generate sales quickly	Based on longer term view of involvement	Combined approach	Not done	Major parallel effort	Long-term impact
Project planning	Done by consultant	Done by Chris	Joint across teams	Detailed plan by project leader	Core e-business team	Project leaders in both areas in parallel

Figure 12.8 Implementation Strategies of Example Companies

EXAMPLES

ASEAN CONSTRUCTION

Due to the wide scope of Asean's e-business effort, several e-business implementation strategy alternatives were defined and developed. The same was carried out for the corporate procurement area. An example at a general level appears in Figure 12.9. Preparing the alternatives was useful to Asean because it gave the managers in the various business units and corporate a chance to review each others' approaches to e-business. This was so successful that the managers then jointly carried out the selection of each of the e-business implementation strategies.

ROGERS COUNTY

The consumer e-business effort required a very limited approach to addressing Web development and marketing/advertising in phases. For the operations the upper rows were as follows:

Area	Phase I Evaluation	Phase II Online ordering	Phase III Full procurement
IT	Competitive assessment	Show winning bids on the Web	Implement package for ordering
Process/ transactions	Identify procedures, exceptions	Automate the dissemination of information	Ordering through receipt of goods; standardize on how people order
Organization	Pick which suppliers	No	Move people to other work; more thinking time on what to order
Purchasing/ merchandising	Assess suppliers; identify issues with suppliers/ purchasing	Notify vendors	—
Web	Nothing	Vendors use web to check orders	Focus on strategic suppliers

Figure 12.9   Example of Simplified E-Business Implementation Strategy for Asean Construction

Groups of Rows		Phases	
Action teams			
IT			
Capabilities			
Benefits			

Figure 12.10   Model for a General E-Business Implementation Strategy

- Software development.
- Quick Hits.
- Policies and procedures.

LESSONS LEARNED

In presenting the e-business strategy tables, it is a good idea to first show a blank table with the rows and columns. People get familiar with the format of the table so that they can concentrate on the content. After this you can proceed to show a table in which the upper part of the table is filled in. This means that the capability rows are left blank. There will be a lot of discussion about this. Indicate in parentheses the opportunities that are covered in each table entry. This will serve as a cross-reference back to the original opportunities. During this activity you should have a great deal of discussion on which column fits specific items. In order to develop the capabilities, you seek to have relatively stable columns.

With this second action you have feedback on the activities and where they fit in phases. Next, you will complete the rows for capabilities. Each explains what the audience will get from the work in the column. For example, the entry in the table for employees and initial Quick Hits indicates what employees can do that they do not do now after the initial phase of Quick Hits has been accomplished. When you discuss capabilities, you should also cover the benefits. In fact, this is so important that we suggest that you might now add a third set of rows for benefits. A model is shown in Figure 12.10. In the benefits rows you place the specific audiences again. The review of this table now helps to again validate both the capabilities and benefits. Why does this discussion appear here and not above? Because it is a valuable lessons learned, but is not absolutely essential.

THE SCORE CARD

Here are some ways to measure how you did with the development of the e-business implementation strategy:

- How many different e-business implementation strategies were generated? If there are too few, then you probably missed some good ones.

- What was the extent of discussion and debate over the tables? In particular, was there a lot of discussion about the capabilities resulting from the Quick Hits?

- Did people propose new opportunities or attempt to make major changes? While some of this is to be expected, if there is too much, then the action team opportunities may be in question.

WHAT TO DO NEXT

Experience has shown that a good way to learn to use the material in this chapter is to develop a simple e-business implementation chart for a limited number of action teams. Do this for two or three action teams. After you have prepared the table, try out the validation steps that were discussed earlier. This will help you analyze the tables later.

Part III

E-Business Transformation

Implement Quick Hits

INTRODUCTION

Quick Hits are short-term improvements that when made can yield their own benefits and lead to e-business. Quick Hits were developed from the collaborative work of the action teams, steering committee, and executive committee. Yet, even with all of this support from employees and management, there can still be resistance and problems. Each Quick Hit is implemented in detail in a unique manner. However, there are some common guidelines that can be provided.

PURPOSE AND SCOPE

BUSINESS OBJECTIVES

The business goal is to implement the Quick Hits to attain the anticipated results. A second goal is to prepare for e-business. Important also is the requirement that the Quick Hit not disrupt the everyday business processes and transactions.

POLITICAL AND CULTURAL OBJECTIVES

A political goal is to show the middle-level managers of the business units that you are serious about change and about implementing e-business. Even though e-business is going to occur further out in the future, people become aware of the changes and how they lead to e-business. The cultural goal is to instill in the organization among the employees and supervisors the value and benefit of change.

Another objective is to increase the faith in management that e-business is a force for positive good. They will see with the Quick Hits that jobs are not disappearing in wholesale lots.

TECHNICAL OBJECTIVES

Most of the Quick Hits are related to the business and not to IT. One may wonder if there are relevant technical objectives to Quick Hits. There are. When you implement Quick Hits, you have an opportunity to collect more detailed information that will help your e-business implementation. You will also see if there is a serious disconnect or misalignment with the Quick Hits and the long-term e-business implementation.

SCOPE

The scope of the Quick Hit implementation extends across all departments that are related to the selected opportunities as reflected in the approved business cases. IT involvement is also part of the scope because you must ensure that IT staff members are culturally enmeshed in the work. This will prepare the way for greater acceptance later when you implement e-business.

END PRODUCTS

While the obvious end products are results that were expected for the opportunities, there are other, more subtle ones:

- Improved morale as employees see the results.
- Preparation for e-business by greater acceptance of change.
- Appreciation for measurement and getting tangible benefits.

Achieving these end products produces several benefits. First, e-business implementation is easier. Second, by focusing on measurement, people tend to better implement change to carry out the opportunities.

APPROACH

PREPARE THE EMPLOYEES FOR CHANGE

One approach to launch the Quick Hit implementation is to have management announce that these changes are coming and that the employees must support them. This is often accompanied by a fuzzy e-business and vague e-business objectives. The result, most of the time, is that the employees are left clueless and confused. What should they do? Do they follow general management or their own supervisors, who push them back to work after the e-business announcements. We have nothing against announcements, but a fundamental rule governing human behavior is that what you do is more important than what you say.

Prior to the announcement, if there is to be one, the core e-business leaders should meet with the supervisors and department managers to go over the opportunities. Of course, they should already be familiar with this through the action teams. Next, the leaders meet with the department employees to go over the current transactions, work, and workflow. The employees who participated in the action teams should be there. Problems with the current methods should be identified. Employees should be given the opportunity to indicate the negative impact of life at work as it is, as well as to pose questions. With the awareness raised, you can now move on to the plan for the Quick Hits. This approach is founded on the same principles of treating drug or alcohol addiction. The first step toward curing someone of these terrible problems is for them to admit that they have a problem.

In Walters 2 the employees were all given information about the approach using the three levels of management as well as the development of Quick Hits. Further preparation occurred during the development of the Quick Hits. So when implementation began, there was anticipation and not dread or fear.

POINTS OF RESISTANCE TO CHANGE

We want to get right into resistance—even before discussing the details of doing a Quick Hit. Here are some points of resistance to change that have been encountered in the past and some tips on what to do about them.

There Is No Time to Make Changes

- *How this arises:* There is certainly a great deal of pressure to perform the work in the departments. Employees may feel that if they devote the time to adopt the change and then carry it out, their manager will punish them.
- *How to prevent it:* The best prevention is to have the business manager and supervisors relate to the employees that the changes are a high priority—as high as doing their normal work.
- *What to do if it arises:* If individuals raise this concern, then you should visit the department manager and straighten this out. If you tell the people that the change is important, it may not matter to them. The line management pays their salaries, so to speak.

We Are Unique and So the Change Does Not Apply

• *How this arises:* The argument here is that the change does not apply to them. However, you find that it does from all of the work of the action teams. People sometimes feel that what they do is an art and craft and not a production process. As a consequence, they treat each piece of work uniquely. In such an environment there are often many exceptions.

• *How to prevent it:* One of the first steps is to review the current methods for handling the work with the employees. In doing this you can point out standardization and the need for change.

• *What to do if it arises:* If someone raises this point, then you can review the workload and indicate that you are not making wholesale changes.

There Is No Benefit from the Change

• *How this arises:* People may like how they do their work now. They do not see the benefit of the change; they only perceive more work.

• *How to prevent it:* At the start when you are reviewing the current work, indicate the impacts of continuing to do the work the same way.

• *What to do if it arises:* Indicate the benefits that were developed during the opportunity analysis.

Change Has Been Tried Before and It Didn't Work

• *How this arises:* This is often heard and it is often true. Many changes are introduced without organization or thought. Without knowing the analysis that went on before, they logically feel the same way.

• *How to prevent it:* Indicate at the start the method for defining and scoring the opportunities. This will demonstrate that an organized method was employed.

• *What to do if it arises:* When someone presents this issue, you should not be defensive. Indicate that this is a natural feeling and that a substantial amount of work was done to ensure that things were thought through. Encourage them to make further suggestions as you go.

The Change Will Disrupt Our Business

• *How this arises:* Supervisors especially are concerned that any change will interfere with the current work. They may feel that they have to be held to two standards.

• *How to prevent it:* Through meetings with department managers and supervisors you can work to minimize any disruption.

- *What to do if it arises:* When this is raised, you want to determine as fast as possible how the work is being disrupted. Then you seek to resolve this with the managers and supervisors.

Why Not Wait until E-Business Is Ready for Implementation?

- *How this arises:* People may want to put off the change and hope that it will go away. They may prefer one huge change.
- *How to prevent it:* You want to explain that change must be carried out in stages so as not to be too disruptive to the business.
- *What to do if it arises:* Return to the same theme that this is an organized approach in which limited changes are better than wholesale change.

What Is in the Change for Me?

- *How this arises:* This gets to the heart of self-interest. This is often un-stated, but it lurks under the surface.
- *How to prevent it:* Indicate what the individual employees will get from the change at the start.
- *What to do if it arises:* Return to the self-interest and address it openly.

DRY RUN THE QUICK HIT IN PRODUCTION

Prior to full-scale implementation of a Quick Hit a valuable step to take is to assemble the employees around the work location. Have the core e-business leaders, the supervisors, and the action team members for that area present. Walk through how the work is performed today and then how it will change. Get any of their concerns out on the table. You will notice that employees have had many chances to provide input and express doubts.

- They were in contact with action team members during the development of opportunities.
- They had a chance to pose questions during the kick-off meeting.
- They have a third opportunity to raise issues in the dry run.

In Walters 2 all Quick Hits had been reviewed in depth by the action teams as well as the steering committee and employees. Prior to implementation each change was reviewed with the department staff across all three shifts of operations in customer service and order processing.

Implement the Quick Hit

Implementation of Quick Hits depends on the type of Quick Hit. This section will consider the common types of changes.

Changes in Procedures

Here a method is changed. For example, a manual logging routine is to be dropped. Another example is that steps in the workflow are to be combined. Another example is the replacement or simplification of a form. You must address the transition to the new procedures. You also should give attention to how the new procedure will be measured. Planning for the effective date of the new procedures is important. After you have changed the procedures, you must monitor the procedures with the supervisors. You want to deal with any very detailed issues immediately. Otherwise, the employees may revert back to the old ways. To reinforce the new ways, it is important to destroy the old methods. You may have to confiscate forms and logs, for example. If you don't kill off the old methods and their support, then you continually risk the possibility that people will revert back to the old methods.

Policy Changes

Procedure changes are sometimes accompanied by changes in department policy. Here you will have to explain why the old policy does not work in the old environment. Then you can explain the new policy. Don't stop there. Go right on to the procedures that are necessary to carry out the new policies. When this is being done, give people a chance to raise issues and questions. From experience most of the questions will revolve around exceptions. Exceptions are addressed below. However, you want to be ready for this by indicating the scope of the policy and the situations to which it applies.

Changes in Interdepartmental Work

In e-business the transactions that you are changing tend to cross departments. In the old workflow transactions would often be logged or counted prior to being handed off to the next department. This is done for defensive reasons. If there is a problem, then people can go to the manual records. For the receiving department of the transactions the same approach is used. The effects are double counting and redundant, useless effort. It is easy to say that this should be killed; it is another thing to do it. You must conduct a joint meeting with the supervisors and action team members from both departments. You will review the problem and indicate how the interface between the two departments will change. After the changes have been made, return often to validate that the changes are in effect. If there is a multishift operation, then you should visit each shift. Don't ever assume that if you change the method during the prime shift, it carries over to the graveyard shift. Human behavior does not work that way.

Minor Systems Changes

There may be some minor systems changes necessary to support the Quick Hit. Of course, any major changes would likely have to wait for e-business. Minor changes could include changes to reports, modifications to screens, and changes to access control. For such changes you will want to ensure that you have detailed requirements. You can generate these by simulating the new workflow with the department staff and action team members. During this session, you should try to eliminate the need for system changes, or at least minimize them because the IT resources are already stretched thin.

Training

You want to reinforce the Quick Hits through training of the current staff and the new staff. In some cases, the change does not require formal training—just orientation at the start of a shift of work. If you are going to undertake training, then you should follow this outline:

- Review the old methods and the problems and their impacts.
- Go over the new methods.
- Indicate the benefits.
- Explain how the new methods will be monitored and measured.

Employees from the department should participate in the training. In that way, there is greater acceptance because the people doing the training are just like the audience. Don't place any stress on e-business. Focus on the change at hand.

Changes in Roles and Responsibilities

Beyond minor procedures, you may have a Quick Hit that involves modifying the roles and responsibilities of the department staff. An example might be to move a specific task in a transaction from one department to another. You will want to address several concerns proactively. For the department that is losing the role and work, there is a concern for staffing levels and job retention. During the implementation of Quick Hits and even the initial implementation of e-business, downsizing is not an option. There can be job shifts later. Stress that the people can redirect their efforts. This can be accomplished by working closely with the supervisor in the department. Moving to the department that is receiving the new role and additional work, you will have to consult in detail with the supervisors to see how this can be done with the current staffing levels. In more extreme situations, you may want to consider transferring one person between departments.

Eliminating an Exception or Workaround

In general, in implementing e-business it is your desire to avoid taking this change on. It can take a great deal of effort to kill off one exception. However, this may be essential in preparation for e-business. How do you eliminate a workaround or exception? First, you have to determine the answers to the following questions:

- What gave rise to the exception or workaround?
- What are the frequencies and volumes of these transactions?
- What are the business rules and policies followed for this work?
- Who handles the workaround and exception?
- What happens if the workaround or exception is not performed and the work is treated like normal work?

Answers here tell you how to kill off the exception and workaround. One approach is to force these transactions through normal work. Another approach is to have any instances of these brought to the supervisor. A key idea here is to remove the resources that perform the workaround or exception and have them perform normal work.

Coping with a Shadow System

A shadow system is a manual set of procedures or a small department-built PC system that is in use in production within a department. Using it has become an ingrained habit. There is almost as much or more dependence on this than on the IT-supplied systems. What do you do? The general approach is the same as for exceptions and workarounds. You seek to provide a substitute for the shadow system through the existing major systems. Alternatively, you can change policies and procedures so that the reason for using the shadow system goes out of existence.

For both exceptions/workarounds and shadow systems you have to be continually vigilant. If you don't monitor what is going on, then employees may start inventing new systems again. Thus, a critical guideline is that you must have the active, not passive, support of the supervisor.

COORDINATE MULTIPLE QUICK HITS

Some Quick Hits are implemented in isolation from others. Other Quick Hits must be executed together. You want to create a very small project team consisting of supervisors, action team members, and employees and follow the methods that have been presented above. In Walters 2 the core e-business team performed the implementation coordination. This was an important task and significant piece of work because a number of the Quick Hits had been bundled together and so had to be sequenced. Policy changes and procedure alterations had to be done at the same time.

PAVE THE WAY FOR LATER QUICK HITS AND E-BUSINESS

By doing the initial Quick Hits you overcome much of the resistance to change. However, if there is a major time gap between these and the next improvements, there is a danger that things could revert back and the old resistance could surface. The technique to support the future is to press for measurements. Another idea is to monitor and visit the departments. A third idea is to hold working sessions with employees to review their new methods. This can be very informal. The agenda is wide open to inputs regarding the work in the department, how the Quick Hits were executed, and additional opportunities. In Walters 2, in the first round of Quick Hits employees were told how the work would lead to other Quick Hits. These later Quick Hits were described and discussed.

MEASURE THE RESULTS OF QUICK HITS

Measurement of even simple changes is important for several reasons. First, it will tend raise morale and confidence for the employees. Second, it will better prepare them for later changes. Third, you can get back to management with the results. The measurement of the Quick Hit involves more than just economic benefits. You also want to answer the following questions:

- What were unexpected points of resistance and problems that were encountered? Answering this will better prepare you for later Quick Hits and e-business.
- Which employees were the most helpful and supportive? You will want to involve these people later on.
- Which employees created the most resistance and problems? In later work, you will want to meet with these people to win them over.
- What were the lessons learned from the transition that can be used later?
- What other opportunities surfaced as a result of implementing the Quick Hit?

As you can see, these speak to positive measurements that you can employ later. The benefits of this are cumulative. As you complete more Quick Hits, you build up more momentum. You become unstoppable!

The first round of Quick Hits for Walters 2 resulted in savings or revenue gains of over $1.4 million. The second round of Quick Hits generated savings in excess of $4.5 million. These Quick Hits more than paid for e-business implementation. Can the Quick Hits be counted in the benefits of e-business? We think so and so did Walters Catalog because they would not likely have been undertaken without the compelling pressure of e-business.

POTENTIAL PROBLEMS THAT CAN ARISE IN QUICK HIT IMPLEMENTATION

Beyond resistance there can be other problems that may surface. One is that of multiple shifts. This was discussed briefly before, but it deserves more discussion. You cannot assume that information and methods that work in one shift automatically transfer to a later shift. A later shift may perform the work slightly differently. They may have more and different exceptions. The lesson learned is to treat each shift individually.

Another problem is that when you actually start to implement the Quick Hit, you find that the situation is in some ways different from that envisioned in the earlier work. What do you do? You cannot go back and reopen the opportunities. Instead, you will have to work with the action team members and the supervisors to address the problem. Here are some specific questions to answer:

- Why did the situation change?
- Why wasn't this discovered before?
- What other things have changed?

Answers can lead you to improvise solutions. In the worse case, you may have to back off from the Quick Hit. However, this is a major decision fraught with peril. Employees who oppose change sense blood and victory. Management will begin to question other opportunities. There is the risk that the effort could unravel. The key lesson learned here is that you must attempt to do as complete an analysis job with the opportunities and involve as many employees as you can to head off this possibility.

STARTUP

Refer to Figure 13.1 for comments on the examples.

INDO FURNITURE

The Quick Hits for Indo Furniture centered on agreements with vendors for software development, computer systems, customer service, and order processing/

			Company			
Subject	Indo Furniture	Diamond Engineering	Asean Construction	Walters Catalog-1	Walters Catalog-2	Rogers County
Prepare employees for change	Family meetings	No preparation was needed	Carried out at the corporate and business unit levels	No preparation was undertaken	Through the action teams and core e-business team	Extensive meetings within operations; introduction among other employees
Resistance to change	Fear of loss of money	None	Fear of loss of jobs	Fear of loss of jobs	None among employees; some fear among middle-level managers	Skepticism of results
Quick Hit implementation	Agreements with vendors; trial shipments	Setup of business	Many Quick Hits across business units	None	Over 65 changes	Changes in policies and procedures

Figure 13.1   Observations from Quick Hits for Example Companies

inventory. In addition, some sample and trial units were prepared for shipment. The factory had to buy a plain paper fax machine. The main concerns of the family members were fear of the new and loss of money. Meetings were held with family members and relatives on the entire project.

DIAMOND ENGINEERING DATA

The major Quick Hits were the setting up of the company and the development of a prototype system. Chris and Mike began sequencing of the work in the form of waves of actions.

EXAMPLES

ASEAN CONSTRUCTION

Employees were prepared for change through many meetings. At these meetings there was little discussion of e-business. Instead, management focused on Quick Hits and the need and benefit for employee input. However, no formal preparation was really needed for the employees. Some of the employees expressed concerns about jobs. Management reassured the employees by indicating that no one would lose their job. However, they indicated that some people would be assigned different and, more likely, more creative jobs. There were many Quick Hits implemented across the business units and corporate. As these were implemented, employees were briefed on the results through presentations by employees who were involved in the implementation. This took away the fear factor.

ROGERS COUNTY

To prepare employees, extensive meetings were conducted with employees to solicit their ideas and concerns. Rather than concerns these meetings elicited even more ideas for improvement. This was very successful. For the consumer part of e-business there was a general announcement made to employees. A prototype was presented to employees. The resistance to e-business was only evident in healthy skepticism. Some employees cited previous efforts and attempts at change that had failed. They worried that this was just another one of these. Examples of success in other organizations were cited in response along with the emphasis on Quick Hits.

Quick Hits consisted mainly of changes in policies and procedures. This required more work than expected. The extra work was due to several factors. First, many employees belonged to a union. The new policies and procedures had to be verified against the union contract. Another source of work was the detail required for development. There also had to be additional training for some employees.

LESSONS LEARNED

A lesson learned in addition to the ones already presented is that efforts must be made to share experiences across all of the Quick Hit efforts. In this regard, it is strongly suggested that you hold regular meetings with the action team members to gather their experience and have them share their problems, concerns, and positive results with each other. This technique continues to boost the morale of the action teams. When you actually start making changes, it may not happen quickly enough for you. You might get depressed. It can cheer you up if you find out that others have had the same problems. You can also encourage action team members to help each other out on a limited scale.

THE SCORE CARD

The basic score card is the list of measurement questions that were posed earlier. You want to not only score the results of the Quick Hits, but also the process of transition to the changes. You also want to measure your progress along the road to e-business, for it is not how far you went, but how far you have to go that matters. Another thing to measure is that of involvement of the employees. A recurring measurement is to verify that people have not returned to their old ways.

WHAT TO DO NEXT

Consider a potential change in your own department. Make a list of the potential problems that you might encounter if you tried to implement change. For each of these examine possible actions that could be taken in advance to prevent the problems from surfacing. Another activity is to find a recent change that was made in a department. Answer the following questions:

- Was an effort made to measure the situation before the change?
- What problems were encountered during the change?
- Could these have been predicted?
- How did the management and employees deal with the problems?
- Was there an effort to measure the results of the change?

Coordinate Your
E-Business Implementation

INTRODUCTION

While much of the work discussed here pertains to the e-business work, we cannot ignore the implementation of Quick Hits. After all, it is the stages of Quick Hit improvements that lead us to e-business. To get an overall picture of what is going on, consider Figure 14.1 for a typical firm. It presents the various parts of the work and shows a high degree of parallel effort. Please note that this figure is not intended to be complete; rather it provides you with an idea of the extent of parallel effort required before going live in e-business.

PURPOSE AND SCOPE

BUSINESS OBJECTIVES

The business objective is to complete the implementation of both Quick Hits and e-business within the schedule and budget that were approved. These are words that sound so simple and yet mean so much. In order to work toward this objective, everyone will, from time to time, have to drop what they are doing and concentrate on implementation. All of the planning is over.

There are other business objectives, including these goals:

- Minimize the disruption to normal business.
- Respond rapidly to issues that are raised during implementation.
- Ensure that there is accountability.
- Verify that training and procedures have been completed.

Area	Phases of work		
Policies and procedures	Quick Hits	Quick Hits	Setup for e-business
Marketing to customers	General approach	Branding, marketing design	Initial marketing effort
Other business departments	Participation in Quick Hits	Participation in Quick Hits	Final readiness steps for e-business
Suppliers	Line up suppliers for pilot	Set up pilot	Conduct pilot
Infrastructure	Design	Installation	Integration and testing
Systems	Acquire/install e-business software	Testing and training	Integration and testing
System development	Design and prototyping	Development and unit testing	Integration and testing
Credit card	Agreements with vendors	Establish credit card link	Integration and testing
Data conversion	Specifications	Data conversion	Data conversion and testing
Web content	Specify products and services	Begin Web setup	Complete Web setup

Figure 14.1   Parts of the E-Business Implementation Effort

POLITICAL AND CULTURAL OBJECTIVES

A major political goal is to use the implementation effort to further build relationships among business departments with each other and with IT. This is a political organization goal. Another political objective is successfully to complete the pilot projects with employees, suppliers, and/or customers. The cultural objective is to instill an atmosphere at lower levels in the organization of collaboration and information sharing. While management can tell people to do this, the real new culture emerges and is carried out through joint work.

TECHNICAL OBJECTIVES

Here are the technical objectives:

- Successfully achieve a working environment for e-business.
- Implement tested and integrated systems.

- Ensure that there is proper security and access control.
- Successfully complete and test the Web content and data conversion.

There are also objectives related to training for business and IT staff, procedures for the business and IT operations, and completion of pilot projects.

SCOPE

The scope, as you can see, is very broad. Just reviewing Figure 14.1 can generate a pause in thinking. It also makes you see how important the initial work on strategy, transactions, and other areas of e-business is and why the original scope must be carefully set. Another by-product is that for startups. While there is probably less integration to do, whole new processes must be established. This is often more work than the Quick Hits.

END PRODUCTS

There are a number of milestones and end products that can be grouped according to their purpose:

- IT and technical end products.
  — Infrastructure and architecture are established.
  — Security and access control have been implemented and tested.
  — Network and systems management functions are in place for operations along with operations and troubleshooting procedures.
  — The e-business software has been developed, tested, and integrated with other software.
  — Data have been converted and Web page content has been setup and evaluated for accuracy and completeness.
- Business departments and employees.
  — There are new policies and procedures in place to support e-business.
  — Employees are trained in the new processes, procedures, and policies.
  — Employees and managers are looking forward to e-business so that there is a positive culture.
  — Certain departments, such as marketing, customer service, etc., have established new or modified business processes to support e-business transactions.
  — A marketing approach has been defined to promote the site and e-business and has been initiated.
  — If there is an intranet system, then it is being used by employees.

- Business departments and employees.
  — Some suppliers have participated in a pilot project and are ready to go into production.
  — Customers may have been sampled or their characteristics analyzed for e-business.
  — With production, suppliers and customers are doing e-business with your firm.
- Management.
  — Management is beginning to get feedback and initial reports from e-business operations.
  — Management is reviewing how the operation is functioning.

APPROACH

MANAGE THE WORK

You will be carrying over the action teams, core e-business team, steering committee, and executive committee into e-business implementation. In addition, there will be subproject teams for IT infrastructure and architecture, systems development, software package implementation, Web content, and data conversion.

Here are some suggestions from experience for managing the implementation work:

- There must be a standardized approach for identifying, organizing, and escalating business and IT issues. Any inconsistency will slow down one part of the project. As you saw in Figure 14.1, if you slow down one part significantly, you risk the overall schedule.
- The core e-business team may have to create temporary committees of action team members, IT, and managers to monitor integration, testing, data conversion, and other higher risk activities.
- The core e-business team members should fan out across the project each day to track what is going on. The core e-business team should meet early in the morning and in the late afternoon to review what is being done.
- Rather than staying focused on progress, the core e-business team should direct their attention toward issues. It is a choice of whether to look at the "glass half full or half empty." Always choose the glass half empty.
- Pay special attention to how each subproject is kicked off. If one starts slow, then you may have difficulty turning around the attitude. Members of the core e-business team should become involved in these meetings to spur people on.
- Gather lessons learned during the major IT related work as well as after Quick Hits are completed. Use these lessons learned in presentations and in giving credit to the teams to raise morale.

How will you review milestones that result from the work? Here are some specific suggestions:

- Further Quick Hits—benefits, effort to implement, time to implement, and unresolved issues.
- Other business changes—schedule, effort, results.
- Systems and IT work—milestones achieved, schedule, cost, and outstanding issues.

How on earth can you evaluate all possible milestones and end products? You can't! Therefore, you must be selective. You must pick milestones that are complex to review and verify and that have an impact on e-business. Here are some examples of milestones of this kind:

- Results of a pilot effort in e-business.
- Setup of Web page content.
- Data conversion.
- System integration and testing of software.
- Testing of the new IT architecture and infrastructure for e-business.
- Quick Hit benefits.

What are some of the types of issues that might arise? There is specific discussion in areas of high risk later. Here you can review these general types:

- An action team encounters a policy or procedure problem that they are not empowered to address. This must be discovered quickly and taken to the appropriate managers or steering committee.
- Technical problems are encountered that were unanticipated. There is insufficient time for in-depth analysis. This is where you want to have an IT team with some technical vendor staff to address these quickly.

You will have to plan out your presentations to management. It is complex to present work and milestones for such a wide variety of projects. Consider instituting a one-page summary approach for each subproject. This should contain the following:

- Purpose of the subproject from a business view.
- Summary Gantt chart showing major summary tasks and milestones.
- Milestones achieved.
- Upcoming milestones.
- Outstanding issues.

The milestones and issues should be expressed in business and management terms, even if they are technical. Now that you have these summaries, you are ready to present an overall summary of the e-business implementation. This summary can take in the following information:

- Summary Gantt chart across the entire effort.
- Milestone summary.
- Significant lessons learned from the recent work.
- Benefits achieved in the work so far (give projected versus actuals).
- Major issues by subproject and what actions management can take.
- Followup from past decisions and actions on key issues.

It does little good to just present information due to the time pressure. You want to use this presentation to get management involved. Focus on three to five issues that they can address. Make sure that you not only identify decisions, but also action items that are required to implement the decisions.

In Walter 1 the burden of managing the work fell on the project leader. The head of the company was forced frequently to intervene to get resources and reset priorities. It was like a series of nightmares. What made things worse is that the people started to view e-business as an IT project. This alienated the employees from involvement. Things improved in Walter 2. There was in-depth support and strength going beyond the core e-business team. There were the action teams. Next, there were the steering and executive committees for review and escalation. Third, there were the employees who were involved in the implementation. It was a real team effort.

FURTHER QUICK HIT IMPLEMENTATION

Some Quick Hits can be easily done. Do them right away. Others require direction, some planning, and thinking through the sequencing of changes. They fit in here. In carrying out these more complex Quick Hits you may encounter some problems. Here are some common ones and what to do about them:

- The action team attempts to implement a Quick Hit in a minimal form. This can be a problem in that there will not only be fewer benefits, but also there has not been sufficient change for e-business. This occurs because there are often different solutions (i.e., "there are many ways to skin a cat"). Press for the action team to examine alternatives with a wider scope.
- In some cases, the Quick Hit cannot be carried out without disrupting the business. You could then just wait until you are close to the time of e-business going live. Don't wait! Sit down with the line managers and supervisors and discuss what can be done now.
- Quick Hits were combined in the analysis if they were highly interdependent. When you get to doing the Quick Hits, you may have to sequence specific actions. In evaluating different sequences consider the process impact, culture impact, and management impact of the change.
- You are still likely to encounter resistance from people who are not on action teams. This often comes from the senior employees in the department who

see their jobs, procedures, and even power threatened. How do you handle this? Review the specific change with the supervisor and action team member from that department ahead of time. Raise this point of resistance and develop a proactive approach. It is important that you and the team not be caught by surprise.

With Walters 1 there were no initial or further Quick Hits. With Walters 2 there were waves of Quick Hits. The second wave occurred during the e-business implementation. Then there were more Quick Hits as new ideas and improvements surfaced.

COORDINATE THE QUICK HITS WITH E-BUSINESS

Measure the Quick Hits as they are implemented. Remember that benefits from these items were estimated. Don't drop the ball. Measure these and report back to management. When you report back, indicate the following information:

- What actions were taken.
- What results were achieved.
- How the Quick Hit supports e-business.
- Lessons learned from the Quick Hit effort.
- Additional actions that can be taken (e.g., more policy changes) to further improve results.

Take along members of the action teams when you make these presentations. They can be very useful by describing what the situation was before and after the Quick Hits. To review the benefits, build on this description and show the differences before and after and their impact.

Coordination of Quick Hits also involves extensive communications within departments. After changes have been made and the desired results achieved, have the department celebrate with the action team. In your room that serves as the command center, create a table on the wall showing Quick Hits by the action teams. Use this to foster a healthy competition among action teams. Hold action team meetings in this room.

In Walters 2 the effort required to coordinate the additional Quick Hits with e-business consumed up to half of the core e-business team's time. This was a surprise to everyone because it was felt that there were fewer interdependencies than there actually were.

MANAGE THE VENDOR EFFORT

When you have time pressure and so many things to do, you will most likely be using various vendors to perform some of the implementation tasks. The chapter on outsourcing provided a detailed discussion of where you might employ outsourcing as well as setting up the outsourcing agreement. Here are some additional guidelines to follow:

• Manage the initial tasks performed by a vendor very closely. Don't stay at arm's length. You want to establish a successful pattern of behavior in working with each vendor.

• Assign many tasks jointly between the IT staff and vendor staff. This will facilitate the transfer of knowledge and lessons learned.

• Involve vendor staff in the lessons-learned meetings. This will further assist in knowledge transfer and collaboration.

• Have regular meetings with vendor management to address issues and problems as well as progress.

What are you trying to accomplish with these steps? You are attempting to erect a collaborative setting for the work. You are trying to get more than the sum of the parts out of this. You are also showing the vendors that you are serious in implementation. You may encounter resistance from the vendor under the excuse that this approach will slow them down. Don't buy into this argument. Insist that these simple guidelines be followed.

In Walters 1 the project leader had to manage developers who worked over 2000 miles away. He had very little time to manage them except through telephone calls, faxes, and e-mails. When he visited the developers, everything was always fine. Then when he returned, he found out that things were not as they seemed. He later found out that the developers met prior to his visit and planned out what they were going to say. He decided to go there unannounced. This helped iron out problems there, but then new problems would surface at home. For Walters 2 there was a coordinated effort to manage vendors. There was the vendor score card. Regular meetings were held with vendor management to go over progress, money, and outstanding issues.

COORDINATE SUPPLIER AND CUSTOMER INVOLVEMENT

If you are going to implement business-to-business e-business you will want to involve selected suppliers. You might do the same for larger commercial customers. Their involvement in pilot projects is a critical success factor for your e-business effort. Their support and experience will later help convince others to become involved in e-business. On the other hand, if they have a negative experience and get turned off, then the whole e-business thrust can be undermined.

How should you involve customers and suppliers? Here are some suggestions:

• Make customers and suppliers members of your e-business steering committee. This will provide a forum for them to give input at the management level.

This will also demonstrate your commitment to e-business and that they are a critical factor in the success of e-business.

- Develop joint detailed plans with the customers and suppliers. This will begin to show their experience in e-business and willingness to assign key resources to the project.
- Involve a number of suppliers and customers in case some drop out later due to pressing internal commitments.
- Hold management meetings at the highest level to show the employees of both companies that the e-business effort is serious.
- Hold review meetings to assess the progress. Share some of the implementation issues with them.

What is going through their minds? Here are some things that you will want to address during their involvement:

- What is in it for the customer or supplier?
- What benefits will they get in terms of pricing, costs, and long-term commitment?
- What has to be done by the supplier and customer?
- What is the level of resource commitment that will be required? If a supplier did this with each customer separately, the company would go broke.
- How will with problems and culture clashes be handled?
- If there is a pressing internal problem, can their involvement be reduced temporarily?

Walters Catalog had their catalog customers at the start of Walters 1. These were marketed to through limited promotions in the catalogs. However, because the catalogs appeared only at intervals of several months, this had limited effectiveness. Web traffic after Walters 1 grew in a very limited way. For Walters 2 the situation was better for several reasons. First, there was a body of existing Web shoppers. Second, there was more experience in doing promotions through the catalogs. Third, limited advertising was done.

Suppliers provided products for Walters Catalog. With a catalog there was a limited number of vendors. Moving to the Web there was a push to line up many more suppliers. This taxed marketing, accounting, and other areas. For marketing the issue was how to give commissions to salespeople who attracted new vendors and products. It was decided to extend the commissions from the catalog to the Web. Next, key suppliers were involved in the rollout of the new Web site. There was some resistance because some firms already sold through their own Web pages. In addition, many potential new suppliers of products lacked Internet and Web expertise. They did not know how best to portray their items. A person was reassigned to marketing to help these suppliers.

IT INFRASTRUCTURE

The IT infrastructure and architecture work encompasses network, hardware, and system software tasks. There are upgrades to current components. These are easy. There are also new software tools and network and hardware components to install. The IT staff have to become familiar with these. This is a good area to consider for outsourcing to the vendor of the products.

There are security and firewall concerns as well as that are handled. Management must make trade-offs in terms of what is reasonable and in common practice. If you insist on excessive security, then there could be negative performance impacts. If you are too light on security, then everything is at risk. There are some specific challenges here for e-business. Here are some examples:

• Establishment of external links to suppliers and customers outside of the Internet and Web.
• Creation of a link with third party network firms.
• Building of links to banks or other firms for credit card authorization and processing.
• Establishing redundant hardware, network, and software for continuous operations.
• Support for operation 24 hours a day, 7 days a week (24/7).

From our experience, these tasks can be major efforts that entail not only hardware, software, and network components, but also IT staffing and computer facilities. The IT infrastructure was basically in place at Walters Catalog. The major addition was to add more network and hardware capacity to handle the additional volume of transactions.

SYSTEM DEVELOPMENT AND INTEGRATION

You want to get this effort going quickly. New software development and testing tools should be installed at the start. Training of the technical staff should also be done then. For the methods and tools follow these guidelines:

• For every tool make sure that there is an established method that the tool supports. Software tools can be employed in many ways. You want the approach that supports the selected method.
• Identify a method and tool expert in the IT group or among vendor staff. This person should serve as a mentor for the IT staff and other vendor staff in using the method and tool.
• Determine the expectations for the method and tool. What are people supposed to get out of using these? What are the benefits? Examples are faster de-

velopment, better quality software, easier to maintain software, and more testable software.

• Identify and address any gaps in the methods and tools. If you fail to do this, there will problems later as people attempt to improvise to fill the gaps individually.

• Walk through how the methods and tools will be employed in an integrated way. In this way the developers understand the integration of the methods and tools with each other.

Here are some additional guidelines for development:

• Implement a configuration management method in which the code is organized and managed centrally.

• Hold lessons-learned meetings on the use of the methods and tools.

• Have the IT and vendor team share initial tasks in development. This will make things easier later and support collaboration.

• Stress reusable code. Before moving into a new area of development the team should sit down and review what code they have developed already and what can be reused.

Let's turn to technical issues. Most of the issues will arise here rather in the infrastructure. What you want to have happen is for the issues to surface at the start of implementation and not at the end. There is a lesson learned here from COBOL programming. Suppose that a programmer is to develop a COBOL program. In terms of lines of code, the data definition part of the project constitutes a high percentage of the total. However, this is very routine work. If the programmer works on this first, he or she can say that they are 40% or more of the way through the work. But they are really not. The risk and exposure lie in the business rules and interfaces. Therefore, in terms of risk, they are probably only 10% of the way through. You can apply this example to technical work in general. You want people to identify and tackle the issues and risks early. A suggestion is to focus all early meetings on issues.

There are additional guidelines for doing a pilot and prototype development. Traditionally, you would develop a prototype to evaluate the user interface and navigation through menus. Often, the prototype would later be thrown away. You cannot afford to do this. The prototype must be working and the eventual software should be based on this prototype system. Here are specific suggestions:

• Center attention on the business rules and interfaces of the software. This is where the risk is. Get this effort going early so that issues start to appear early.

• Make the Graphical User Interface (GUI) simple and in black and white. Don't aim for making it pretty. If you spend time here, you are avoiding the business rules and interfaces. Do the GUI at the end. This has the effect of giving more stress to the objective rules and interfaces, rather than to the subjective user interface, over which there can be endless arguments.

- Involve action team members in the design and development of the software. These people know both the Quick Hits and the business processes. If you rely on others who only know the current procedures, you may be developing software that is rendered obsolete by the Quick Hits.

The IT group in Walters Catalog had limited Web experience in Walters 2. They had outsourced the development in Walters 1 so that there was limited experience gained. Additional IT staff had to be hired.

ADDRESS TESTING AND QUALITY ASSURANCE

It is possible to write whole volumes on testing and quality assurance. Also, this is not a book on these subjects. Here are some useful guidelines to use:

- Treat testing and quality assurance as a separate subproject. This will ensure that it receives adequate attention.
- Make someone separate from the programmers in charge of quality assurance. This person should report to the IT manager.
- Build the test plan and start creating test cases from the action teams right away. Don't wait. It will hold up the project.
- Create test cases that concentrate on areas of exposure including interfaces and integration along with business rules. This is appropriate because in the approach to e-business you will not be automating many exceptions.
- Employ the action teams and other employees in departments in testing.
- Encourage the discovery of errors and problems. A big mistake is that firms treat errors as the fault of the testers.
- Test business policies and procedures and not just systems.
- Test the usability, accuracy, and completeness of operations procedures and training materials.

If you learn one thing in regard to the technical side of e-business implementation, it is that testing and quality assurance play key roles. In one case a customer was able to combine discounts and get merchandise free. He then posted this in a chat room. Within days, the firm had lost several million dollars because they had to ship the merchandise. It is surprising, but true, that many firms neglect testing and the test environment. They can deal with production and development, but fail to see the need for quality assurance. The marketing of testing and quality assurance was a continuing struggle in Walters 2.

DATA CONVERSION AND WEB CONTENT

Experience has shown that people don't pay sufficient attention to data conversion and Web content. When you implement e-business, management will want to know what results were achieved. How you do this is to implement reporting from both old and new software. This not only requires integration, but also data conversion. Don't take people's word about the quality of the data. In e-business you get down to individual transactions. This is often a level below that which the organization has employed. The summary can be just fine; the devil is in the detail, as they say.

Turning to Web content, it seems so simple. You photograph the product and add descriptive material and put it on a Web page. Ah, if life were so simple. The standards for accuracy and descriptive material are higher than in paper catalogs. You have to make the item look attractive. Consider several luggage manufacturer sites. Their black luggage shows up as a black blob. They don't show the interior of the luggage, which is a critical factor in deciding which luggage to buy. The luggage vendor assumes that you know it! Setting up one item consumes substantial time and many steps. In one case, one item took on average 4 hours. The steps include photography, digital rendering and preparation, preparing the description, reviewing the description, etc. If you make a mistake, you could pay dearly. An example occurred with a computer manufacturer who put a new laptop computer on their Web site. They received thousands of orders. They were at first elated and later depressed when they found out that someone had left out three zeros in the price. They had to ship laptops with a major loss being incurred.

In Walters 1 this issue did not really surface because of the limited number of products on the Web. In Walters 2 the setup of Web content became a major issue. In the end this had to be outsourced to cope with the volume of products that had to be established on the Web. Data conversion and interfaces were a problem at Walters Catalog during Walter 2. There was a client-server system for customer service and an Internet system for Web sales. There were constant interface efforts to keep the interfaces synchronized. In addition, to get management reports on profits and sales, information had to extracted and massaged from four different systems.

COPE WITH DOCUMENTATION

In an academic setting there is a tendency to document everything. This is a good idea. Unfortunately, it does not work in the real world. It is extremely difficult to adhere to documentation standards imposed by standards organizations, for example. What is our basic guideline? Document as little possible. Even then you will produce a great deal of documentation. Always answer the following questions before documenting something:

- If you don't do the documentation, what is the risk? How can you be damaged?
- Who will develop the documentation?
- Who will review the documentation?
- What level of detailed review will be employed?
- How will the documentation be employed?
- How will the documentation be updated?

As a result of experience, you tend to document where you have risk. You should develop documentation using a successive outline approach. The person developing the documentation provides more detailed outlines at each stage. In that way, you have a better understanding than sending the person off to do documentation and then having them return a month later with an unsuitable product. Another guideline relates to the review of documentation. You cannot afford to read an entire document and hope to find problems. An alternative approach is to have the person who created the document present it to a group in a lessons-learned session. Carefully watch their body language, listen to their tone of voice, and detect where they go into little detail. This will help you identify areas to review based on risk.

In some firms there is an emphasis of ISO 9000 and other standards. These standards are a good idea and well intentioned. However, they can create an enormous burden of documentation at the same time that other IT activities are being undertaken with high priority. For some the only choice is to call the e-business effort a prototype and to consider the documentation requirements later.

CHANGE THE E-BUSINESS STRATEGY AND PLAN

During the e-business implementation you will have to revise the plan and to review the e-business—especially if the schedule is slipping. In previous chapters, the use of an e-business project template was emphasized for both the overall project and for the subprojects. This is now where the template becomes invaluable. You can carry out many changes in the detail of the schedule without affecting the template project structure. This provides stability and consistency. Even so, a recommendation is that you make only discrete changes to the schedule as opposed to making minor changes. Reasons for changes in tasks should be given in text fields in the schedule.

In terms of the e-business strategy, it is unlikely that you can change the basic strategy in midstream. However, it does not hurt to review the e-business vision, objectives, and strategy with management and the action teams.

STARTUP

Refer to Figure 14.2 for a table with comments on the examples.

INDO FURNITURE

The key in managing the work lay in coordinating with the Indo factory on production planning, shipping, and complaints. There were instances of damage and even sabotage. Claims had to be initiated to recover funds. Further Quick Hits were often based around testing the interfaces among the systems of the various vendors. These efforts required substantial time and coordination across many different time zones. The first tests were based on batch files. When on-line testing was done, there were many problems. It was then decided to keep the interface in a batch mode with fairly frequent updates. For commercial customers the challenge was to line up dealers. Some samples of the furniture were shown at furniture trade shows. This was successful. However, some dealers did not use the Internet or Web so that resort was made to the fax machines.

DIAMOND ENGINEERING DATA

The division of managing the work at Diamond was natural. Chris handled the business end while Mike dealt with engineers and the setup of the knowledge base and the software. Further Quick Hits involved system development and testing. Also, there was the establishment of accounting and other business practices. There was also a limited marketing effort.

EXAMPLES

ASEAN CONSTRUCTION

Managing the work was actually quite easy because there was the organization infrastructure for e-business in the core e-business teams, the action teams, and coordination among the various business units and corporate. An issues database was established along with regular gathering of lessons learned. Experiences were shared across business units. The Quick Hits just kept coming. This was good because it gave the teams more time to implement e-business. One division

Subject	Company					
	Indo Furniture	**Diamond Engineering**	**Asean Construction**	**Walters Catalog-1**	**Walters Catalog-2**	**Rogers County**
Manage the work	Coordination with the factory	Chris managed the business; Mike worked on the knowledge base and supervised development	Through the various project leaders	Burden fell on the project leader	Core e-business team, implementation teams	Two core teams for operations and consumer
Further Quick Hits	Test runs with the interfaces	Development, testing	These just kept coming	Not applicable	Second wave of Quick Hits	Development of the lessons learned and wizards
Customers/ suppliers	Lining up of dealers	Lining up engineers; contacting potential customers	Contacts with suppliers; some advertisements with customers	Limited effort except for some advertising in the catalogs	More proactive contact with customers and suppliers	Some limited advertisements

Figure 14.2 E-Business Implementation Comments for Example Companies

considered concentrating on Quick Hits and not pursuing e-business due to the benefits and effort required. They were discouraged from this, but not entirely. The division just scaled back their e-business effort.

The major focus at the corporate level was on business-to-business e-business. Several suppliers totally endorsed e-business and supported the implementation. In the area of gathering and using lessons learned about engineering and construction projects, considerable time was spent in structuring the information for later use. Then the issue arose as to how to encourage the engineers to use the database of experience. The approach that was employed was to require that lessons learned be reviewed at each step of the way in an engineering project.

ROGERS COUNTY

The internal operations e-business effort and that for consumers were managed separately. There was little coordination required except in IT systems because the activities were so diverse. This made the management easier. The major software development for operations was the development of the forms software, with many business rules being incorporated into the software. This was a challenge because during this work a number of shadow systems surfaced. Another software development effort was directed toward the development of wizards. No one had experience in this area so that it was learn as you go.

In addition to this work, operations also had to collect lessons learned from employees. This was perceived to be a major hurdle at the start. However, it turned out to be a nonevent because many employees started volunteering things from their experience. What was underestimated was the manual, labor-intensive effort to turn raw experience into structured lessons learned.

LESSONS LEARNED

Here are some lessons learned from past efforts:

- Test the approach for handling issues by beginning with those that surfaced in the definition of the Quick Hits.
- Set aside one room as a command center for e-business implementation. Put the schedule on the walls. Also, post key issues along with the creation dates and priorities.
- During the work, core e-business team members should provide a brief update of what other teams are doing when they meet with individual groups.
- Have the meetings of the steering and executive committees held in the room that serves as a command center. This will not only indicate the degree

of activity, but will also be useful when you have to refer to specific issues or subprojects.

THE SCORE CARD

Here are some of the relevant measures to take during implementation in the form of questions:

• Are the Quick Hits yielding the benefits that were anticipated? If there are fewer benefits, then you have to question the earlier analysis. However, it may also be that the action teams are not fully implementing the Quick Hits.

• Are action teams getting bogged down in specific issues related to Quick Hits? This could delay the project if they are getting sidetracked.

• Are any issues showing up in the technical work that are surprises? There is no problem if surprises come up at the start. The problem occurs when they surface late in the project when there is little time.

WHAT TO DO NEXT

Because you haven't started implementing e-business yet, you might want to review the magazines and literature to find lessons learned from other companies' experiences in e-business implementation. Use these to add to your lessons-learned and issues databases. Another idea is to make a list of potential e-business implementation issues by reviewing your current business activities. This will better prepare you for implementation.

Chapter 15

Manage Your E-Business Operations

INTRODUCTION

E-business operations are complex. You must not only support e-business, but also the normal business processes. However, e-business places many urgent demands on the IT group as well as business departments such as customer service, accounting, fulfillment, and marketing. There is the day-to-day coordination with suppliers as well as dealing with customers. There can be even more pressing are changes and requests:

• Marketing designs a new promotion that requires coordination with many different departments.
• The competition is embarking on a new program that appears to be successful. You have to respond.
• There are continued issues between e-business and regular business transactions.

E-business tends to take on a life of its own. Figure 15.1 provides a picture of what is involved in e-business operations. In this diagram you can see the pressures of four major external factors:

• *Technology.* New technology and products continue to emerge. The challenge is not only selection, but also integration with what you have.
• *Customers and suppliers.* Establishing deeper relationships carries with it more responsibilities.
• *Management.* Not only does management place demands on the business and e-business, but there are the challenges of resource management and allocation and measurement of the transactions and processes.

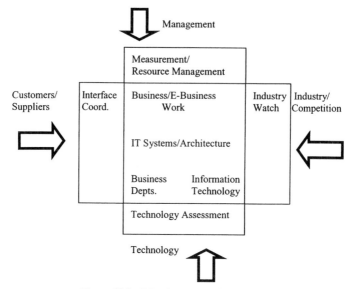

Figure 15.1 E-Business Operations Diagram

• *Industry and competition.* You have to watch the marketplace and determine what actions you need to take.

For each of the four forces, there is a coordination and management box. These help organize the internal response and proactive direction to these forces. At the core are the business and e-business transactions supported by the systems and IT architecture, the business departments, and the IT organization. It is interesting to note that IT is placed on a level with the business departments. In the past the IT organization would most likely have been shown to be supportive of the departments. While this is still true, it is also a fact that e-business requires more direct involvement in the business processes and transactions.

PURPOSE AND SCOPE

BUSINESS OBJECTIVES

The business objective is to support the expansion and competitive position of the enterprise overall, including both e-business and regular business. An additional goal is to be able to pursue new initiatives and growth in e-business. This can mean new products and services, expansion of e-business transactions, increase in the number of suppliers and/or customers involved in e-business, and increased collaboration and information sharing among employees.

POLITICAL AND CULTURAL OBJECTIVES

In traditional business, there is dependence on key employees in departments. When you move into e-business, you discover that there is reliance on the IT staff. A political goal is that the IT group must become more flexible and responsive to e-business. A cultural objective is to have department staff work together operationally on a daily basis to address specific questions and actions on a timely basis. You want to achieve this without substantial management intervention.

TECHNICAL OBJECTIVES

IT must support the operation of the transactions as well as provide resources to address new demands. Outsourcing vendors have to be managed. Outsourcing agreements may have to be created or modified. IT must also deal with new technology. As an example, suppose that you have a working Web site based on Hypertext Markup Language (HTML) and linking to back office systems. Then XML and mobile communications emerge as critical. You can be faced with rewriting what has been done.

SCOPE

E-business operations include the following elements of scope:

- Support and operation of standard business transactions in parallel with e-business.
- Operation of the network, hardware, and software to support both e-business and regular business.
- Software maintenance and enhancement to handle business demands related to regular and e-business.
- Creativity in figuring out ways to improve e-business and expand its benefits.

Do you notice something in these bulleted items? Both business and e-business are treated together. They are combined. That is the way it is with e-business. This is even true with a startup firm in which there are new standard, non-e-business processes. Another thing to notice is that there is a larger role for IT. You can see this by contrasting the ideas above with those in early chapters in this book.

END PRODUCTS

There are a number of technical and business end products, including:

- Successful operation of both regular and e-business.
- Implementation of changes and enhancements to existing transactions.
- Expansion of e-business to reach new customers and suppliers.
- Enhancement of e-business to handle new marketing and other opportunities.
- Incorporation of new technologies to increase the flexibility, reliability, and efficiency as well as to reduce costs.

APPROACH

COORDINATE E-BUSINESS

E-business requires coordination on an ongoing basis. There must be coordination across departments. Doing this work is full-time. Experience shows that it is a good idea to appoint an e-business coordinator. Duties include the following responsibilities:

- Collect information on the business activities and issue measurement score cards.
- Survey the industry as well as analyze internal data to discover new e-business opportunities.
- Review infrastructure and organization issues related to the business activities (this includes requests for changes as well as analysis findings).
- Recommend and design specific changes and improvements to management as well as alerting management to problems.
- Manage the implementation of change.
- Coordinate the training of new staff in the activities and collect the experience and knowledge of departing staff.

Except for smaller organizations, this is too much for one person. Moreover, while you want to have someone center post e-business on a routine basis, you also desire to have departments involved in reviewing and surveying what is going on in industry (following the guidelines of Chapter 6). Your objective is to involve many business departments in being aware and involved in e-business. In order to support coordination and achieve this goal, consider having one department assigned as a coordination department. This is a rotational role that is in addition to normal business. Every 6 months another department would take over the responsibilities. Here are some duties of the department coordination role:

- Collect information on the industry and competition.
- Review technology and systems from a business perspective.
- Support the coordination of management requests.
- Identify requirements generated by customers and suppliers.
- Build on the database of lessons learned with respect to e-business by gathering experience internally.
- Organize the assumption and rotation of the role.

Do these business departments have a lot of time to devote to this? No, of course not. This is a limited activity. It should, however, be performed by as many employees in the department as possible.

For Walters 1 there was no coordination. The default was to have support fall back to the IT group. In Walters 2 the core e-business team slimmed down to two people. One remained as coordinator for a year and the other for 6 months. At the end of the six months, a new coordinator was appointed for a year. The steering committee and executive committee continued. Another level of coordination was instituted in Walters 2 by having departments monitor the Web and competition. Of particular interest were various promotions and deals. The first group that volunteered was customer service. It was decided to have the coordination role rotate to another department after 6 months.

Support E-Business Operations

E-business operation includes the following components:

- Business departments
  — Being involved in handling Web-generated orders and requests on a daily basis.
  — Handling exceptions that e-business does not address.
  — Responding to Web customers and suppliers.
  — Enforcing policies for both Web and regular business.
  — Identifying potential problems to be dealt with by the e-business coordinator.
  — Synchronizing e-business and regular business work.
  — Handling peak volumes generated by e-business.
- Management
  — Monitoring e-business and regular business.
  — Defining priorities for resources overall so that demands of both the regular and e-business are met.
  — Keeping the business organization and IT focused on business goals, e-business goals, and the e-business vision.
  — Reviewing the e-business strategy to ensure that it is an appropriate approach for attaining the goals and vision of e-business.

- IT organization
  — Maintaining the IT architecture to ensure reliability, availability, and maintainability.
  — Ensuring that there is adequate capacity to handle growth.
  — Enhancing current and e-business systems to deal with demand.
  — Investigating new systems and technology in terms of its potential benefit in the business.
  — Managing IT resources so that the most pressing work is performed.

Within these bulleted components there are many trade-offs that have to be performed. Here are some guidelines and challenges:

- Maintenance must be controlled and probably reduced to free up resources for important enhancements.
- IT skills must be updated to support new systems and technology.
- Management must be more involved and supportive of the condition and upgrading of the hardware, network, and software in the IT infrastructure and architecture.
- Business departments and IT must work more closely together.
- Business departments must actively consider e-business at all times.

ADDRESS E-BUSINESS ISSUES

Many issues can arise during operations. Here are some examples:

- Organization problems surface. Marketing problems are often the most numerous.
- Software cannot support the new marketing Web promotions and discounts—delaying the marketing and affecting your competitive position.
- People are tired from the implementation and innovation stops.
- Customer complaints are unheeded and grow.
- Benefits of the new processes are not measured—the old and new cannot be compared.
- The implementation was not complete so that new workarounds and shadow systems have to be created.
- Surrounding systems and processes change, impacting e-business without planning.
- There is a need to assess and quickly define some specific new technology to determine how it might fit within your IT architecture and support e-business.
- Consultants who helped in implementation leave—taking their knowledge with them.

- Competitors change and you do not respond.
- Organization changes do not occur—affecting the effectiveness of e-business.
- Management wants to start some new initiative. It may rob resources from operational support of e-business.

There must be a coordinated approach to handling issues and opportunities. An issues database was discussed earlier. This database can serve as a repository for potential problems and opportunities. Key data elements include priority of the issue, status of the issue, impact of the issue if it is not addressed, potential benefits of resolving the issues, and how these benefits are measured. In addition, when an issue is resolved, the details of the resolution should be entered into the database. Include the date of resolution, decisions made, actions taken, and follow-up after the actions. Issues should be coordinated centrally through the e-business coordinator. In some cases, this role has been expanded to include regular business issues that impact e-business indirectly or directly. The e-business coordinator should conduct regular meetings on issues.

In Walters 1 there was no effort to analyze issues in a structured way. Walters 2 took a much more organized approach. Starting a checklist of over 150 issues, the issues database began to grow. Issues were regularly analyzed by the e-business coordinators and then reviewed with the steering committee.

MEASURE E-BUSINESS

Why carry out measurement if e-business is working? Because you want to determine how e-business is doing. Here you will be measuring at a more detailed level. In the next section, you will move up to your e-business strategy, vision, and goals. Here are questions to get you thinking. These are purposely across a range of activities.

- What is the level of customer service being provided?
- What are the nature and number of complaints being received?
- How easy is it for customers or suppliers to navigate the Web site?
- What is the volume of sales or work being performed via e-business versus traditional business?
- What is the cost of transactions performed through the Web?
- What are competitors doing with their Web sites? What else can you do to improve your competitive position on the Web?
- What is the performance of the systems in handling peak volumes of customer or supplier activity?

Perform Cost and Benefit Analysis

Measurement data can be employed in estimating the costs and benefits of e-business. Tangible costs in such areas as infrastructure and IT can be identified. It is much more difficult to estimate the labor hours that were spent on e-business implementation. For benefits you can start with those of the Quick Hits. Then you can consider the process scoreboards to get additional benefits in labor savings and productivity gains. Some of these, of course, overlap the Quick Hit benefits. Then there may be increased sales due to the Web.

Do companies perform payback analysis? Some surveys indicate that about one-third of their sample expected payback in 1 year or less. Almost half did not perform return on investment (ROM) calculations. Most indicated that they had to get into e-business. There was little choice. Walters 2 was one of these companies. They did develop analysis that indicated that the benefits of the Quick Hits easily paid for the e-business implementation.

Review Your E-Business Strategy, Vision, and Goals

You want to examine current operations in order to reassess your e-business strategy, vision, and goals. Here are some basic questions to answer:

• Do the new e-business activities and changes support the business and e-business visions as well as the e-business objectives?
• Does the e-business implementation change the organization and infrastructure as desired?
• Do the e-business activities support flexibility in the business?
• What are the impacts of the new e-business activities internally on morale?
• How do the new E-business activities help management direct work better?
• Do the new e-business activities have an impact on the external community (e.g., suppliers, customers, investors, and regulators)?

In order to do an assessment, you can return to some of the tables that were presented earlier. Examine the changes that have occurred in the business and IT as a result of the e-business implementation. In Walters 2 a review was conducted and the strategy for e-business was left unchanged.

Expand E-Business

In addition to maintenance and enhancement work in the next section, you want to consider how to expand e-business. The ideas that seem good to you will then result in more enhancements that can be addressed using the methods in the next section.

How can you expand e-business? Here are some examples:

- Extend e-business to more suppliers. You might desire to approach new suppliers or get existing ones on e-business.
- Extend e-business to address more customers. You might want to reach customers in a new geographic area.
  - Add new products and services for e-business.
  - Add in-depth functions to address individual customers. This could include target marketing.
- Implement a broader range of supply chain or customer relationship management systems and capabilities.
- Start to take advantage of the information gathered from e-business transactions.
- Make changes in business infrastructure for e-business growth (warehouses, offices, etc.).
- Begin to change the organization and culture to have fewer layers for e-business.

Now you can represent each of these as a dimension on a graph. You can use this graph to trade-off between different approaches for expansion. You can base approaches on:

- E-business for its own sake—set yourself up long-term for e-business.
- Customers.
- Expansion of business in general.

Of course, you can think of many more sources for expansion. Figure 15.2 shows how these three directions for expansion might impact each of the dimensions listed above. Note that this is subjective. The purpose of this diagram is to support collaboration and communications. You will then generate a series of ideas for expansion. In order to evaluate these, you can employ the following criteria:

- Risk to the current business.
- Risk to e-business.
- Cost of implementation.
- Elapsed time for implementation.
- Sales and profits estimated that result from the expansion idea.
- Impact on the organization and culture.
- Impact on IT.
- Resources required.

Then you can employ the chart in Figure 15.3 to evaluate each idea. The good ideas then generate specific enhancements in the following areas:

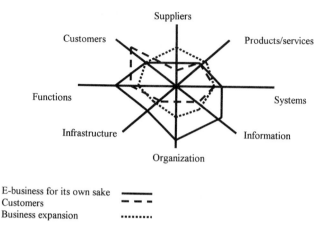

Figure 15.2 Graph of Areas for E-Business Expansion

- Business policies.
- Business processes and procedures.
- IT architecture.
- IT systems.
- Management.
- Business infrastructure.

What is the organization process for deciding what to do? The e-business coordinators assemble potential ideas and coordinate the generation of opportunities. Rather than have many action teams, there can be one action team that crosses

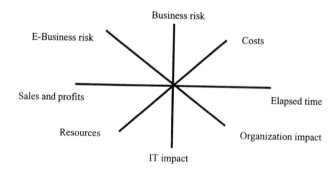

Figure 15.3 Evaluation of E-Business Expansion

the major departments that are involved in e-business. The action team can prepare opportunities and vote. The winners rise to the steering committee. Business cases are then prepared. The same method of review is used as before. How often do you want to go through this? In traditional business this would be performed on an annual basis. With the faster pace of e-business, you should consider intervals of four or six months. This gives IT, management, and business units to propose new e-business initiatives in an organized manner. If you did it on an annual basis, then the current work will probably be disrupted due to high-priority demands.

In Walters 2 this approach was used with a 4-month interval. There were some changes:

- New promotions.
- Extension to new types of products.
- Expansion of e-business internationally on a limited scale.

IMPLEMENT E-BUSINESS ENHANCEMENTS

Maintenance for e-business is different from e-business enhancements. You have both for the business and for IT. In e-business maintenance you move to address situations that impede the current operation of the normal and e-business. Here are some examples of e-business maintenance:

- Installing new releases of network software and other system software to reduce potential exposure to operations.
- Increase hardware server capacity to handle the same functions, but higher volume of work.
- Fix errors and problems in the application software.
- Repair a system interface due to a change being made in one system.
- Enhance the network routers and gateways to ensure that the performance of the network is adequate.
- Correct pictures and descriptions on Web pages.
- Reassign business staff to handle peaks in workload due to e-business.

Enhancements are quite different. You are responding to a new business situation or taking advantage of new technology. Here are some examples:

- Implement new quality assurance and testing software.
- Move to a new programming language with a new set of libraries.
- Install a major new software release for a software package that you are using.
- Perform a major upgrade to the systems.
- Select and install new e-business software.

- Implement new policy changes for the business and e-business.
- Introduce procedure changes for efficiency and streamlining.

Note that some of these appeared before, during initial implementation. Here they are expanded or extended.

You have several ways to manage this effort. The business departments and IT can make changes independently. Not a good idea. You can deal with these changes as you go—on an ad hoc basis. Again, another bad idea. What is a better way to manage change? There are several levels of management. Every 2–3 months, there should be a meeting of the e-business steering committee to review what is going on and what potential new improvements are possible. IT and the e-business coordinator should work together with the e-business coordination department to analyze these potential changes and current activities. Analysis steps that can be pursued for the current work and maintenance are given in Figure 15.4. Steps for the potential enhancements are shown in Figure 15.5.

After preparing this information, you can now proceed to trade-offs. How would resources be reallocated if you performed the enhancements? Here it is suggested that you prepare a table of resources versus impact. An example is

Prepare a table of what people are working on.

Resource	Primary activity	Secondary activities	Comments

Next, identify the various projects and efforts that are ongoing.

Activity/project	Purpose	Benefits	Schedule	Comments

A third table relates to outstanding maintenance requests. This is the backlog of maintenance work.

Maintenance	Purpose	Effort required	Resources	Comments

You will use these tables to identify opportunities where resources can be shifted from maintenance and regular work into enhancements.

Figure 15.4   Steps in Assessing Current Work and Maintenance

Recall that an enhancement can be business or e-business oriented or both. For each enhancement, you should prepare the following list of considerations:

- Description of the enhancement (what)
- Who would do the enhancement and who would be involved (how)
- How long the enhancement would take to implement (how long)
- Benefits of the enhancement to regular business (why)
- Benefits of the enhancement to e-business (why)
- Impact to the normal business if the enhancement is not done (priority)
- Impact to e-business if the enhancement is not performed (priority)
- Potential risks and uncertainty factors in the enhancement (exposure)
- Additional changes in other areas that are required by the enhancement (cross-impacts)
- How the benefits will be measured (benefits achieved)
- Follow-up activities necessary to ensure that the enhancement is successful

Is all of this necessary? It is if you don't want unpleasant surprises.

Figure 15.5   Steps in Evaluating Potential E-Business-Related Enhancements

shown in Figure 15.6. You can now develop a recommended plan of attack. After this preparation, you are now ready for the steering committee review. It is possible that you will get different directions than what you went in with. You may get some enhancements turned down and others approved. Academically, this is fine. In real life this can be a disaster. What if the steering committee approves a number of policy, procedure, and systems changes, but the network and hardware upgrades are turned down? It turns out that these upgrades are essential to the other enhancements. That is why you have to present and emphasize that these are to be evaluated as a group or bundle.

TAKE ADVANTAGE OF NEW TECHNOLOGY

It is not possible to make a list of all new technologies and products. Here we can provide some guidelines for assessing new technology:

- Look at technologies from not only the supply (vendor) view, but also from the demand view in terms of functions and performance.
- Pay attention to software that can assist in managing networks, improving security, and supporting both configuration management and capacity planning.
- Have a list of potential new systems and technology available at all times. This assists in providing focus to your efforts.
- Consider making technology improvements in releases or groups. Here you would bundle a series of changes to the IT architecture and systems. This will minimize the impact and disruption on the business.
- Consider what can be done to improve testing and quality assurance.

Resources	Current activities	Enhancement activities	Impacts	Comments

Figure 15.6   Table of Resource Allocation

- Examine the literature to gather examples of what products firms have used.
- Get advice and opinions from your consultants and outsourcing vendors.

On a regular basis, it is valuable to have a formal review of the systems and IT architecture. Here are some ideas:

- *Step 1:* Show the original architecture and issues prior to e-business.
- *Step 2:* Reveal the current IT architecture that supports e-business.
- *Step 3:* Identify the known issues and concerns in reference to this diagram.
- *Step 4:* Present a list of potential technology products and solutions.
- *Step 5:* Indicate how some of the solutions could resolve the issues in the diagram in Step 3.

In doing this, you may gain support for taking action. You must be ready for this. The major problem is resource conflicts. Implementing any new system or technology will take time from critical IT staff. Therefore, be prepared to address resource allocation and management. You will want to consider what activities can be dropped or given lower priority. The impact may be to provide lower service levels until the new systems or technology are implemented.

STARTUP

Refer to Figure 15.7 for the table for the example firms.

INDO FURNITURE

There was no desire to really expand the Web site and e-business. This was due to the limited manufacturing capacity at the factory. In fact, the chests became very popular, but there was only a limited number of carvers that could do the work with sufficient quality. So the chests had to be removed from the Web site. Beds did not require the same skills because there was no carving required. There has been some consideration of adding chairs that are not carved. An additional

Subject	Company						
	Indo Furniture	Diamond Engineering	Asean Construction	Walters Catalog-1	Walters Catalog-2	Rogers County	
Coordination	Through the consultant	Chris coordinated the business; Mike, the engineers	Through the established teams	None	Through the core e-business team	Through the established teams	
Support	Another person hired for support	Vendor supplied; a person was hired to support Mike	IT and the core e-business teams	IT support; it was viewed as an IT project	Action teams with new members	Operations project team	
Issues	How to manufacture more furniture	How to get more experience	Slow supplier involvement	Too many to list	How to get enough Quick Hits implemented	Public acceptance was initially limited	
Measurement	Sales/profits	Sales	Employee involvement; number of suppliers	On-line sales	On-line sales; process score cards	Multiple score cards	
Enhancements	Consideration of additional furniture items	More information for the knowledge base	Expansion into other areas	None	Extension of Quick Hits to major changes	Extension of the operations system	

Figure 15.7 E-Business Expansion for Example Companies

person has been hired for support. This was due to the requirements for coordination. The new employee worked in logistics support and in tracking problems with the vendors.

DIAMOND ENGINEERING DATA

At Diamond the engineering knowledge base grew slowly. The user base also grew at a slow rate. Both of these things were taken into account in the original business plan. A person was hired to help Mike. This was a junior engineer who assisted in the maintenance of the knowledge base and answered user questions. This freed up Mike to concentrate on marketing.

EXAMPLES

ASEAN CONSTRUCTION

Coordination of e-business was undertaken by the established teams and committees. Support for e-business was provided by the core e-business team and action teams. At the corporate level, the suppliers were brought into e-business at a good pace for the core of the suppliers. Expansion to other suppliers proceeded more slowly. Work continues, but at a reduced pace. However, there have been many benefits by involving the key suppliers.

ROGERS COUNTY

The consumer part of e-business was placed into production and continues to expand. Public interest was initially limited. For operations, the lessons-learned database expanded. The forms were either automated or were simplified and eliminated or consolidated. Score cards were employed for measurement on a consistent basis. The operations approach was extended to other areas of the county government.

LESSONS LEARNED

Here are some lessons learned from e-business operations:

• Consider appointing overlapping coordinators for e-business. That is, suppose that the function is assigned to someone for a year. Six months into this period another person is appointed for a term of a year. This provides overlap and continuity. Moreover, it actually gives you two coordinators.

- In terms of issues, you must avoid the temptation to rush in and solve an issue. Most of the time you take no action. Instead, you continue to monitor the issue and its impact. Issue management requires a fine sense of timing. If you run to management with each issue, you risk looking like the "kid who cried wolf." Organize the issues and present them in groups to management. Make sure that when you present issues, you identify not only alternatives, but also the actions and impacts on resources.

THE SCORE CARD

Revisiting the tables, as was suggested earlier, is one good method. Gathering information to complete the tables provides you with insight and opinion of employees. Here are some questions to address during operations of e-business:

- How do employees view their jobs? What is different about their work? Is it less routine?
- What is the awareness of e-business among employees?
- Is it easier for new employees to begin to do their assigned work?
- Is management sensitive to the demands of e-business?
- What is the level of management awareness of the outside forces highlighted in Figure 15.1?

WHAT TO DO NEXT

One action to take is to examine the literature and review the lessons learned and experience of different companies in e-business. Use this to add to your lessons-learned database. Use the Web sites and references that are included in Appendices 3 and 4, respectively, as a starting point. You can begin with measurement of your current Web site. Here are some questions to address:

- Is there a strategy for the Web site?
- Is the site updated regularly?
- How are visitor comments handled?
- What has been the impact of the Web site on the processes?
- What is the volume of Web site traffic?
- What features and capabilities does the Web site have?
- What is the status of information on the Web site?
- How is the content on the site maintained?
- What role do employees play in the Web site?

SOME CONCLUSIONS

You have just taken a journey through transforming your business into e-business. Like many trips, it is an adventure that is worth pursuing. More than almost anything in recent times, e-business offers great potential for management, customers, suppliers, and employees. E-business is the next natural step in the evolution of the application of systems and technology. E-business, as we have said tirelessly, is a long-term program, not a one-time project. As with any journey you want to travel it well. You want to do it right. The approach and lessons learned have provided a roadmap and guidelines for your voyage. Bon Voyage!

Appendix 1

The Magic Cross Reference

The letters "ff" indicate the reader should also see the following pages.

Area	Topic	Pages
E-business	Trends	7–8
	Goals	10
	Barriers	10–11
E-business implementation	Quick Hits and e-business	257–258
	Management	254–257
	Vendors	257–258
	Customers and suppliers	258–259
	System implementation	261–264
E-business implementation strategy	Grouping opportunities	219–220
	Alternative strategies	224–225
	Implementation plan	227–228
	Resistance to change	239–241
	Quick Hit implementation	242–243
	Measure Quick Hit results	245–246
E-business IT architecture	Systems issues	128–130
	Staffing issues	130–131
	New architecture	132–134
E-business objectives	Objectives	70–72
E-business operations	Coordination	272–273
	Support	274–275
	Measurement	275–276
	Expansion	276–278
	Implement enhancements	279–280

Area	Topic	Pages
E-business organization	Organization	177–178
	Opportunities	181–183
	Business cases	183–186
E-business project	Planning	197–199
	Coordination	205–206
	Resource management	207–209
	Implementation score cards	211–217
E-business software	Evaluation	131–133
E-business strategies	Definition	87ff
	Overlay	90–91
	Separation	93–95
	Replacement	95–97
	Integration	97–99
E-business vision	Definition	68ff
Outsourcing	Identify opportunities	143–146
	Objectives	152
	Select opportunities	152–154
	Preparation	154–157

Appendix 2
The E-Business Project Template

Here is a list of over 200 tasks that are appropriate for your e-business effort. These can serve as the starting point for your e-business planning.

- 1000 Overall e-business vision, objectives, and plan
  - 1100 Develop e-business vision
  - 1200 Define e-business objectives
  - 1300 E-business management
    - 1310 Identify issues management approach
    - 1320 Identify management approach
    - 1330 Establish project steering committee
    - 1340 Establish the e-business executive committee
    - 1350 Identify project leaders
  - 1400 Identify organization roles
- 2000 E-business strategy
  - 2100 Define overall e-business goals
  - 2200 Determine mission of organization with e-business
  - 2300 Identify alternative strategies
  - 2400 Perform strategy evaluation
  - 2500 Document/present strategy
  - 2600 Strategy review
- 3000 Implementation approach
  - 3100 Evaluate the vision of the organization
  - 3200 Assess supplier alliances and relations
  - 3300 Assess current marketing initiatives
  - 3400 Approach to technology
  - 3500 Perform comparative analysis
  - 3600 Define approach
  - 3700 Review approach

4000   Identify e-business processes
    4100   Define core processes to support e-business
    4200   Group processes to include related processes
    4300   Create comparison tables for processes
    4400   Identify finalists
    4500   Evaluate finalist processes
    4600   Make final selection
5000   Competitive and marketplace assessment
    5100   Define ongoing competitive assessment approach
    5200   Identify internal resources to participate
    5300   Investigate benchmarking
    5400   Identify specific sources of information
    5500   Define evaluation methods
    5600   Collect information
    5700   Organize information for long-term use
    5800   Perform analysis
    5900   Present results of analysis
6000   Technology assessment
    6100   Evaluate hardware in terms of e-business
        6110   Suitability and support of e-business
        6120   Identify missing hardware components
    6200   Network assessment for e-business
        6210   Internal network capacity and performance
        6220   Security available and required
        6230   Extranet/intranet requirements
    6300   System software assessment
        6310   core operating systems
        6320   Database management systems
        6330   Desktop systems
        6340   Utility software
    6400   Test environment
        6410   Test hardware
        6420   Test network
        6430   Test software tools
    6500   Development environment
        6510   Development hardware
        6520   Development network
        6530   Development software tools, languages, libraries,
                environment
    6600   Identification of alternatives for e-business support
        6610   Hardware
        6620   Operating systems

          6630   Network software/management/security
          6640   Development environment
          6650   Test environment
     6700   Define technology direction for e-business
          6710   Hardware
          6720   Operating systems
          6730   Network software/management/security
          6740   Development environment
          6750   Test environment
          6760   Interfaces with legacy and existing systems
          6770   New software
     6800   IT staffing
     6900   Develop comparative tables
     6A00   Documentation of technology assessment
7000   Gather information on current processes
     7100   Direct observation of processes
     7200   Identification of issues in processes
     7300   Interdepartmental interfaces
     7400   Review of process documentation
     7500   Assess current Web activities
     7600   Perform analysis and develop comparative tables
     7700   Determine fit with e-business
     7800   Documentation
     7900   Review current processes
8000   Define the new e-business processes
     8100   Generate alternatives for new processes
     8200   Assess alternatives in terms of regular/e-business
     8300   Develop comparative tables
     8400   Technology requirements for new processes
     8500   Staffing requirements for new processes
     8600   Compare new with current processes
     8700   Documentation
     8800   Review new processes
          8810   Current business
          8820   E-business
9000   Measurement
     9100   Identify areas of risk
     9200   Define e-business measurement approach
     9300   Infrastructure/technology/support
     9400   Measurement of current business
     9500   Measurement of Web business
     9600   Measurement of Web visitors

10000   Develop the implementation strategy
       10100   Define alternative strategies for processes
       10200   Define alternative strategies for technology
       10300   Define alternative strategies for organization/policies
       10400   Define alternatives for marketing
       10500   Conduct assessment of alternatives
       10600   Develop overall implementation strategy
       10700   Define prototype/pilot activity
       10800   Define phases for implementation
       10900   Review implementation strategy
11000   Define the implementation plan
       11100   Define implementation plan template
       11200   Identify specific implementation issues
       11300   Assess the project management process
       11400   Determine implementation leaders/team composition
       11500   Develop detailed plan and subprojects
       11600   Analyze the completed plan
12000   Implementation
       12100   Hardware setup for e-business
       12200   Network setup and testing for e-business
       12300   Firewall/extranet/security
       12400   Development environment setup
       12500   Test environment setup
       12600   Establishment of development standards
       12700   Setup of quality assurance
       12800   Installation of e-business software packages
       12900   Establishment of external links
       12A00   Testing of e-business software for production
       12B00   Changes to current application software
       12C00   Interfaces between current and e-business software
       12D00   Implementation of marketing changes
       12E00   Marketing campaigns
       12F00   Setup of Web content
       12G00   Software development
       12H00   Integration and testing
       12I00   Quality assurance and integrated testing
       12J00   Procedures and training materials
       12K00   Operations procedures
       12L00   Network procedures
       12M00   Changes to current processes and workflow
       12N00   Address current customers and suppliers
       12O00   Conduct test of workflow and processes

13000 Postimplementation assessment
      13100 Gather lessons learned
      13200 Identify unresolved issues
      13300 Conduct usability assessment
      13400 Conduct performance evaluation
      13500 Assess impact on current processes
      13600 Assess customer–supplier relationships
      13700 Perform cost–benefit analysis
      13800 Define recommendations for later work
      13900 Conduct review

Appendix 3

Web Sites

Here are some Web sites of interest to e-business. Note that these are examples. The lists are not intended to be complete.

Collaboration Tools

- PlaceWare Conference Center 2000—Web conferencing facility
- intranets.com—Set up intranet
- www.response-o-matic.com—Set up forms
- www.beseen.com—Message boards
- www.server.com-insert—Message boards
- hotoffice.com—Scheduling
- Daytracker.com—Scheduling
- Webex.com—Scheduling
- scheduleonline.com—Scheduling

Use Bookmarks

- Backflip.com—Download applet to browser; add to Yahoo page
- Blink.com—Create account and upload bookmarks
- Clip2.com—Public topic guides; can subscribe
- Desktop.com—Bookmark manager, e-mail, recipe box, photo album
- Etour.com—Call up selected categories
- Hotlinks.com—Share bookmarks

Business-to-Business

- Bluestone.com—Range of software products
- Calico.com—Customizable pricing and features, personalization

- Exceloncorp.com—Portal, content management, and publishing
- Ironside.com—Sell-side wholesaling
- Microsoft.com—Biztalk server
- Objectspace.com—OpenBusiness integrates with trading partners

Voice on Web

- Deltathree.com—Clickit is PC-phone service link
- Eshare.com—Net agent and contact center services support voice, e-mail, and live chat
- Facetime.com—Instant customer/instant messaging, text, voice chat
- HearMe.com—VoiceCreator adds voice, VoiceNetwork; hosts and manages all voice traffic
- Lipstream.com—Real-time voice communications
- Vocaltec.com—Surf/call network services; ASP integrated voice, cobrowsing, text chat, form completion

Customer Relationship Management

- Goldmine Software (www.goldmine.com)
- Interact Commerce Corp. (www.interactcommerce.com)
- Multiactive Software (www.multiactive.com)
- Sales force automation (salesforce.com, upshot.com)

Customer Support

- Liveperson.com—Customers chat through text in real time
- Lipstream.com—Voice over IP
- Hipbone.com—Shared browsing, post pages to customer's browser
- Net2phone.com—Call back

E-Retailing

- ECongo.com—Free commerce builder, free service
- Digitalstorefronts.com—Commerce enable an existing site: Retail Pro
- Openmarket.com, bluemartini.com—Large systems, e-business suite
- Stamps.com—Fulfill on-line orders
- Ibill.com—Billing
- Warrantynow.com—Warranty: WarrantyNow
- Thereturnexchange.com—Returns: The Return Exchange

Competitive Intelligence Vendors

- Cartia.com—Organizes information
- Cipher-sys.com—Organizes and distributes information
- Compassware.com—Distributes to sales staff
- Currentanalysis.com—News and analysis on telecom
- Delfin.com—Assesses relationships between places, products, and events
- EHNC-aptex.com—Reads content of customer e-mail and routes
- Knowx.com—Searches public records
- Netcurrents.com—Chat rooms, Web sites, bulletin boards, e-mail newsletters
- Corporateinformation.com—Direct link to 350,000 profiles
- Company.sleuth.com
- Hooversonline.com
- Netmind.com
- EoMonitor-havElink.com/cat2main.htm
- Direct search-gwis2.circ.gwu.edu/~gprice/direct.htm
- Edgar-online.com
- Lexis-nexis.com
- Thomasregister.com
- Members.aol.com/kudzukat/kks__pepl.html—Kudzukat's people search

Marts and Exchanges

- Buildpoint.com—Exchange for construction materials, labor (2% fee)
- Cephren.com—Exchange for construction material and labor (0.88% to sellers)
- Chemdex.com—Chemicals and laboratory supplies (negotiable)
- Esteel.com—Steel industry (0.3–0.88%)
- Ironmax.com—Construction equipment ($30/lead; 1%)
- Metalshare.com—Metals; (0.25–1% for product guide purchases)
- Medsite.com—Reseller of medical supplies and equipment
- Paperexchange.com—Papermaking materials and equipment
- Plasticsnet.com—Materials and equipment for plastics industry
- Redladder.com—Construction material (0.5–3%)
- Verticalnet.com—Multiple industries

E-Business Magazine Web Sites

- www.zdnet/enterprise/e-business—Internet magazine
- www.zdnet/enterprise/e-business/bphome/—Best practices

- www.canadianebusiness.com
- www.asia.internet.com
- www.thestandardeurope.com
- www.japaninc.net
- www.i-on.com/know/know.asp
- www.ebusiness.about.com/industry/ebusiness
- www.advisor.com
- www.webpractices.com/ebizpubs.html
- www.dmoz.org/business/e-commerce

Appendix 4
Bibliography

Constantine, Larry. *Constantine on Peopleware.* Prentice-Hall, New Jersey, 1995.

Garside, John. *Plan to Win: A Definite Guide to Business Processes.* Purdue University Press, Purdue, 1999.

Kalakota, R., M. Robinson, and D. Tapscott. *E-Business Roadmap for Success.* Addison Wesley, Reading, Mass., 1999.

Liantiaud, Bernard, and Mark Hammond. *E-Business Intelligence.* McGraw-Hill Professional Publishing, New York, 2000.

Lientz, B. P., and K. P. Rea. *Breakthrough Technology Project Management,* 2nd Ed. Academic Press, San Diego, 2001.

Lientz, B. P., and K. P. Rea. *Dynamic E-Business Implementation Management.* Academic Press, San Diego, 2000.

Lientz, B. P., and K. P. Rea. *Start Right in E-Business.* Academic Press, San Diego, 2000.

Lientz, B. P., and K. P. Rea. *Professional's Guide to Process Improvement.* Aspen Publishing, New York, 2001.

May, Paul Richard. *Business of E-Commerce.* Cambridge University Press, London, 2000.

Porter, Michael. *Competitive Strategy Techniques for Analyzing Industries and Competitors.* Free Press, New York, 1998.

Swift, Ronald S. *Accelerating Customer Relationship: Using CRM and Relational Technologies.* Prentice-Hall, New Jersey, 2000.

Tyndall, G. R. *et al. Supercharging Supply Chains.* John Wiley and Sons, New York, 1998.

Appendix 5

Tables for Examples

Subject	Company					
	Indo Furniture	Diamond Engineering	Asean Construction	Walters Catalog-1	Walters Catalog-2	Rogers County
Business goals	Stability, low risk; low cost; minimal technology	Need to define precise benefits and use of knowledge base; establish sustainable business	Maintain relations with government; maintain competitive position; increase collaboration across diverse business units	Business goals unclear; goals are too general	Focus on integration of e-business and regular business	County government must be efficient and run with limited staff; use technology as much as possible
Business processes	Manufacturing, shipping	Knowledge base, wizards, payments, customer database	Many different processes—some cross business units	Focus on sales	Focus on customer service as well as sales	Focus on customer service delivery and operations
Organization/ infrastructure	Family business, thermal paper fax	Nothing	Major data center serving business units; dispersed business infrastructure	Centralized business	Centralized business	Distributed across the county

Products and services	Western-oriented products	Knowledge base	Public work; housing; toll roads	Everything	Focus on limited products on the Web	Scheduling and operations
IT plan	All external	Nothing	Overall plan to upgrade architecture for e-business	Lack of plan	Plan that emphasizes fixing problems	Existing plan is not intranet oriented
IT architecture	Use others as remote user	None	Modern, but needs Web components	Many systems issues; frequent breaks	Limited modernization was done	Basically in place to support intranets
IT staffing	No one	One person knows IT	Regular IT group	Very limited	Very limited	Management is traditional IT; staff lack Web skills
Direction— e-business	Get basic logistics, order processing, and customer service in place	Focus on customer and on support for knowledge base	Need to pursue some e-business initiatives across business units as well as within	None	Service and fulfillment as well as sales	Focus on intranets that involve largest number of employees for maximum impact

Subject	Company					
	Indo Furniture	Diamond Engineering	Asean Construction	Walters Catalog-1	Walters Catalog-2	Rogers County
Cross-impact of transactions	Ordering and customer service at different locations need to be addressed	The knowledge-base transactions need to be integrated	Transactions such as purchasing have to be made consistent across business units	Lack of coordination	Integration from ordering to customer service	New intranet systems must be useful across operations
Mapping goals into processes	Ordering, payments, shipping, returns are key	Knowledge-base transactions are of greatest importance	Purchasing across business units; b-c within units	Not done	Ordering, customer service, accounting, marketing	Sharing knowledge, forms automation
Quick Hits	Set up company; arrange for ordering and service	Set up company; build knowledge base	Streamline purchasing; centralize purchasing for many items	Not done	Pursue the key opportunities	Forms automation
Costs and benefits	Obvious	Obvious	Collaboration; some reduced costs in labor	Not done	Increased sales; reduced cost of sales	Reduced labor; improved productivity
Presentation	Business plan to get limited funding	Business plan to get limited funding	Collaboration among business unit managers	Not done	Get support at the lower levels	Get support within operations

Subject	Company					
	Indo Furniture	Diamond Engineering	Asean Construction	Walters Catalog-1	Walters Catalog-2	Rogers County
Alternative e-business visions	Revenue, culture, business alternative visions developed	Knowledge, business, and customer alternative visions developed	Developed at both the company and business unit levels	Not formally done	Comprehensive vision elements defined	Alternatives provided to many employees; voting
Settle vision	Revenue and culture vision	Provide growing and most useful knowledge	Reconcile different visions	Developed during a planning session	Many planning sessions concurrent with e-business objectives	Vision developed through consensus
Alternative e-business objectives	Extensive list generated	Developed list of e-business objectives	Developed lists for both company and business units	Not formally done	Developed for each vision alternative	Developed in a collaborative way
E-business objectives	Selected through mapping to vision	Selected by partners	Selection through voting	Not formally done; no clear e-business objectives	One set linked to vision	Developed with management and selected employees

Subject		Company				
	Indo Furniture	Diamond Engineering	Asean Construction	Walters Catalog-1	Walters Catalog-2	Rogers County
Overlay strategy	Can create problems with local customers	Not appropriate	Possible in several business units	Tried this first	Rejected the second time	Possible in some areas
Separation strategy	Possible, but lack of resources	That is what a startup is in this case	Not appropriate	Never considered	Strongly considered due to the problems the first time	Not appropriate
Replacement strategy	Not really except for manufacturing	Not appropriate	Possible for parts of toll-way operations	Never considered	Not appropriate	Long term possibility
Integration strategy	Capitalize on limited resources	Not appropriate	Good for corporate in purchasing	Dropped due to perceived time pressure	First time showed need for integration	Possible for b–c
Selection	Integration— easiest initially	Separation	Combination	Overlay strategy	Integration strategy	Integration for b–c; overlay for employees; eventually replacement
Impacts	Overseas orders impact business	Thinking this through helped provide focus and improve the business plan	Involve more people	Confusion during the project	More people in the business involved	Involve more people

Subject	Company					
	Indo Furniture	Diamond Engineering	Asean Construction	Walters Catalog-1	Walters Catalog-2	Rogers County
Initial industry assessment	Surveys of potential suppliers and furniture suppliers	Extensive surveys of knowledge-based services; engineering sources	Survey of similar firms in other countries	Nothing	Review of other catalog firms	Surveys of other government agencies
Ongoing industry assessment	Furniture suppliers; magazines	Ongoing search for engineering data and sources	Ongoing surveys of firms	—	Assessment of promotion and marketing	Search for new applications

Subject	Company						
	Indo Furniture	Diamond Engineering	Asean Construction	Walters Catalog-1	Walters Catalog-2	Rogers County
Current IT systems and architecture	None	None	In place	Accepted as is	Problems in network capacity and weak workstations	Adequate
IT staffing/ work	None; contracted	None; contracted	Retraining of some IT staff	None	Use vendors to improve internal skills	Additional staff training for IT
Ongoing technology assessment	None	None	Within IT	None	IT and core e-business team	Within IT and operations
E-business architecture	Through the vendors	Limited	In place	No formal structure	Use the existing architecture with enhancements	Established
IT projects and action items	Integration	Focus on software development and knowledge base	Expansion of the network across the company; links to suppliers	Enhancements for security	Add hardware and network capacity	Improved security

Chapter 8

Subject		Company				
	Indo Furniture	Diamond Engineering	Asean Construction	Walters Catalog-1	Walters Catalog-2	Rogers County
What can be outsourced?	Virtually everything	Computer systems; Web development	Consulting; Web development	Web content	Web content; process improvement	Software packages; software development
Objectives of outsourcing	Stability; low cost	Growth; low cost	Expertise; speed up implementation	Web site development	Save time; expertise	Quality development; stability
Evaluation/ selection	Integration; cost	Stability; low cost	Experience	No real criteria except cost	Experience	Experience
Cleanup of processes	Accounting	Not applicable	Many Quick Hits	Did not occur- overlay strategy	15 key processes	Operations processes
Prepare for outsourcing	Planning	Planning; joint work	IT network	Lack of preparation	Prepare information on products	Define requirements

Subject	Company					
	Indo Furniture	**Diamond Engineering**	**Asean Construction**	**Walters Catalog-1**	**Walters Catalog-2**	**Rogers County**
Employees	No problem	Not applicable	Joint participation in planning and implementation	As needed	Action teams, opportunities, Quick Hits	Through participation
Marketing	Limited	Limited	Limited	Not addressed	Limited organization change	Changes in thinking about promotions
Customers	Through direct contacts	Through advertising and direct contact	Advertising and incentives	Not addressed except through advertising	Through advertising	Through advertisements
Suppliers	Not applicable	Direct contact	Direct contacts	Not addressed	E-business experienced suppliers	Selected suppliers

Chapter 10

Subject	Company					
	Indo Furniture	Diamond Engineering	Asean Construction	Walters Catalog-1	Walters Catalog-2	Rogers County
Management approach	Remote support and management; family steering committee	Two-person approach and then investors	Same as in chapter with steering committee in each business unit	Project leader reporting to president	Action teams, steering committees, executive committees	Steering committee, action teams, informal executive committee
Team approach	Issues based	Daily meeting	Teams in business units and corporate	Ad hoc teams	As in chapter	Issues based
Issues	Communications across time zones	Maintained issues manually	Issues database	No structured approach	Overcome the past perceptions	No formal method

Subject	Company					
	Indo Furniture	Diamond Engineering	Asean Construction	Walters Catalog-1	Walters Catalog-2	Rogers County
Project managers	Manager	Owners	Two people from each country	Junior person	Two project leaders	Two project leaders
Team members	Family members; technical support; consultant	Owners	Action teams and others for implementation	Lack of team member identification	Action teams and others for implementation	Many across operations and separately for consumer e-business
Planning	Use of templates	Linked to business plan	Use of templates	Overdetailed project plan	Use of templates	Use of templates
Coordination	Everything in writing for clarity	Informal	Informal	Ad hoc	Through the action teams	Through the project teams
Resource management	Informal	Informal	Through the project leaders and line management	Ad hoc	Through the project leaders and line management	Through the project leaders and line management

Chapter 12

Subject	Company					
	Indo Furniture	Diamond Engineering	Asean Construction	Walters Catalog-1	Walters Catalog-2	Rogers County
Group into phases	Setup; growth	Setup; growth	Within business units and coordinated with corporate	Not done	Customer service, development, marketing, order processing; Quick Hits	Software development; Quick Hits; policies and procedures
Organize technical work	Coordination with vendors	Mike did this	IT with the core e-business team	IT group	IT group with the core e-business team	IT group with operations
Alternative e-business implementation strategies	Business versus IT	Knowledge base versus software development	Quick Hits versus long term	Not done	IT versus business versus combination	Automation of clerical functions versus new applications
Selection of e-business implementation strategies	Based on need to generate sales quickly	Based on longer term view of involvement	Combined approach	Not done	Major parallel effort	Long-term impact
Project planning	Done by consultant	Done by Chris	Joint across teams	Detailed plan by project leader	Core e-business team	Project leaders in both areas in parallel

313

Chapter 13

Subject			Company			
	Indo Furniture	Diamond Engineering	Asean Construction	Walters Catalog-1	Walters Catalog-2	Rogers County
Prepare employees for change	Family meetings	No preparation was needed	Carried out at the corporate and business unit levels	No preparation was undertaken	Through the action teams and core e-business team	Extensive meetings within operations; introduction among other employees
Resistance to change	Fear of loss of money	None	Fear of loss of jobs	Fear of loss of jobs	None among employees; some fear among middle-level managers	Skepticism of results
Quick Hit implementation	Agreements with vendors; trial shipments	Setup of business	Many Quick Hits across business units	None	Over 65 changes	Changes in policies and procedures

Chapter 14

Subject	Company					
	Indo Furniture	Diamond Engineering	Asean Construction	Walters Catalog-1	Walters Catalog-2	Rogers County
Manage the work	Coordination with the factory	Chris managed the business; Mike worked on the knowledge base and supervised development	Through the various project leaders	Burden fell on the project leader	Core e-business team, implementation teams	Two core teams for operations and consumer
Further Quick Hits	Test runs with the interfaces	Development, testing	These just kept coming	Not applicable	Second wave of Quick Hits	Development of the lessons learned and wizards
Customers/ suppliers	Lining up of dealers	Lining up engineers; contacting potential customers	Contacts with suppliers; some advertisements with customers	Limited effort except for some advertising in the catalogs	More proactive contact with customers and suppliers	Some limited advertisements

	Company						
Subject	**Indo Furniture**	**Diamond Engineering**	**Asean Construction**	**Walters Catalog-1**	**Walters Catalog-2**	**Rogers County**	
Coordination	Through the consultant	Chris coordinated the business; Mike, the engineers	Through the established teams	None	Through the core e-business team	Through the established teams	
Support	Another person hired for support	Vendor supplied; a person was hired to support Mike	IT and the core e-business teams	IT support; it was viewed as an IT project	Action teams with new members	Operations project team	
Issues	How to manufacture more furniture	How to get more experience	Slow supplier involvement	Too many to list	How to get enough Quick Hits implemented	Public acceptance was initially limited	
Measurement	Sales/profits	Sales	Employee involvement; number of suppliers	On-line sales	On-line sales; process score cards	Multiple score cards	
Enhancements	Consideration of additional furniture items	More information for the knowledge base	Expansion into other areas	None	Extension of Quick Hits to major changes	Extension of the operations system	

Index

The letters "ff" indicate the reader should also see the following pages.